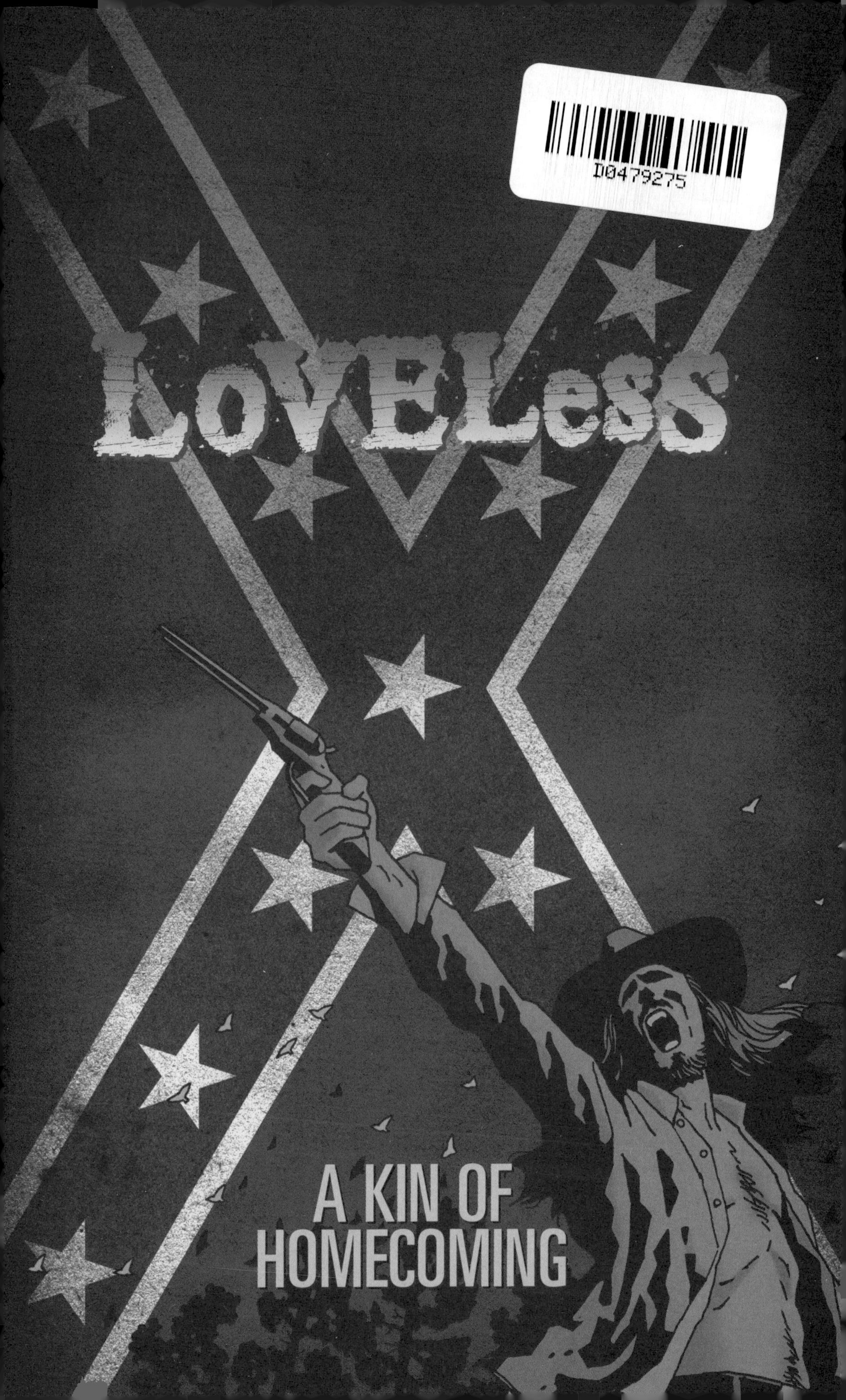
LOVELESS
A KIN OF
HOMECOMING

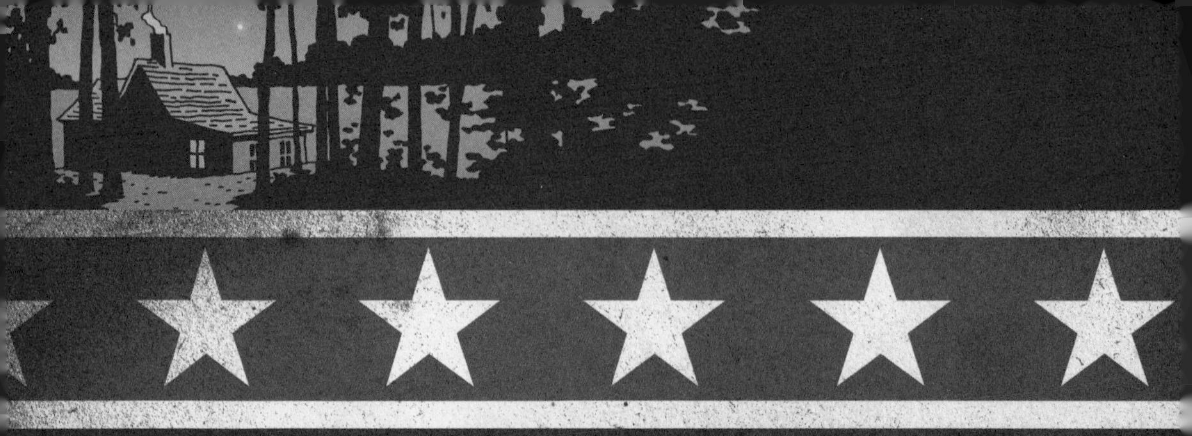

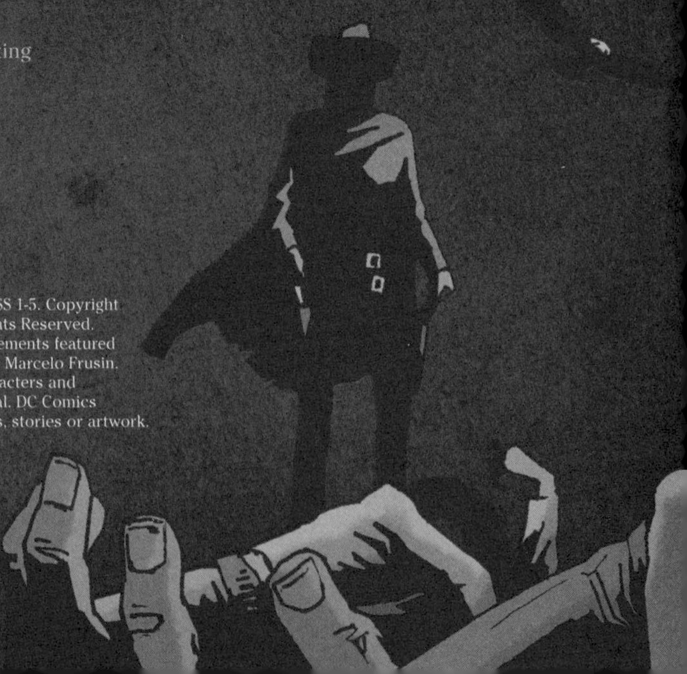

LOVELESS: A KIN OF HOMECOMING

DC Comics, 1700 Broadway, New York, NY 10019
A Warner Bros. Entertainment Company
Printed in Canada. First Printing.
ISBN: 1-4012-1061-9. ISBN 13: 978-1-4012-1061-8.
Cover illustration by Marcelo Frusin
Publication design by Brainchild Studios/NYC

BRIAN **AZZARELLO** MARCELO **FRUSIN**

PATRICIA MULVIHILL
colorist

CLEM ROBINS
letterer

MARCELO FRUSIN
covers

LOVELESS™

A KIN OF HOMECOMING

Loveless created by

BRIAN AZZARELLO *and* MARCELO FRUSIN

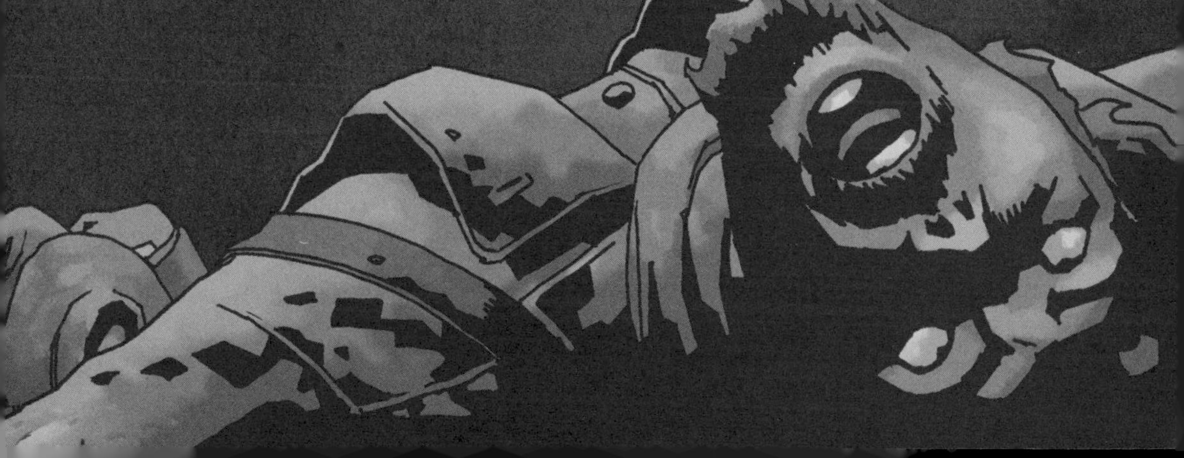

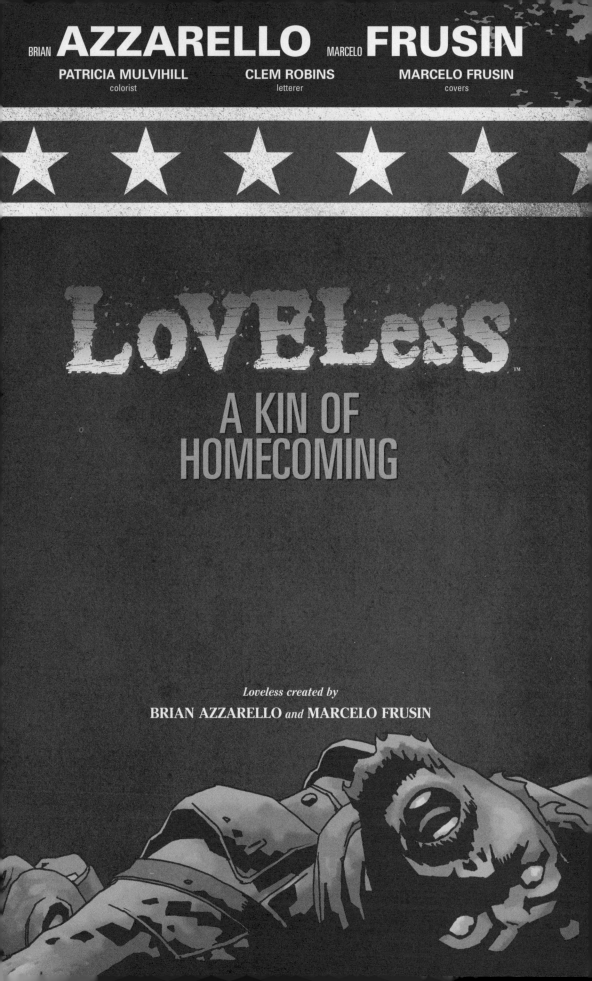

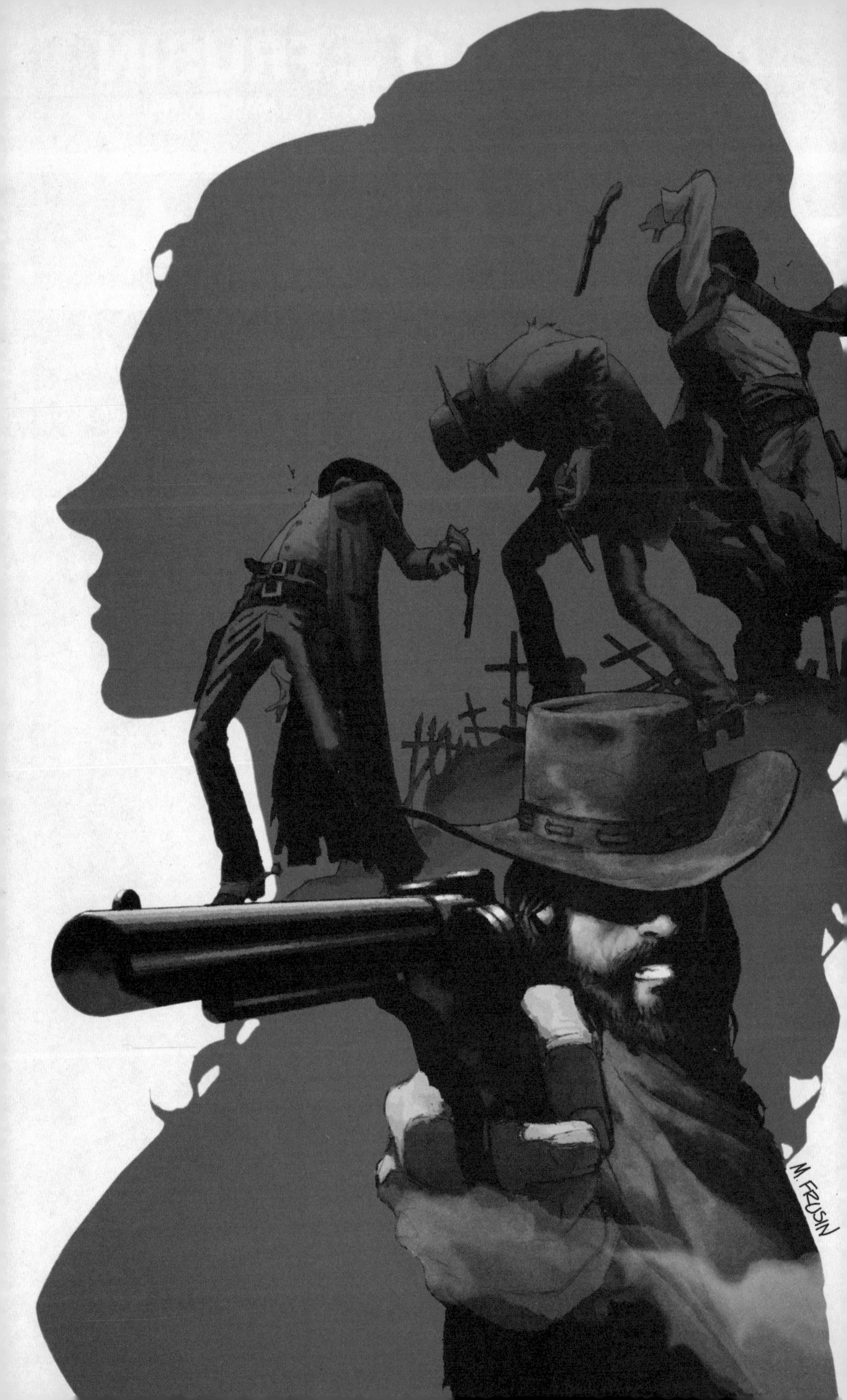
M. FRUSIN

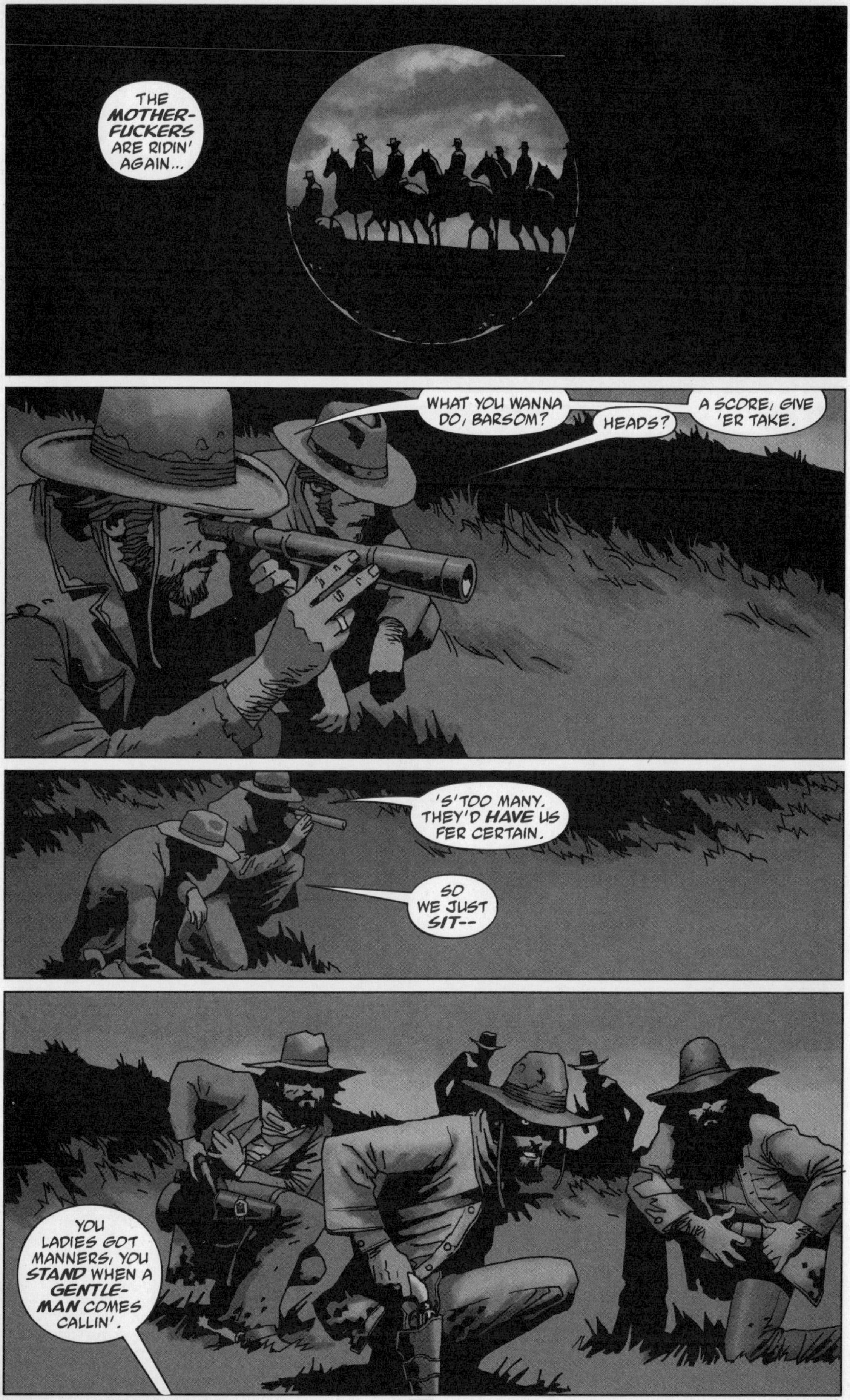

THE MOTHER-FUCKERS ARE RIDIN' AGAIN...
WHAT YOU WANNA DO, BARSOM?
HEADS?
A SCORE, GIVE 'ER TAKE.
'S'TOO MANY. THEY'D HAVE US FER CERTAIN.
SO WE JUST SIT--
YOU LADIES GOT MANNERS, YOU STAND WHEN A GENTLE-MAN COMES CALLIN'.

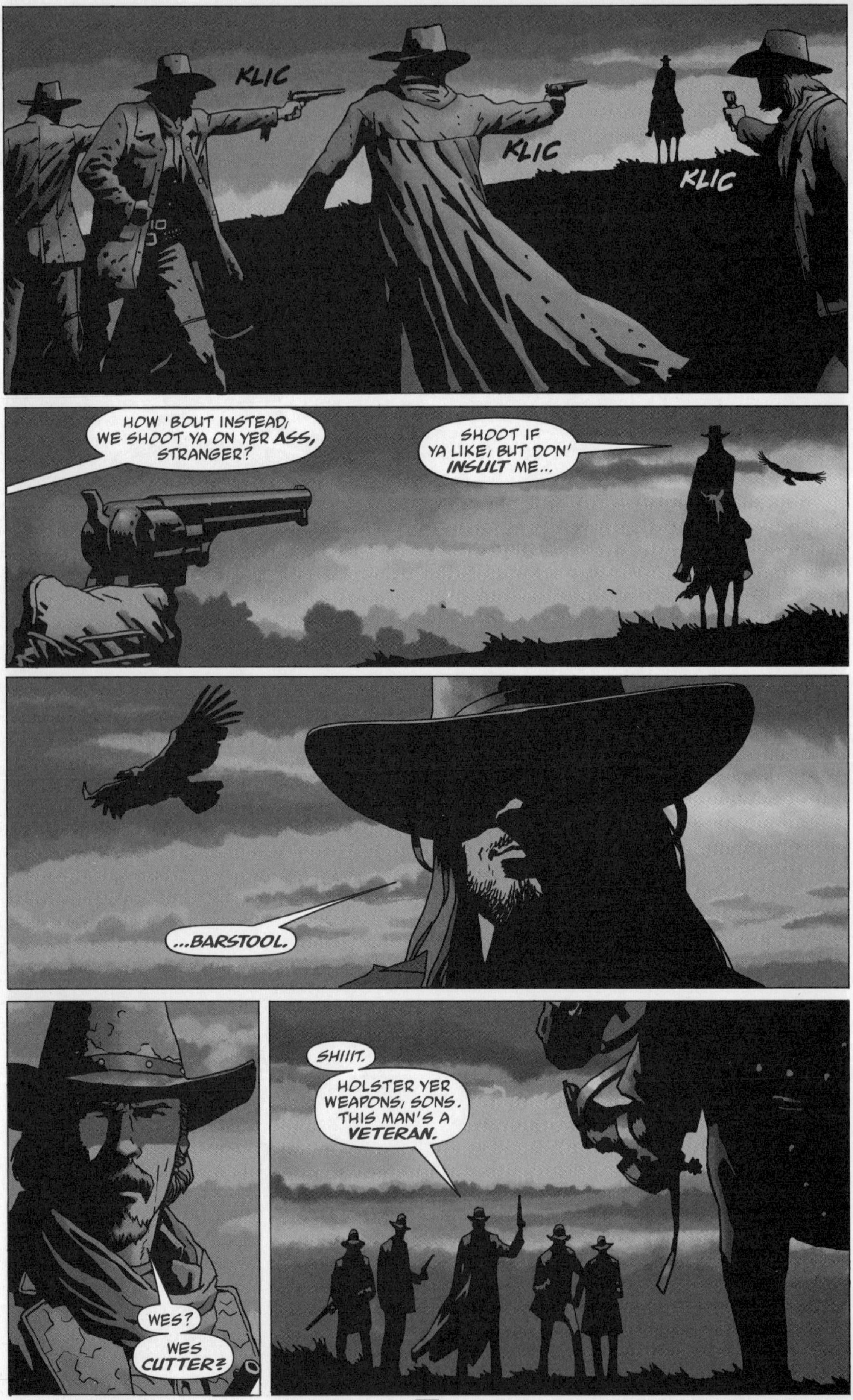
KLIC
KLIC
KLIC
HOW 'BOUT INSTEAD, WE SHOOT YA ON YER ASS, STRANGER?
SHOOT IF YA LIKE, BUT DON' INSULT ME...
...BARSTOOL.
WES?
WES CUTTER?
SHIIIT.
HOLSTER YER WEAPONS, SONS. THIS MAN'S A VETERAN.

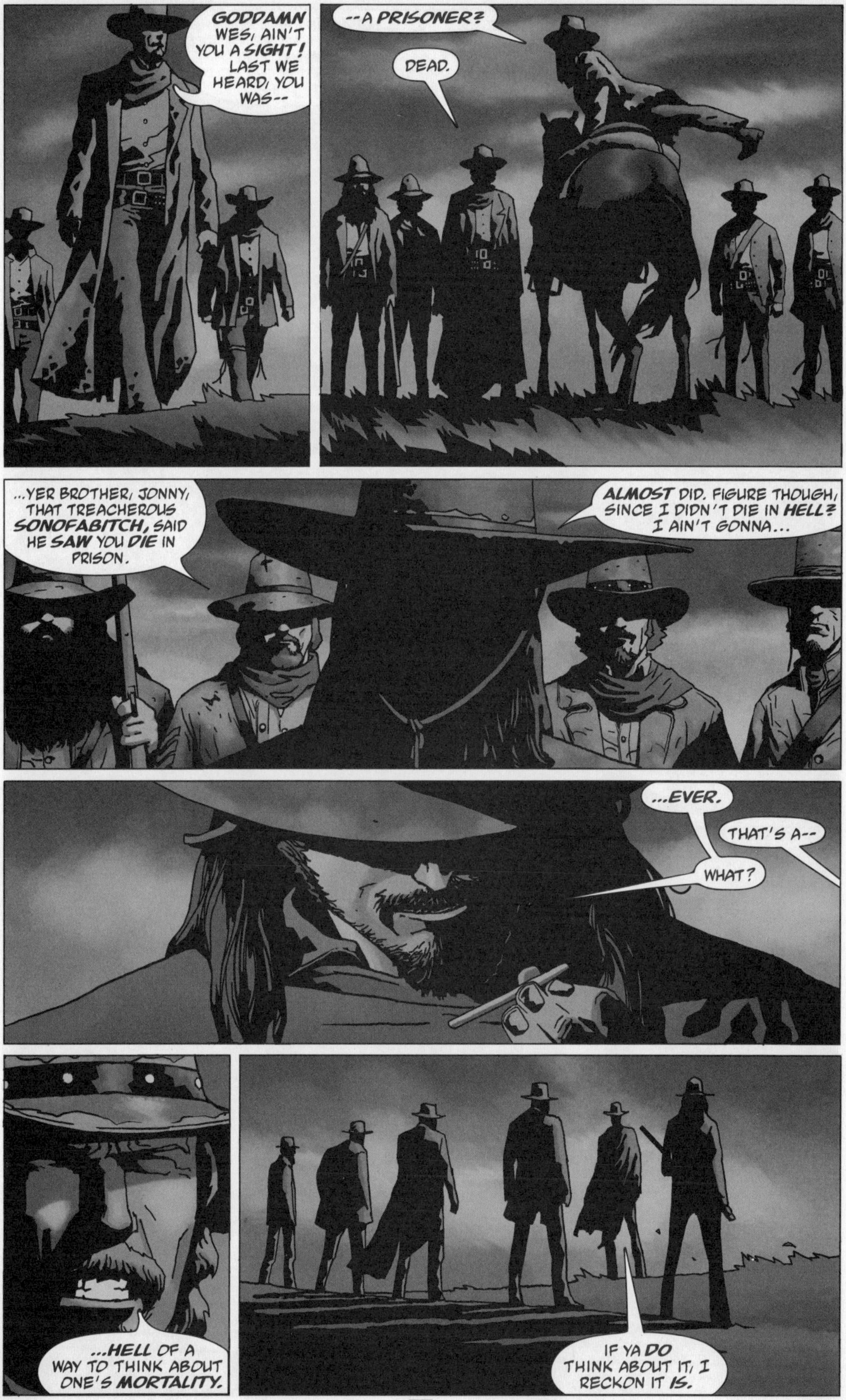
GODDAMN WES, AIN'T YOU A SIGHT! LAST WE HEARD, YOU WAS--
--A PRISONER?
DEAD.
...YER BROTHER, JONNY, THAT TREACHEROUS SONOFABITCH, SAID HE SAW YOU DIE IN PRISON.
ALMOST DID. FIGURE THOUGH, SINCE I DIDN'T DIE IN HELL? I AIN'T GONNA...
...EVER.
THAT'S A--
WHAT?
...HELL OF A WAY TO THINK ABOUT ONE'S MORTALITY.
IF YA DO THINK ABOUT IT, I RECKON IT IS.

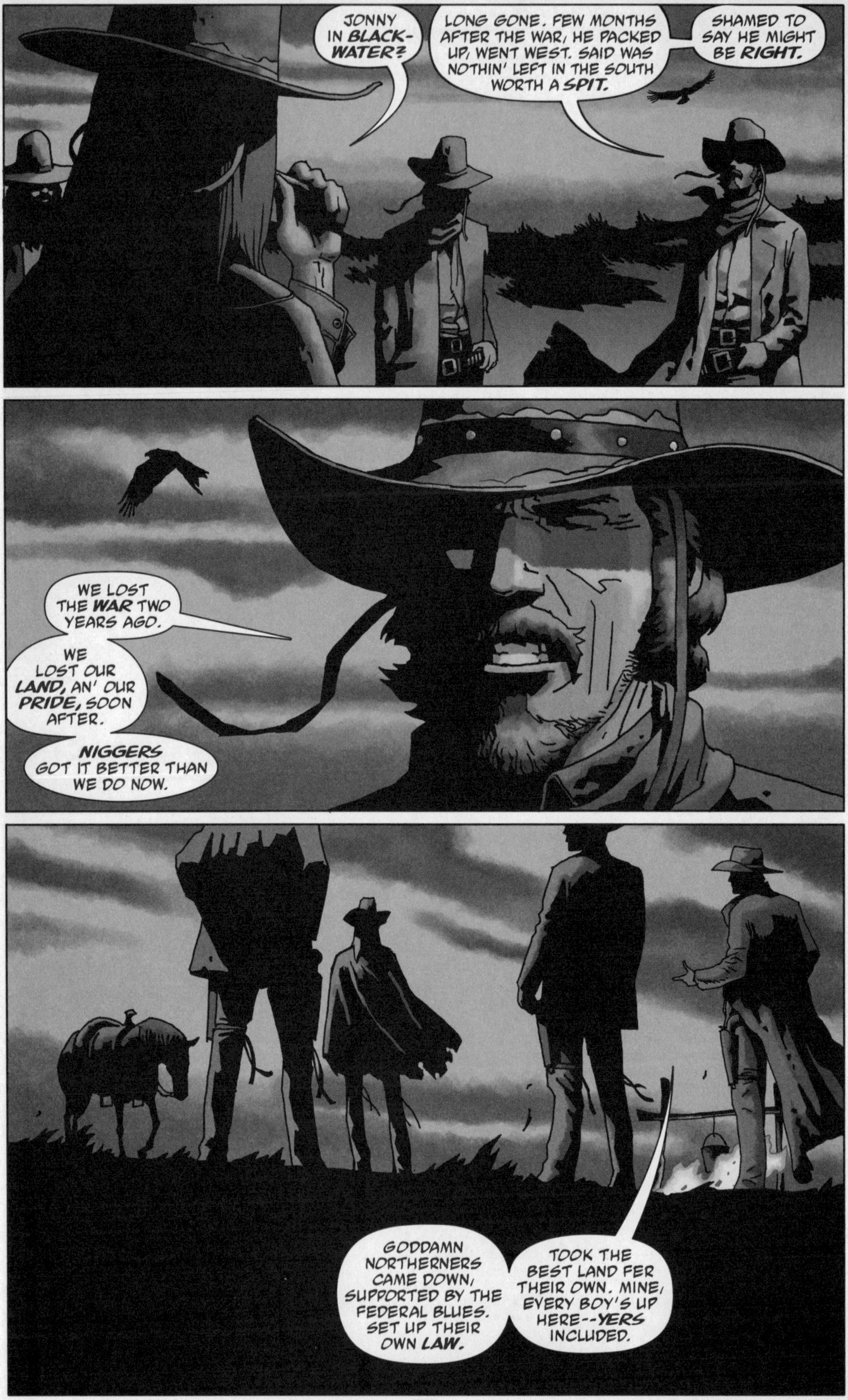

JONNY IN BLACKWATER?
LONG GONE. FEW MONTHS AFTER THE WAR, HE PACKED UP, WENT WEST. SAID WAS NOTHIN' LEFT IN THE SOUTH WORTH A SPIT.
SHAMED TO SAY HE MIGHT BE RIGHT.
WE LOST THE WAR TWO YEARS AGO.
WE LOST OUR LAND, AN' OUR PRIDE, SOON AFTER.
NIGGERS GOT IT BETTER THAN WE DO NOW.
GODDAMN NORTHERNERS CAME DOWN, SUPPORTED BY THE FEDERAL BLUES. SET UP THEIR OWN LAW.
TOOK THE BEST LAND FER THEIR OWN. MINE, EVERY BOY'S UP HERE--YERS INCLUDED.

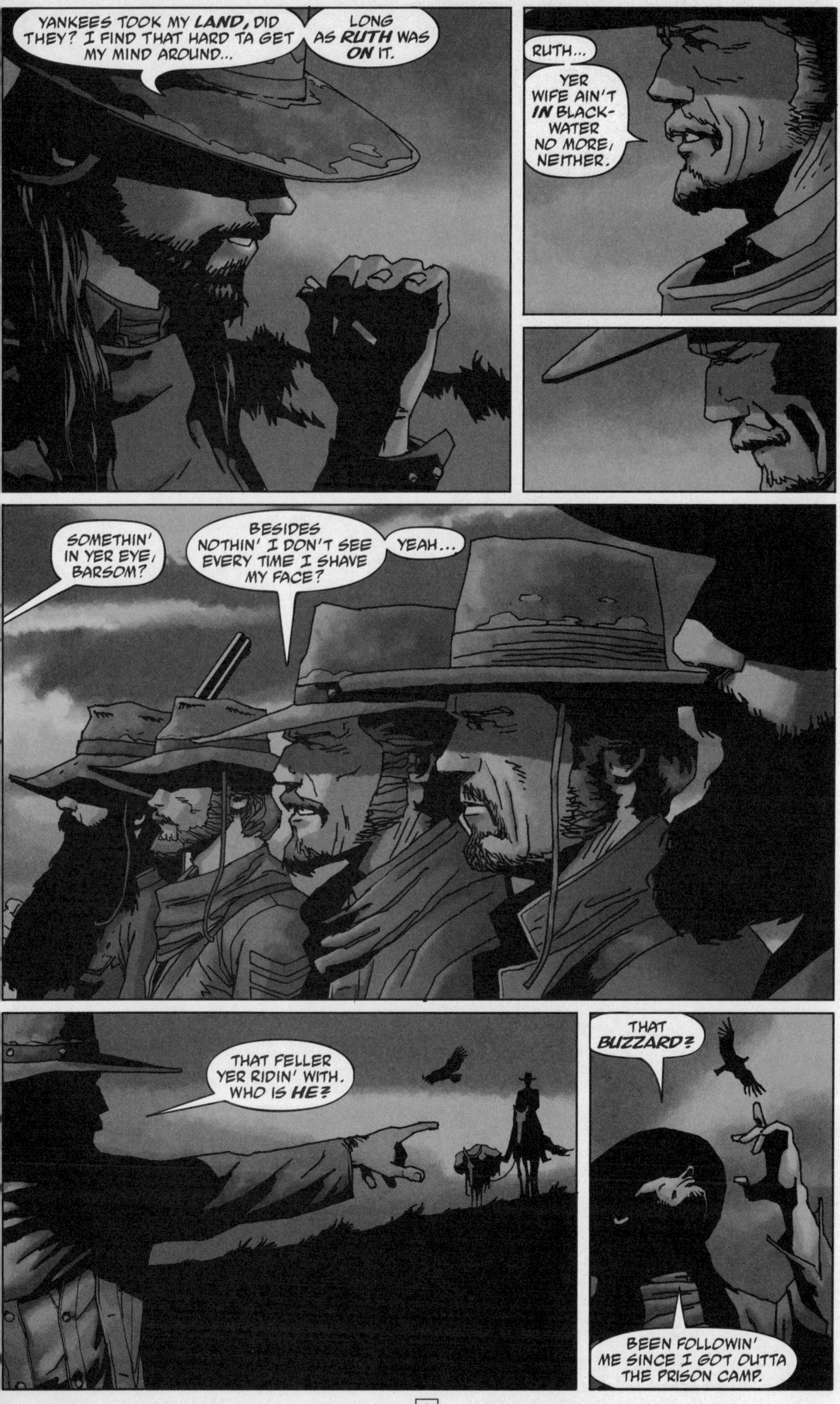
YANKEES TOOK MY LAND, DID THEY? I FIND THAT HARD TA GET MY MIND AROUND...
LONG AS RUTH WAS ON IT.
RUTH...
YER WIFE AIN'T IN BLACK-WATER NO MORE, NEITHER.
SOMETHIN' IN YER EYE, BARSOM?
BESIDES NOTHIN' I DON'T SEE EVERY TIME I SHAVE MY FACE?
YEAH...
THAT FELLER YER RIDIN' WITH. WHO IS HE?
THAT BUZZARD?
BEEN FOLLOWIN' ME SINCE I GOT OUTTA THE PRISON CAMP.

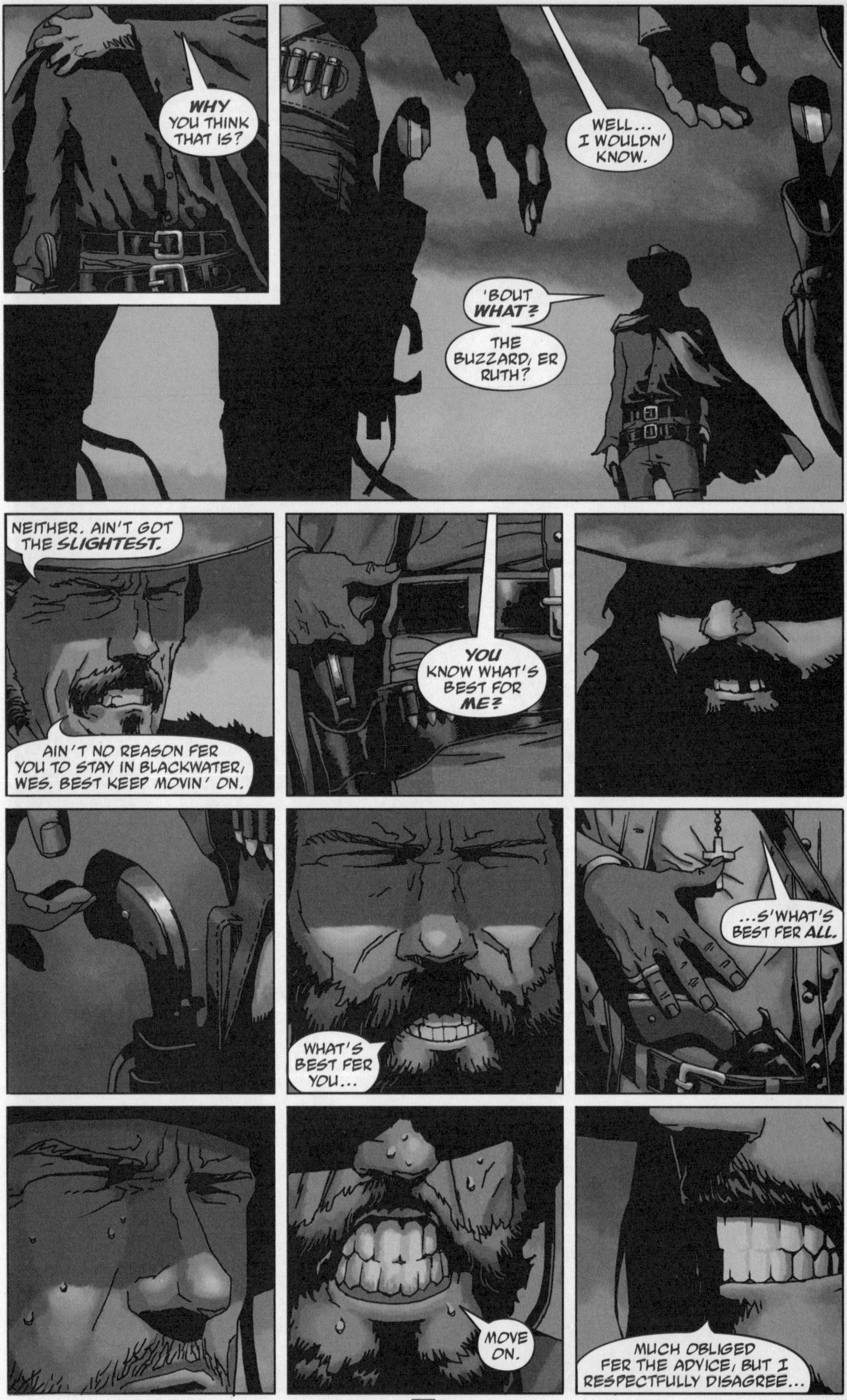

WHY YOU THINK THAT IS?
WELL... I WOULDN' KNOW.
'BOUT WHAT?
THE BUZZARD, ER RUTH?
NEITHER. AIN'T GOT THE SLIGHTEST.
AIN'T NO REASON FER YOU TO STAY IN BLACKWATER, WES. BEST KEEP MOVIN' ON.
YOU KNOW WHAT'S BEST FOR ME?
WHAT'S BEST FER YOU...
...S'WHAT'S BEST FER ALL.
MOVE ON.
MUCH OBLIGED FER THE ADVICE, BUT I RESPECTFULLY DISAGREE...

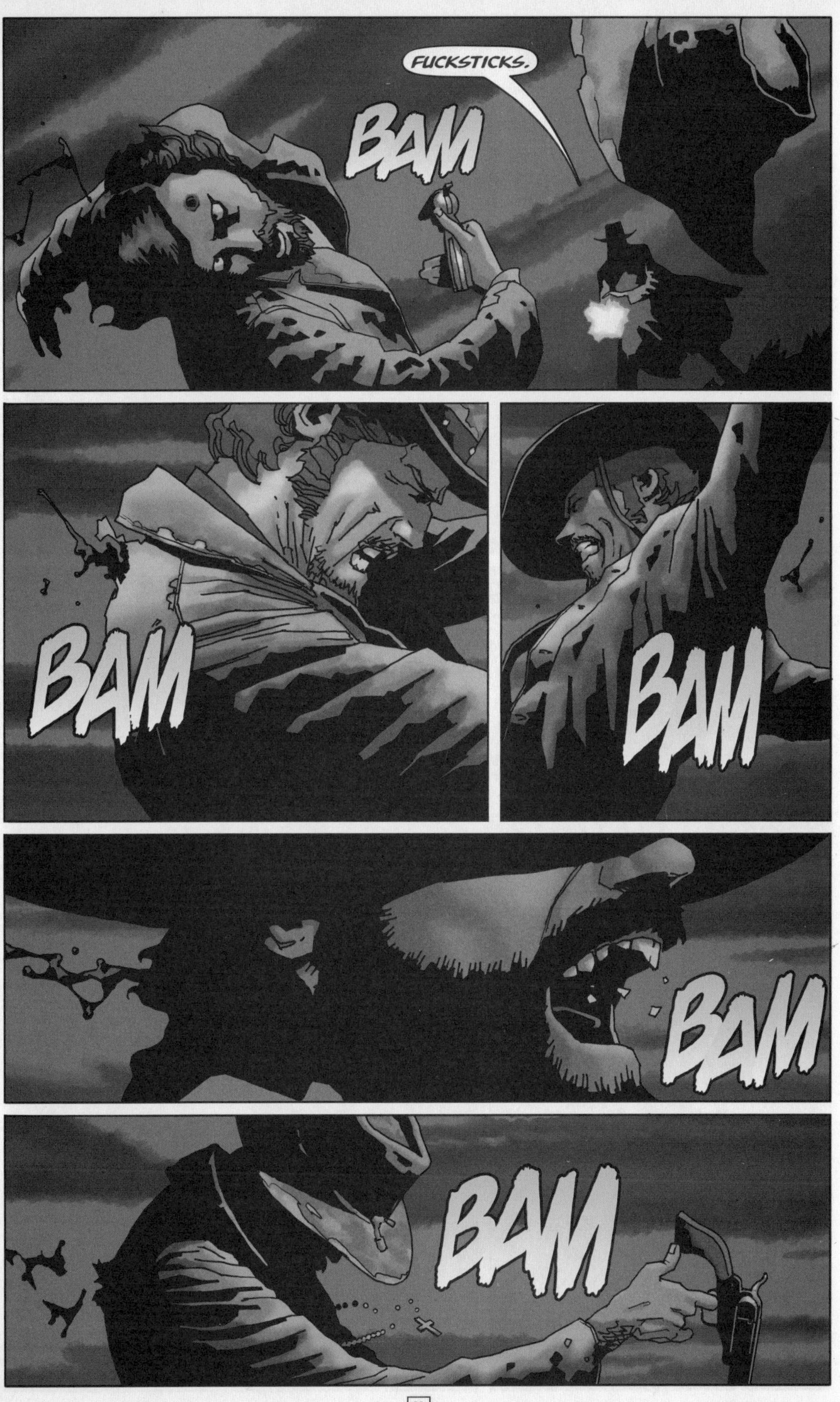
FUCKSTICKS.
BAM
BAM
BAM
BAM
BAM

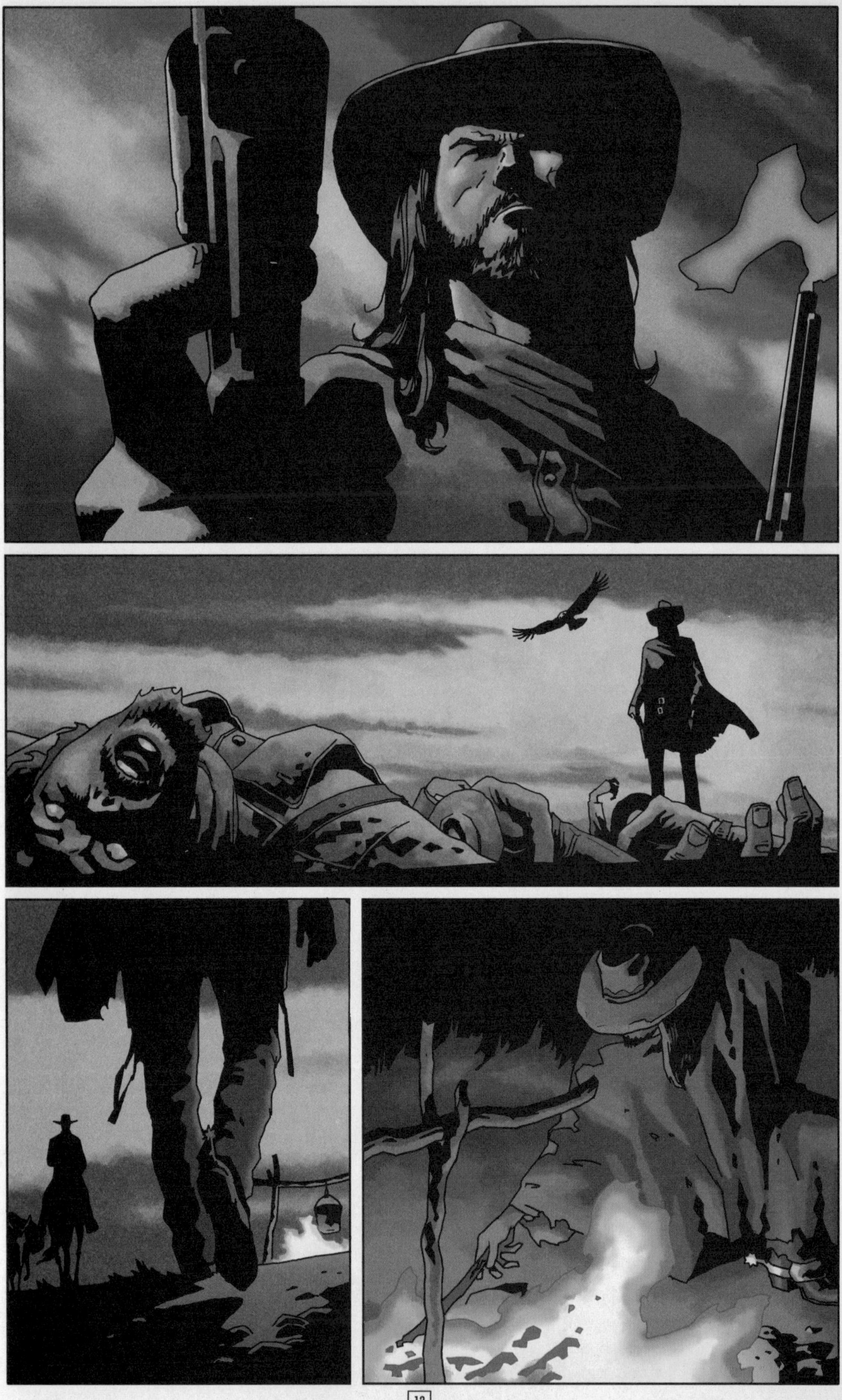

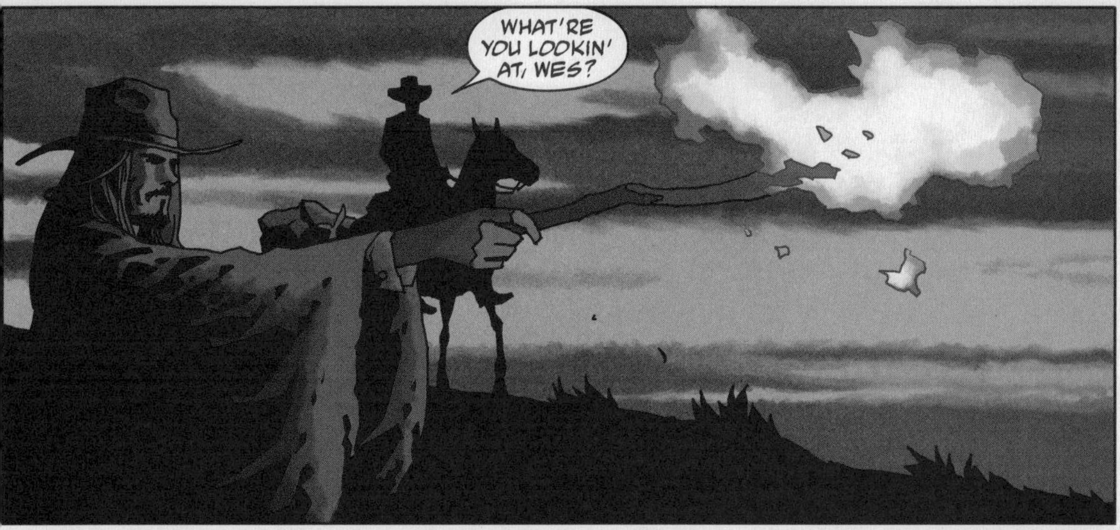
WHAT'RE YOU LOOKIN' AT, WES?

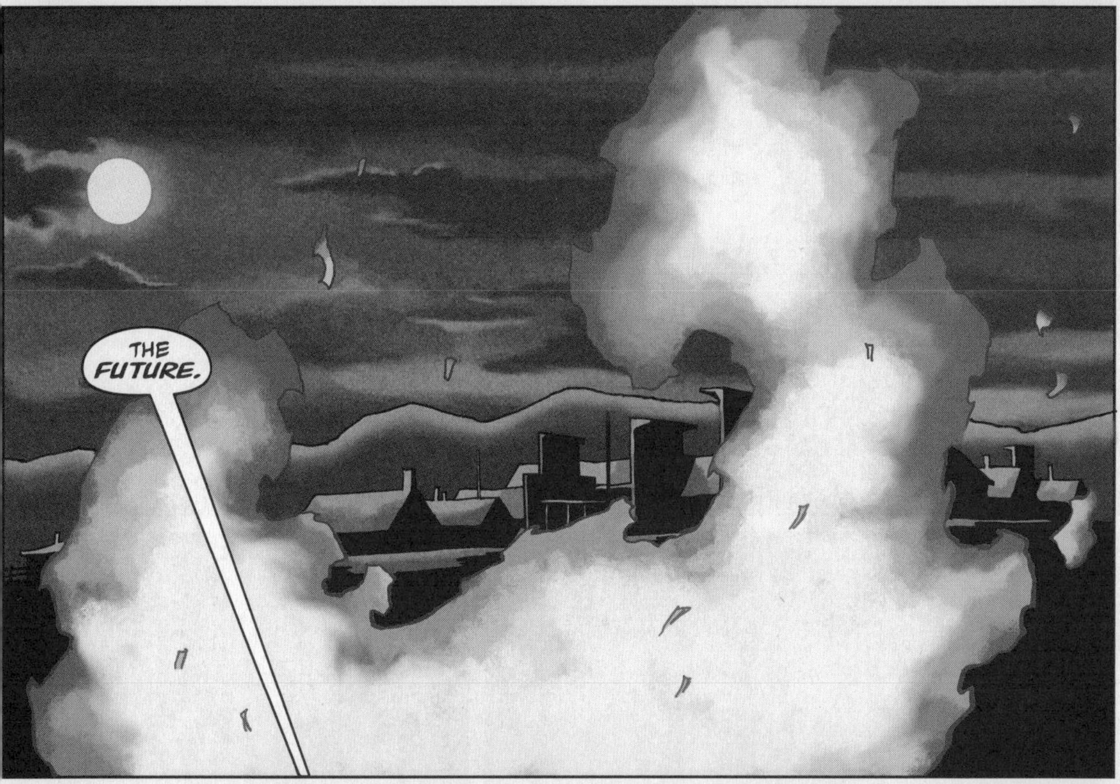
THE FUTURE.

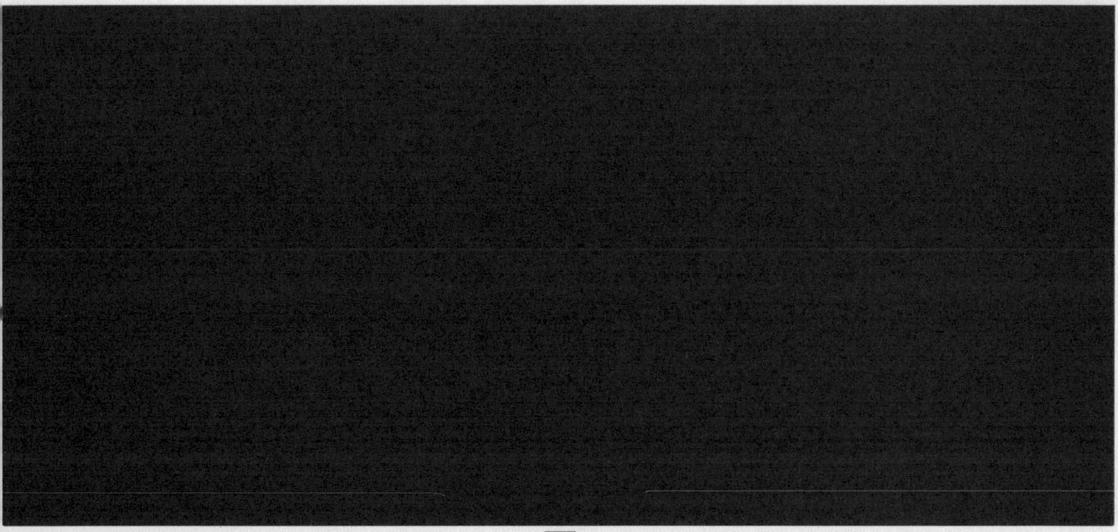

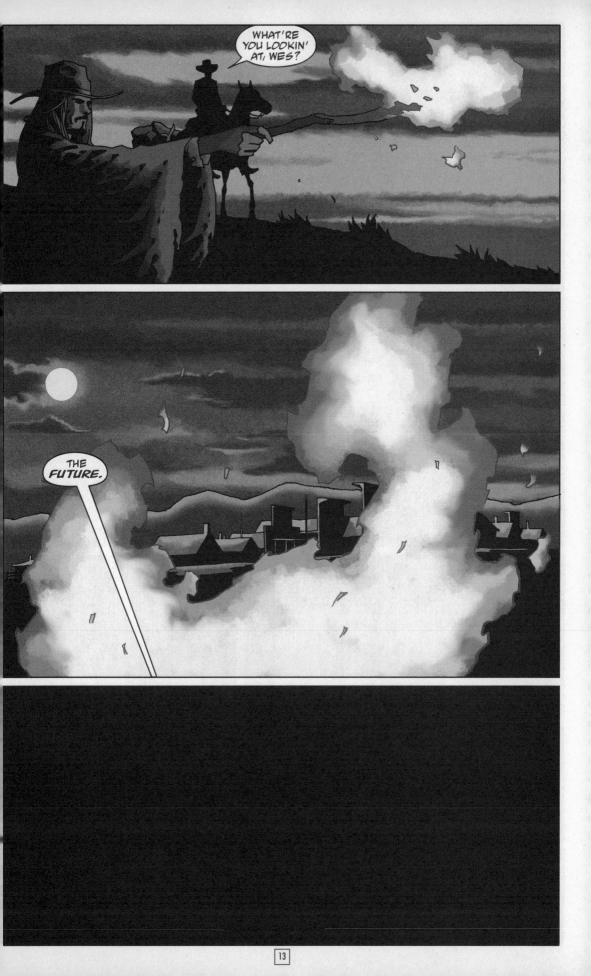

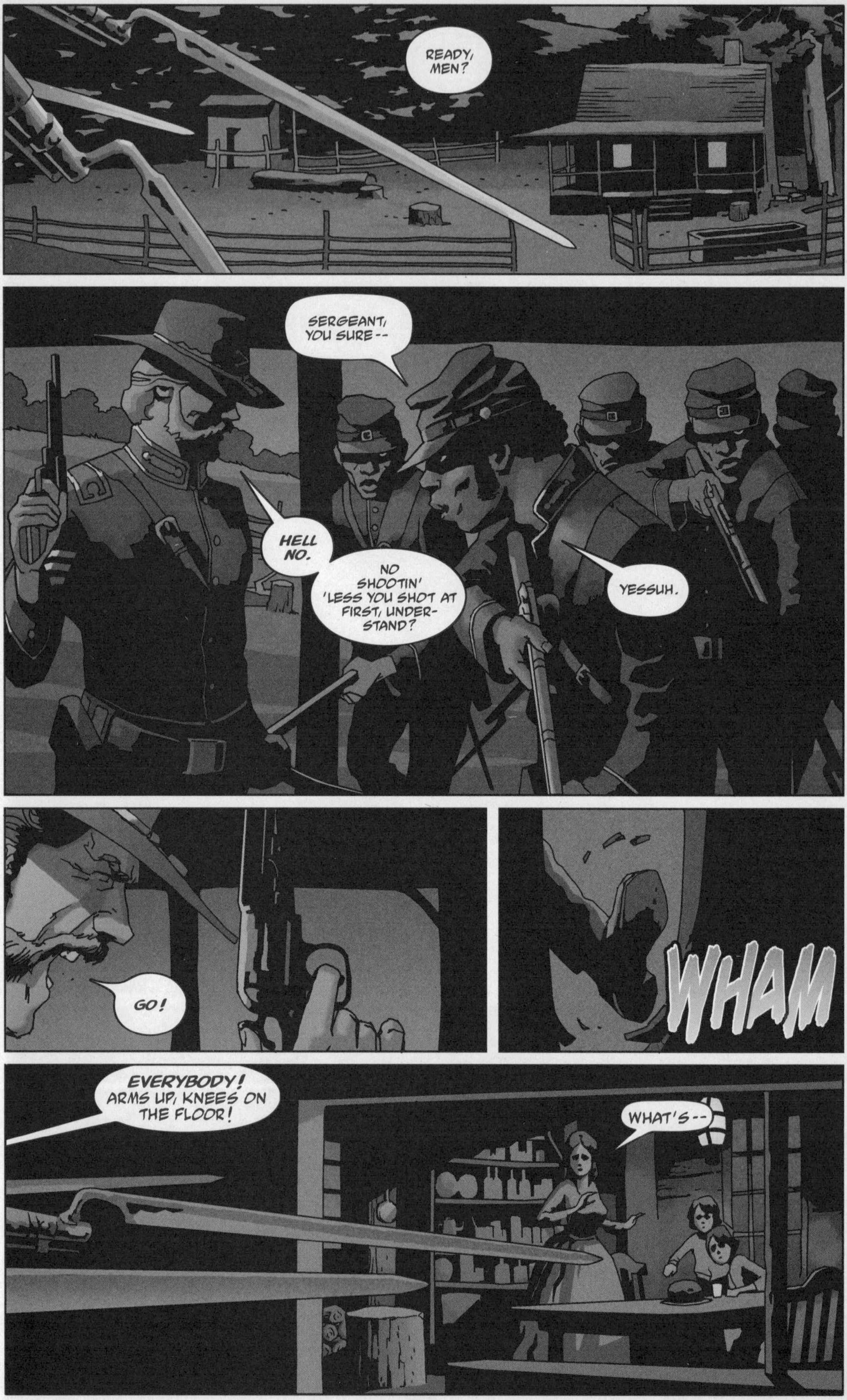
READY, MEN?
SERGEANT, YOU SURE--
HELL NO.
NO SHOOTIN' 'LESS YOU SHOT AT FIRST, UNDER-STAND?
YESSUH.
GO!
WHAM
EVERYBODY! ARMS UP, KNEES ON THE FLOOR!
WHAT'S--

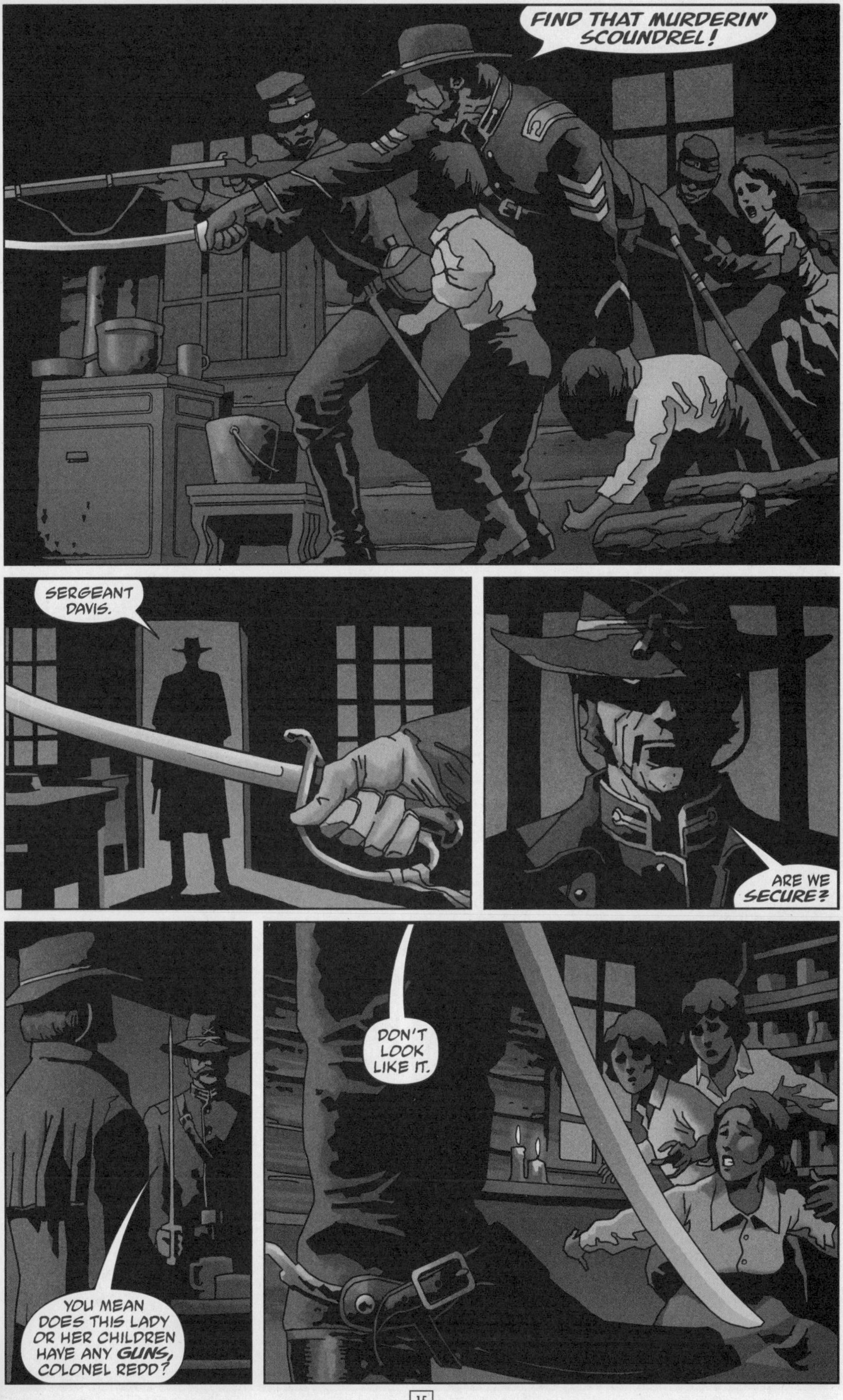
FIND THAT MURDERIN' SCOUNDREL!
SERGEANT DAVIS.
ARE WE SECURE?
YOU MEAN DOES THIS LADY OR HER CHILDREN HAVE ANY GUNS, COLONEL REDD?
DON'T LOOK LIKE IT.

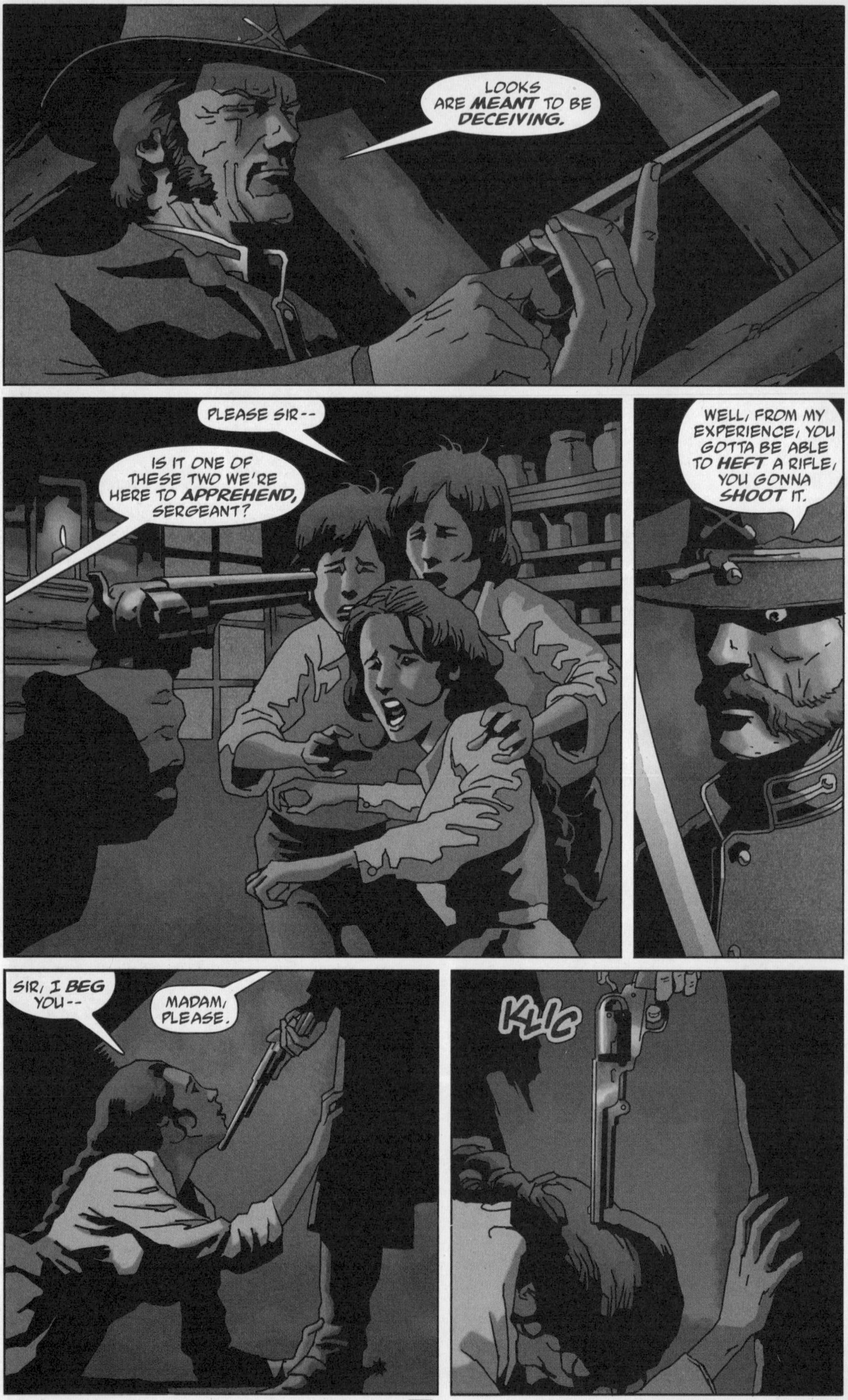
LOOKS ARE MEANT TO BE DECEIVING.
PLEASE SIR--
IS IT ONE OF THESE TWO WE'RE HERE TO APPREHEND, SERGEANT?
WELL, FROM MY EXPERIENCE, YOU GOTTA BE ABLE TO HEFT A RIFLE, YOU GONNA SHOOT IT.
SIR, I BEG YOU--
MADAM, PLEASE.
KLIC

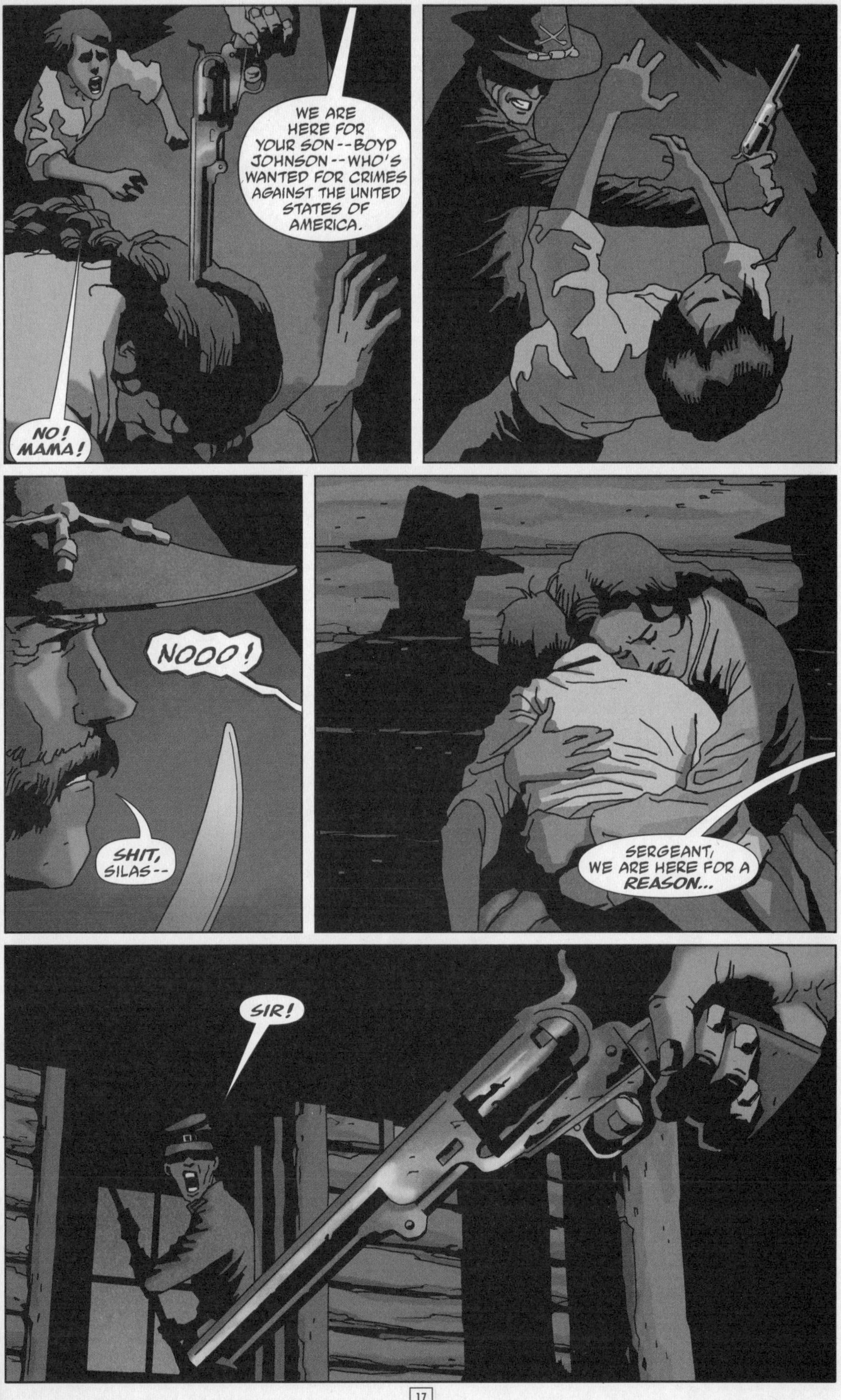
WE ARE HERE FOR YOUR SON--BOYD JOHNSON--WHO'S WANTED FOR CRIMES AGAINST THE UNITED STATES OF AMERICA.
NO! MAMA!
NOOO!
SHIT, SILAS--
SERGEANT, WE ARE HERE FOR A REASON...
SIR!

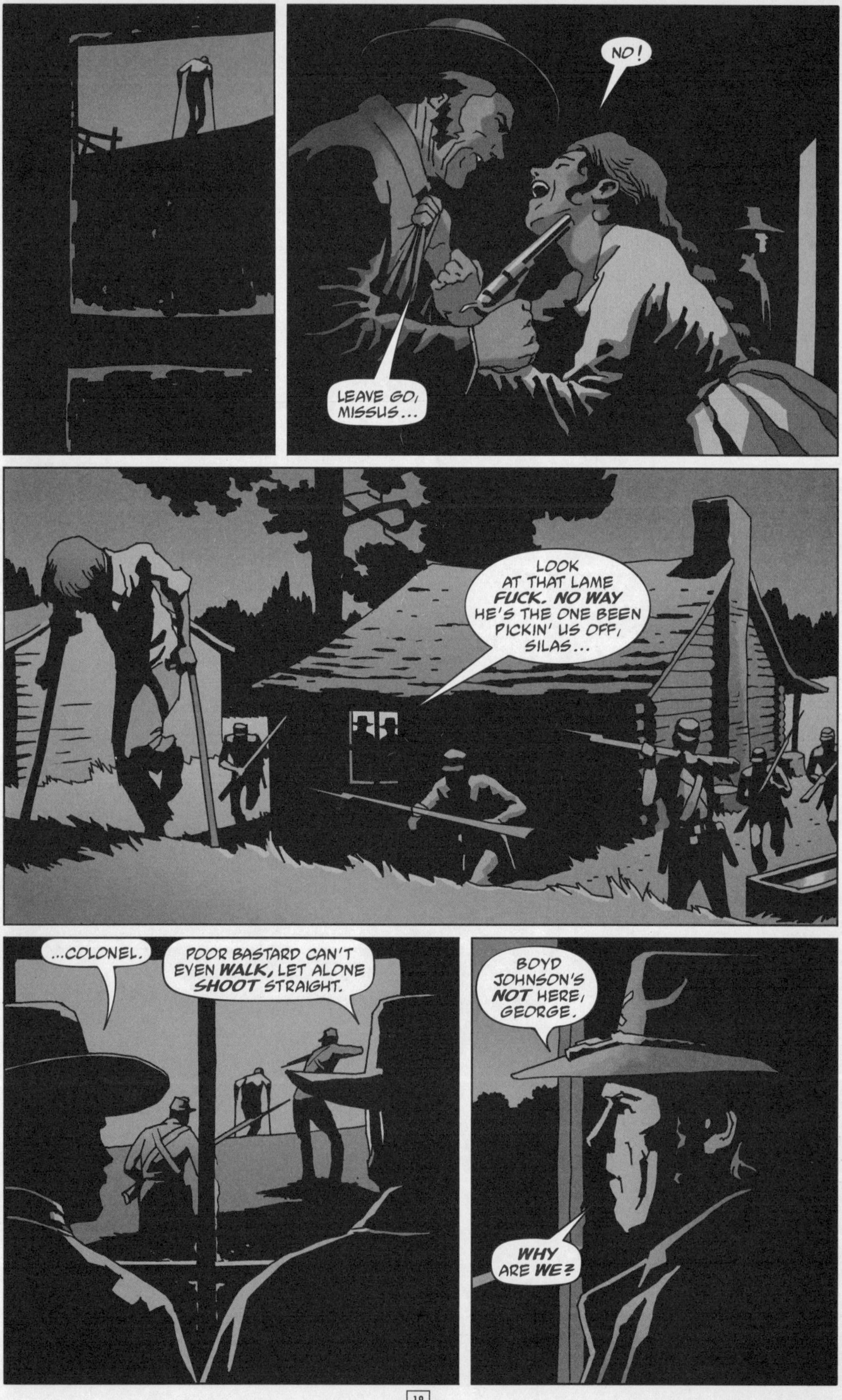
NO!
LEAVE GO, MISSUS...
LOOK AT THAT LAME FUCK. NO WAY HE'S THE ONE BEEN PICKIN' US OFF, SILAS...
...COLONEL.
POOR BASTARD CAN'T EVEN WALK, LET ALONE SHOOT STRAIGHT.
BOYD JOHNSON'S NOT HERE, GEORGE.
WHY ARE WE?

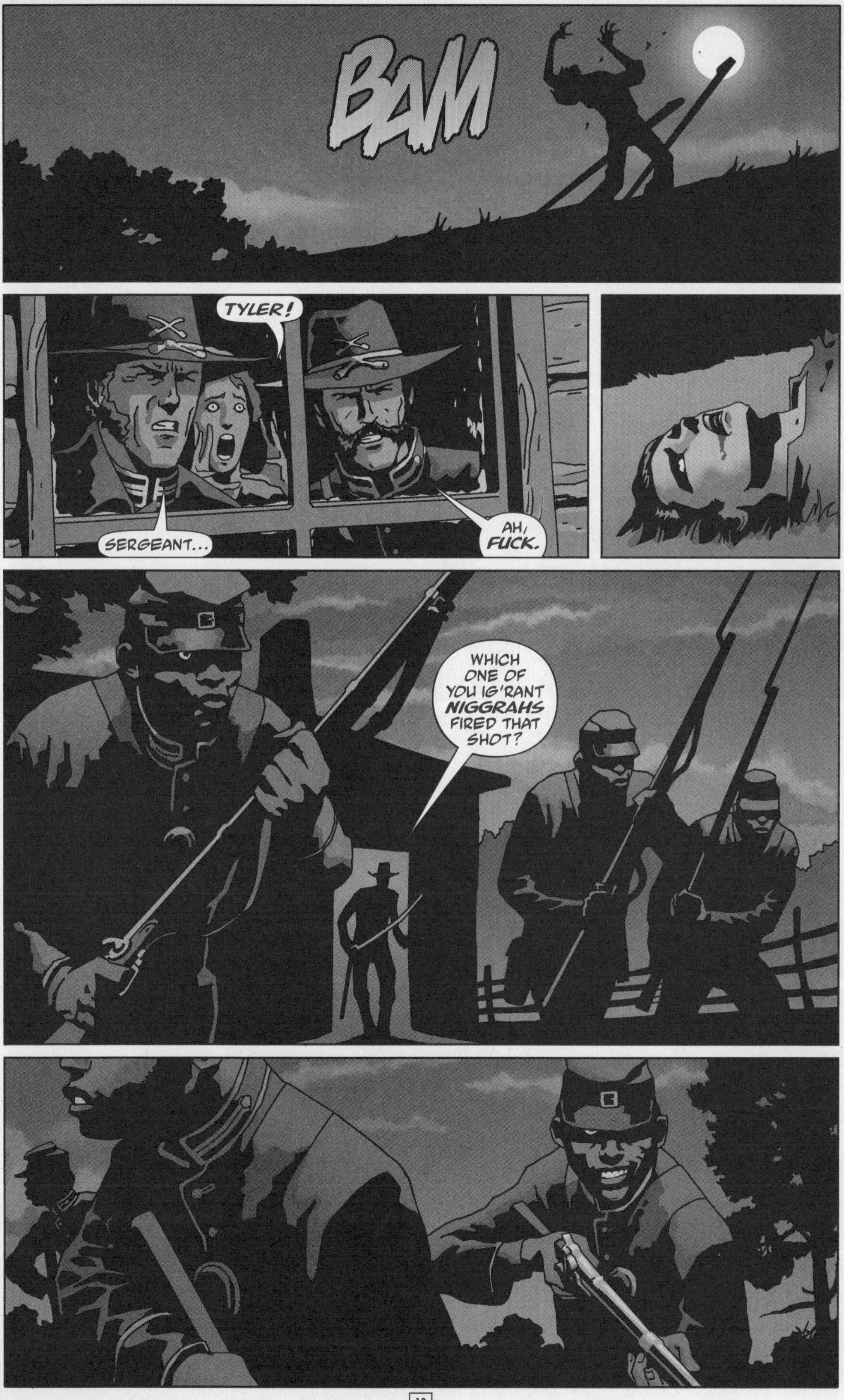
BAM
TYLER!
SERGEANT...
AH, FUCK.
WHICH ONE OF YOU IG'RANT NIGGRAHS FIRED THAT SHOT?

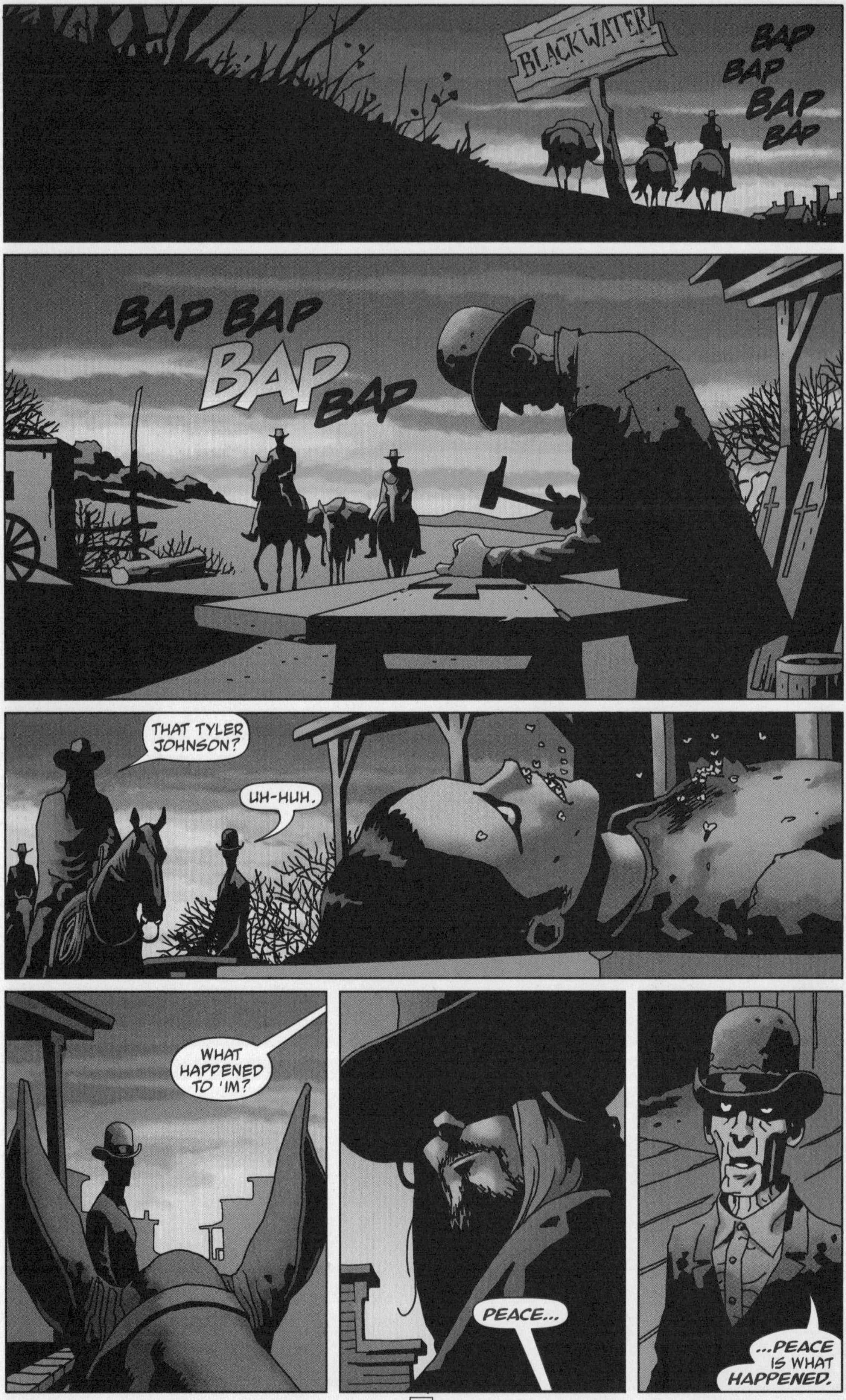
BLACKWATER
BAP
BAP
BAP
BAP
BAP BAP
BAP
BAP
THAT TYLER JOHNSON?
UH-HUH.
WHAT HAPPENED TO 'IM?
PEACE...
...PEACE IS WHAT HAPPENED.

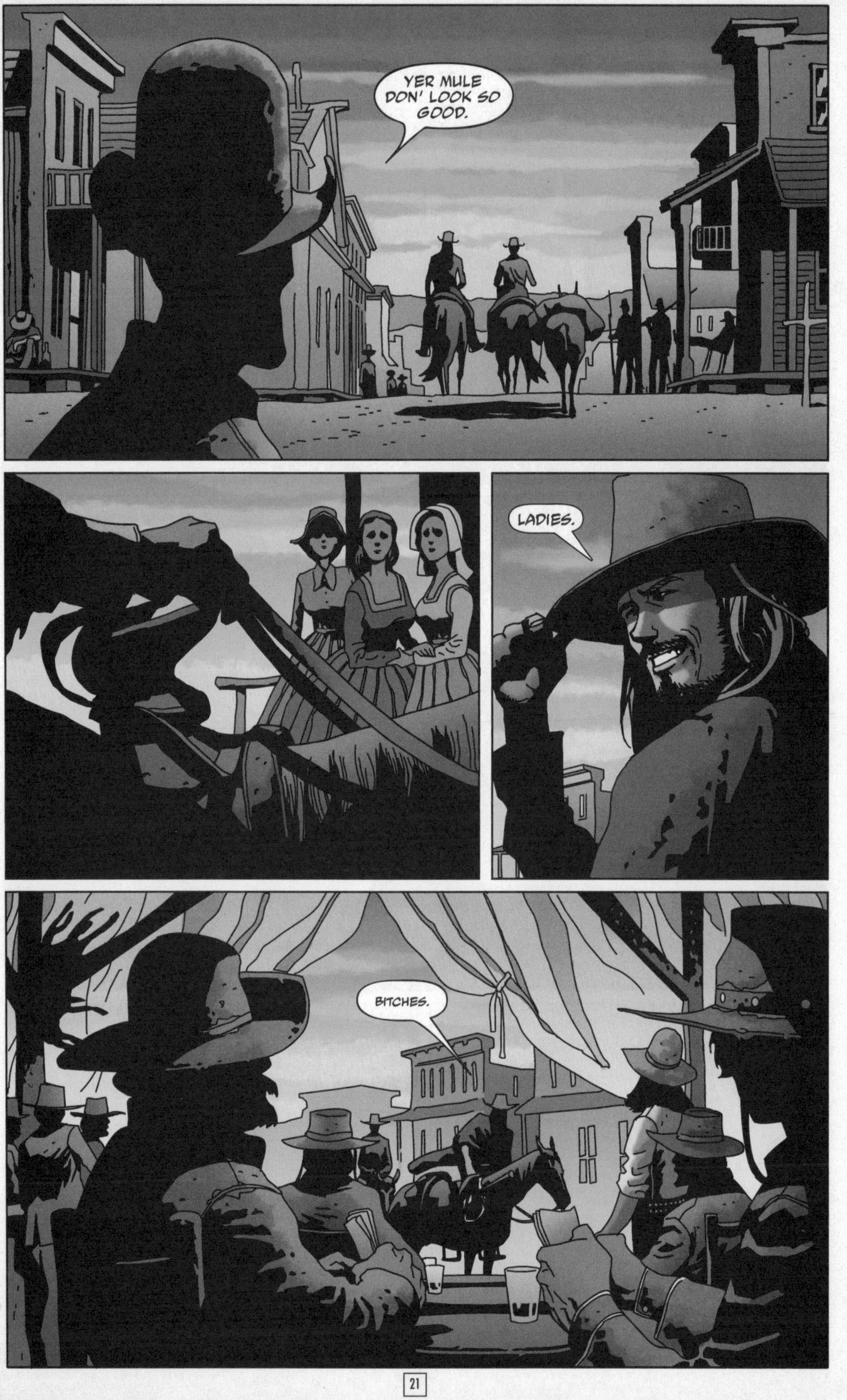
YER MULE DON' LOOK SO GOOD.
LADIES.
BITCHES.

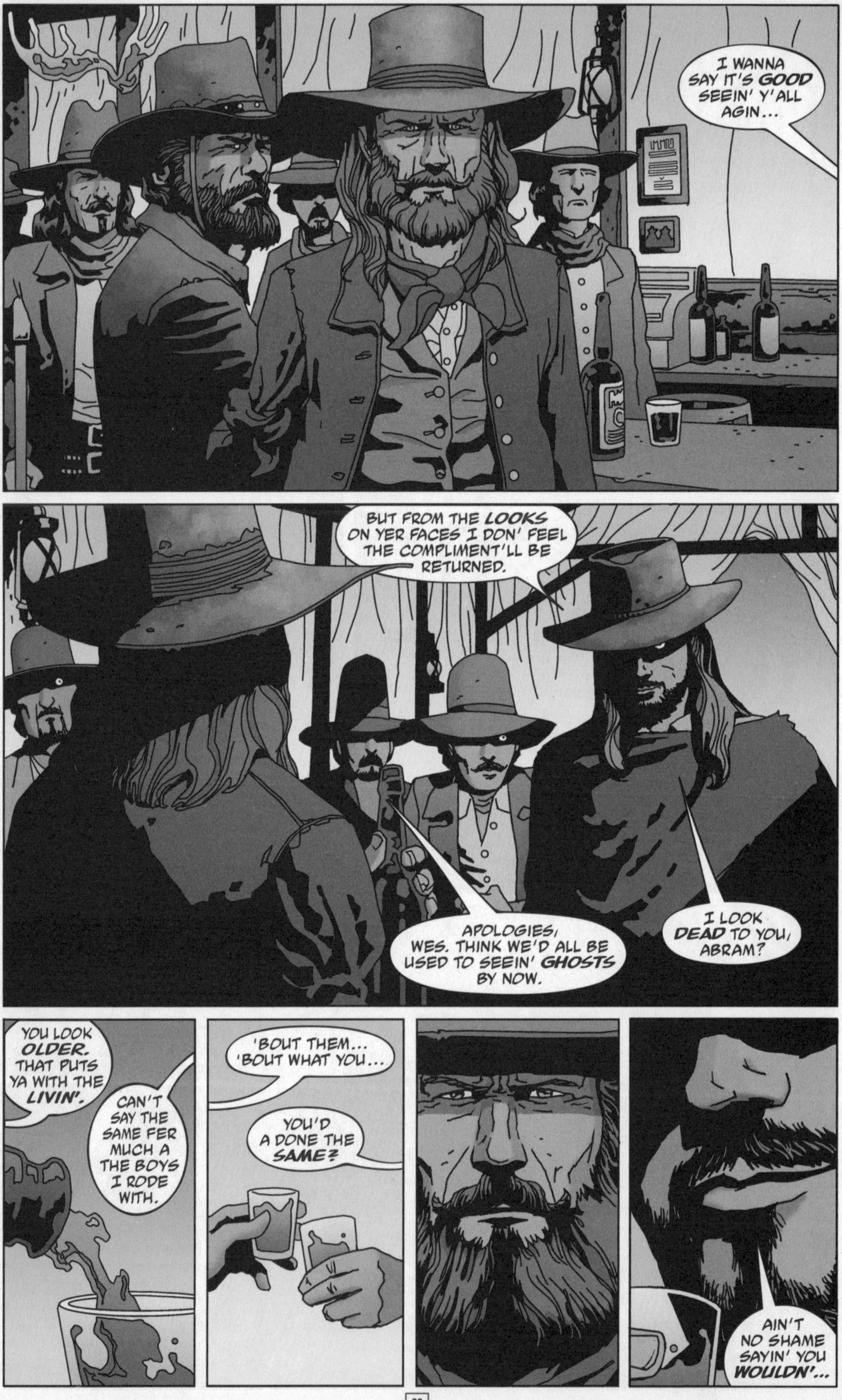
I WANNA SAY IT'S **GOOD** SEEIN' Y'ALL AGIN...
BUT FROM THE **LOOKS** ON YER FACES I DON' FEEL THE COMPLIMENT'LL BE RETURNED.
APOLOGIES, WES. THINK WE'D ALL BE USED TO SEEIN' **GHOSTS** BY NOW.
I LOOK **DEAD** TO YOU, ABRAM?
YOU LOOK **OLDER.** THAT PUTS YA WITH THE **LIVIN'.**
CAN'T SAY THE SAME FER MUCH A THE BOYS I RODE WITH.
'BOUT THEM... 'BOUT WHAT YOU...
YOU'D A DONE THE **SAME?**
AIN'T NO SHAME SAYIN' YOU **WOULDN'...**

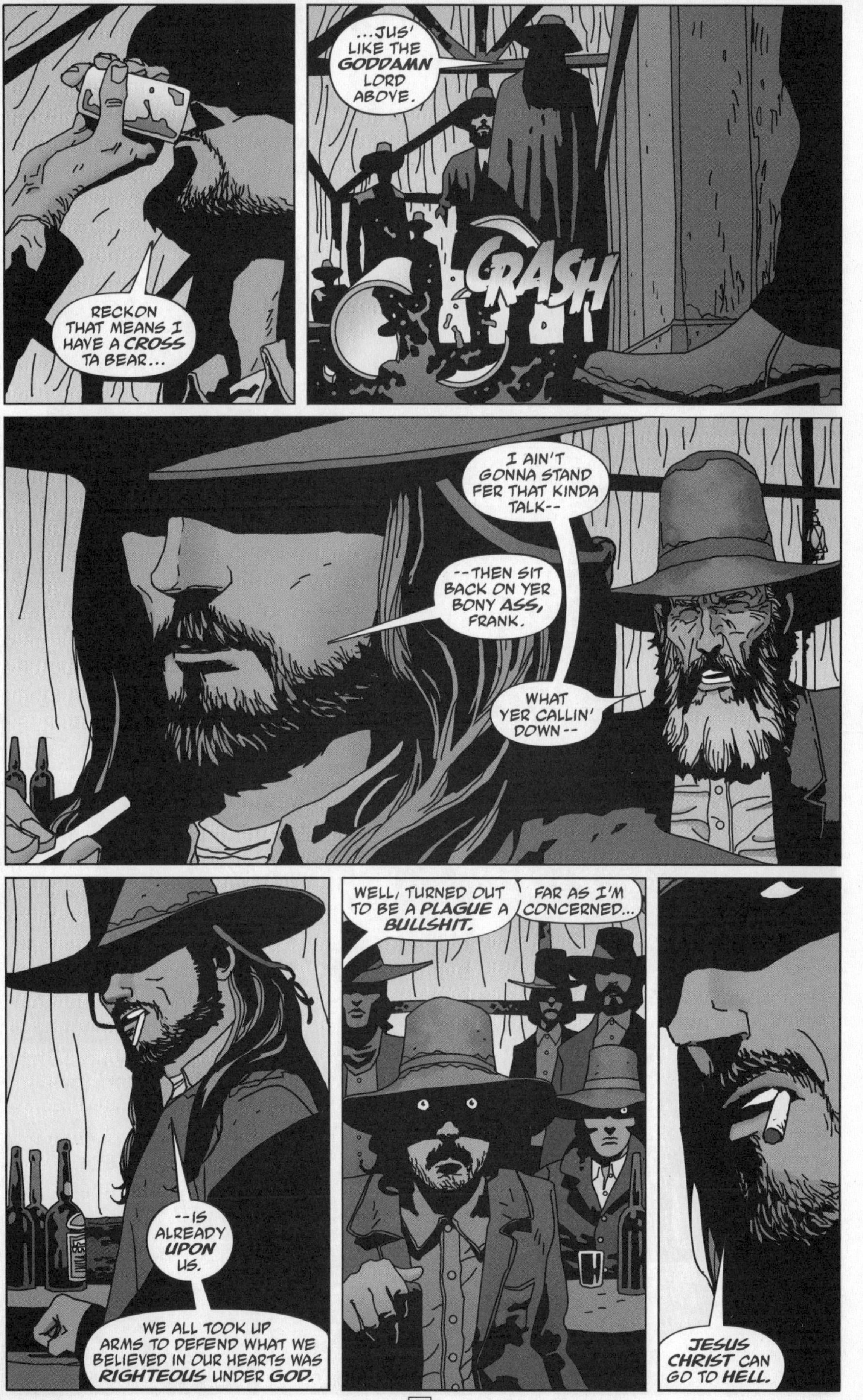
RECKON THAT MEANS I HAVE A CROSS TA BEAR...
...JUS' LIKE THE GODDAMN LORD ABOVE.
CRASH
I AIN'T GONNA STAND FER THAT KINDA TALK--
--THEN SIT BACK ON YER BONY ASS, FRANK.
WHAT YER CALLIN' DOWN--
--IS ALREADY UPON US.
WE ALL TOOK UP ARMS TO DEFEND WHAT WE BELIEVED IN OUR HEARTS WAS RIGHTEOUS UNDER GOD.
WELL, TURNED OUT TO BE A PLAGUE A BULLSHIT.
FAR AS I'M CONCERNED...
JESUS CHRIST CAN GO TO HELL.

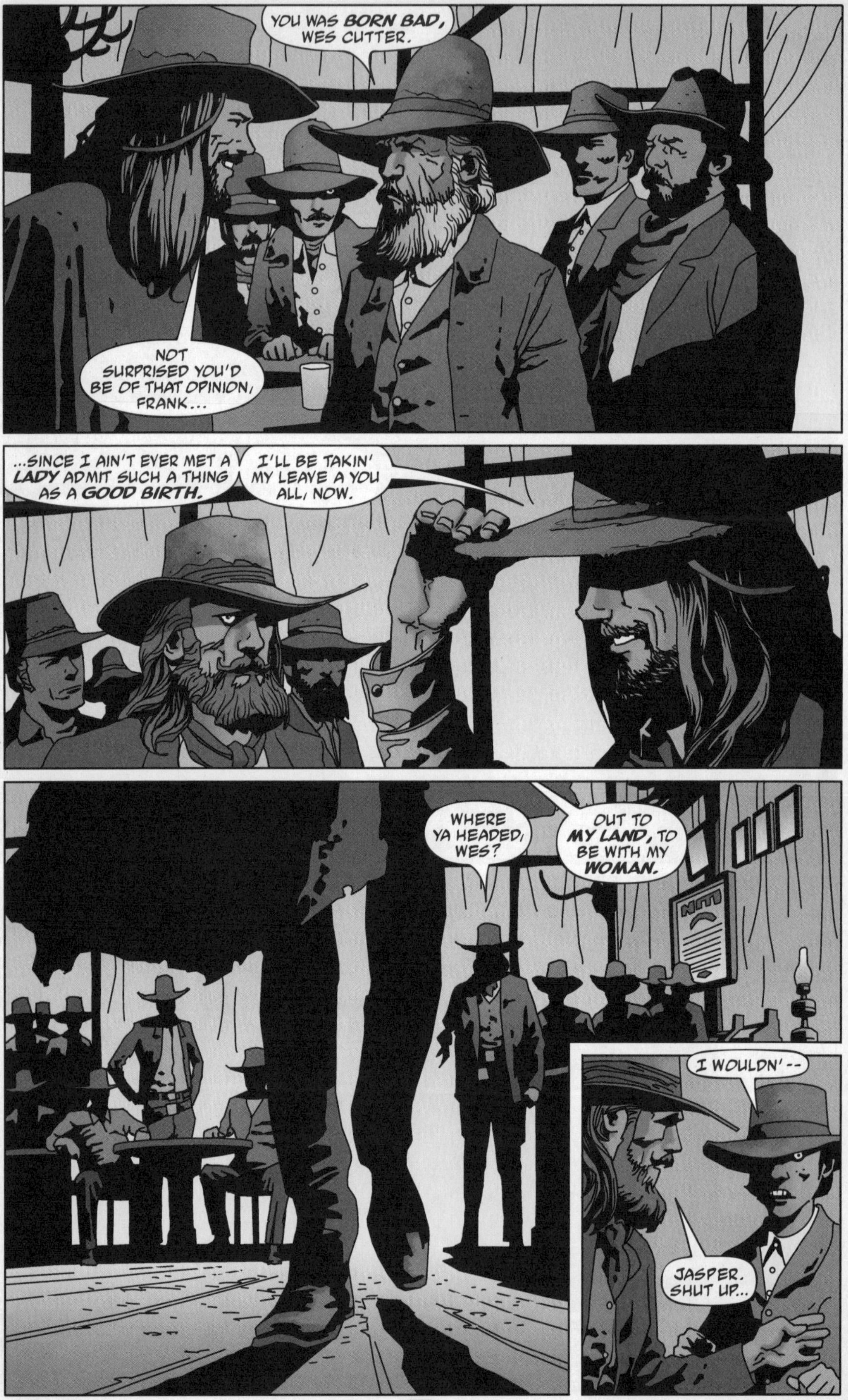
YOU WAS BORN BAD, WES CUTTER.
NOT SURPRISED YOU'D BE OF THAT OPINION, FRANK...
...SINCE I AIN'T EVER MET A LADY ADMIT SUCH A THING AS A GOOD BIRTH.
I'LL BE TAKIN' MY LEAVE A YOU ALL, NOW.
WHERE YA HEADED, WES?
OUT TO MY LAND, TO BE WITH MY WOMAN.
I WOULDN' --
JASPER. SHUT UP...

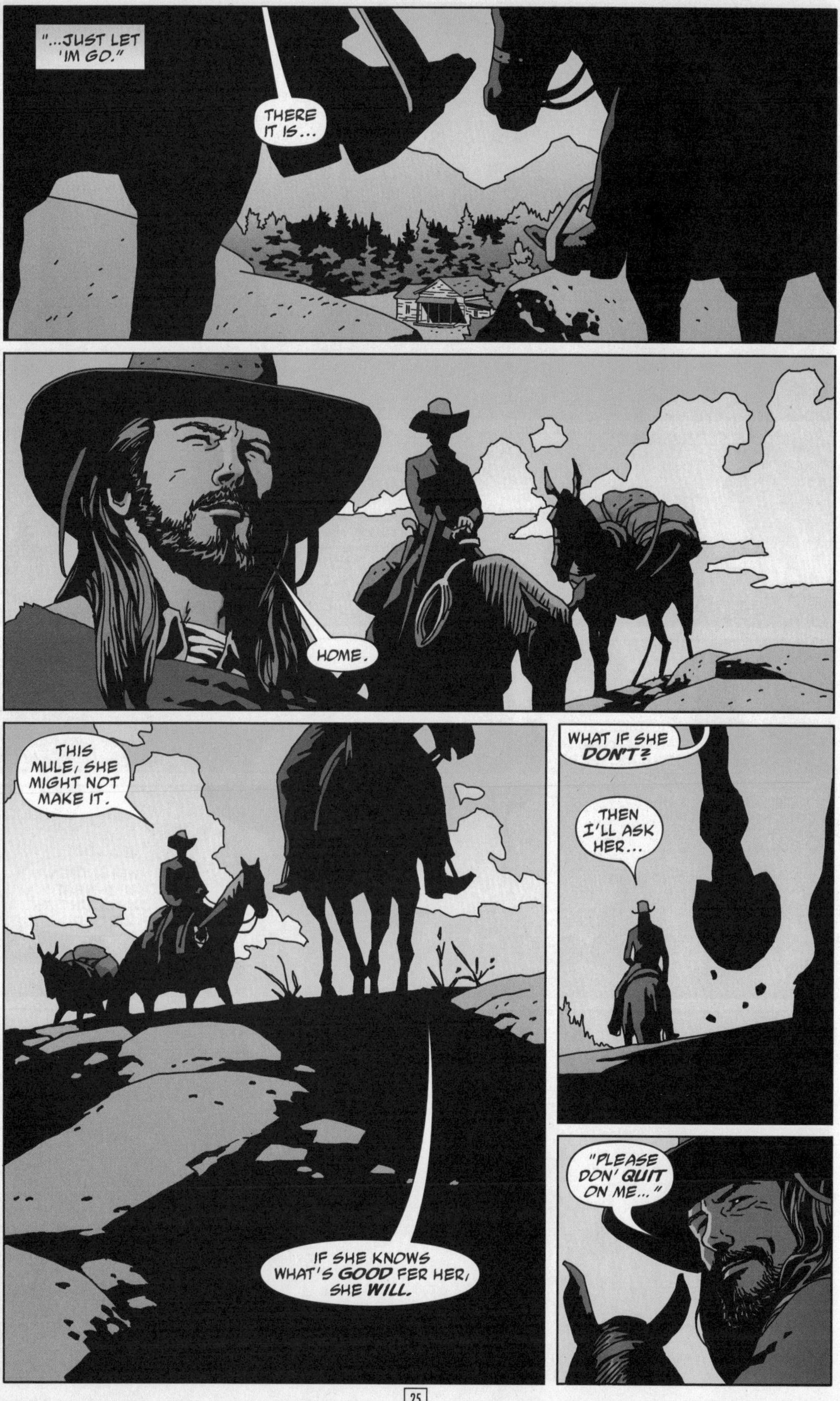
"...JUST LET 'IM GO."
THERE IT IS...
HOME.
THIS MULE, SHE MIGHT NOT MAKE IT.
IF SHE KNOWS WHAT'S **GOOD** FER HER, SHE **WILL.**
WHAT IF SHE **DON'T?**
THEN I'LL ASK HER...
"PLEASE DON' **QUIT** ON ME..."

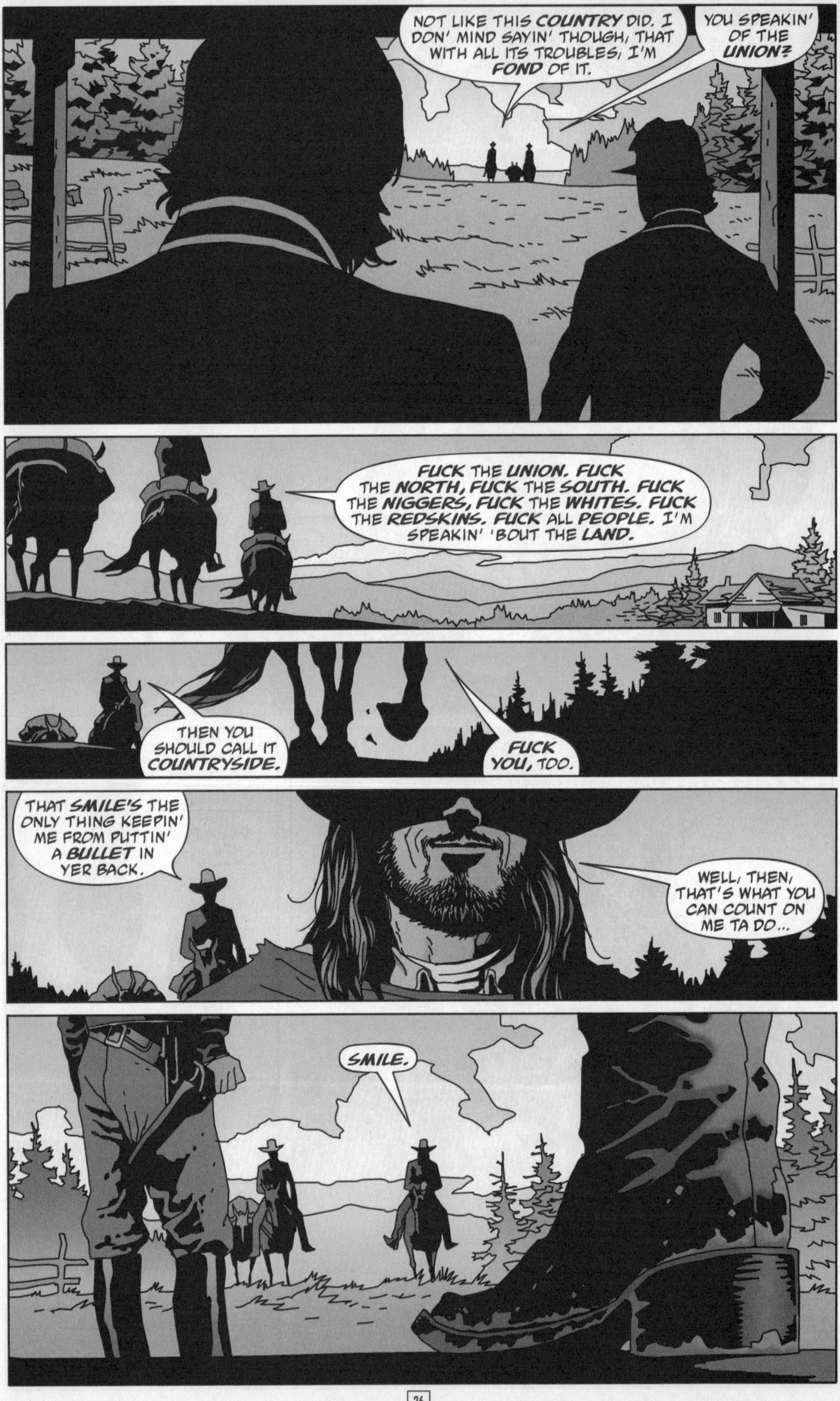
NOT LIKE THIS **COUNTRY** DID. I DON' MIND SAYIN' THOUGH, THAT WITH ALL ITS TROUBLES, I'M **FOND** OF IT.
YOU SPEAKIN' OF THE **UNION?**
FUCK THE **UNION. FUCK** THE **NORTH, FUCK** THE **SOUTH. FUCK** THE **NIGGERS, FUCK** THE **WHITES. FUCK** THE **REDSKINS. FUCK** ALL **PEOPLE.** I'M SPEAKIN' 'BOUT THE **LAND.**
THEN YOU SHOULD CALL IT **COUNTRYSIDE.**
FUCK YOU, TOO.
THAT **SMILE'S** THE ONLY THING KEEPIN' ME FROM PUTTIN' A **BULLET** IN YER BACK.
WELL, THEN, THAT'S WHAT YOU CAN COUNT ON ME TA DO...
SMILE.

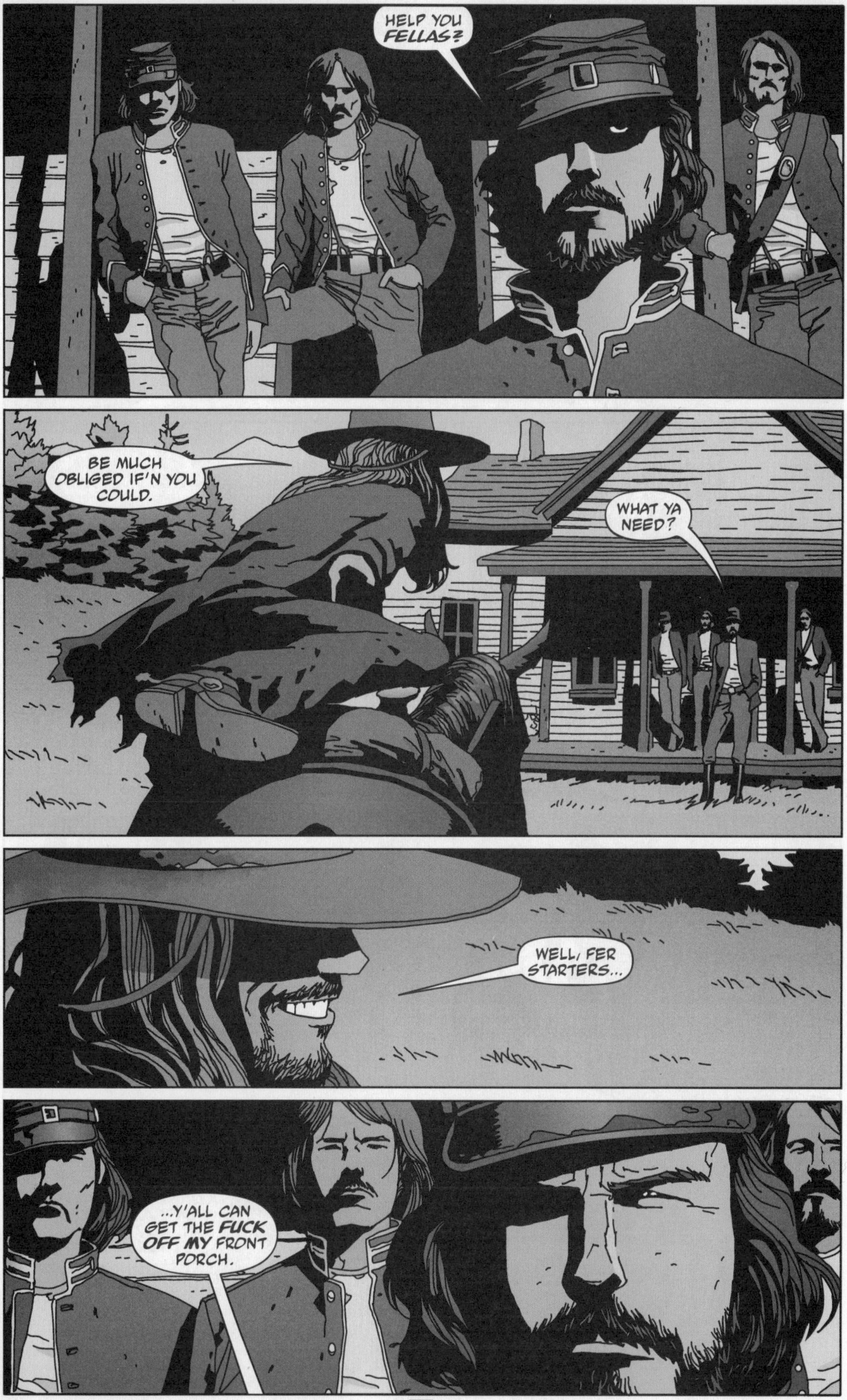
HELP YOU FELLAS?
BE MUCH OBLIGED IF'N YOU COULD.
WHAT YA NEED?
WELL, FER STARTERS...
...Y'ALL CAN GET THE FUCK OFF MY FRONT PORCH.

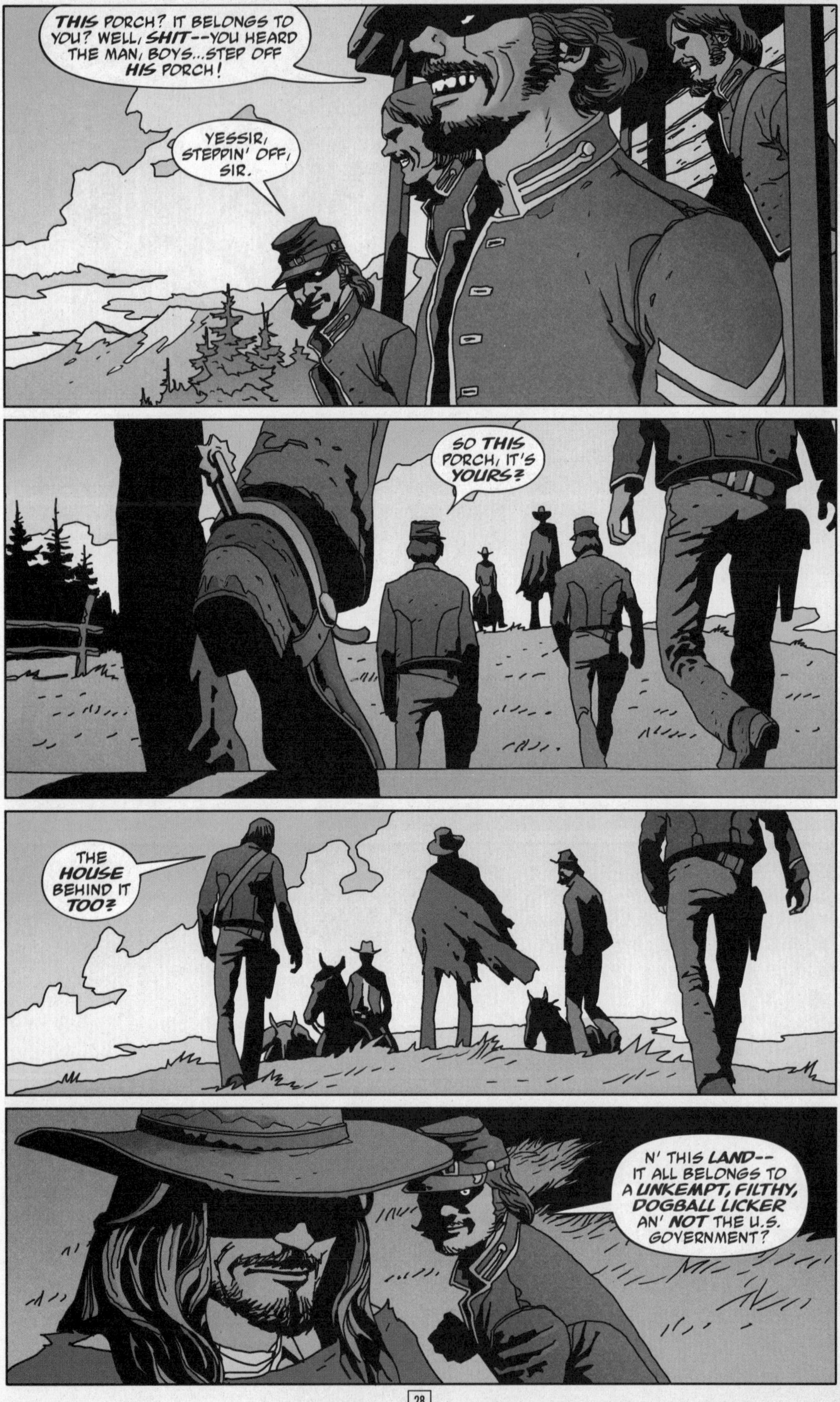
THIS PORCH? IT BELONGS TO YOU? WELL, SHIT--YOU HEARD THE MAN, BOYS...STEP OFF HIS PORCH!
YESSIR, STEPPIN' OFF, SIR.
SO THIS PORCH, IT'S YOURS?
THE HOUSE BEHIND IT TOO?
N' THIS LAND-- IT ALL BELONGS TO A UNKEMPT, FILTHY, DOGBALL LICKER AN' NOT THE U.S. GOVERNMENT?

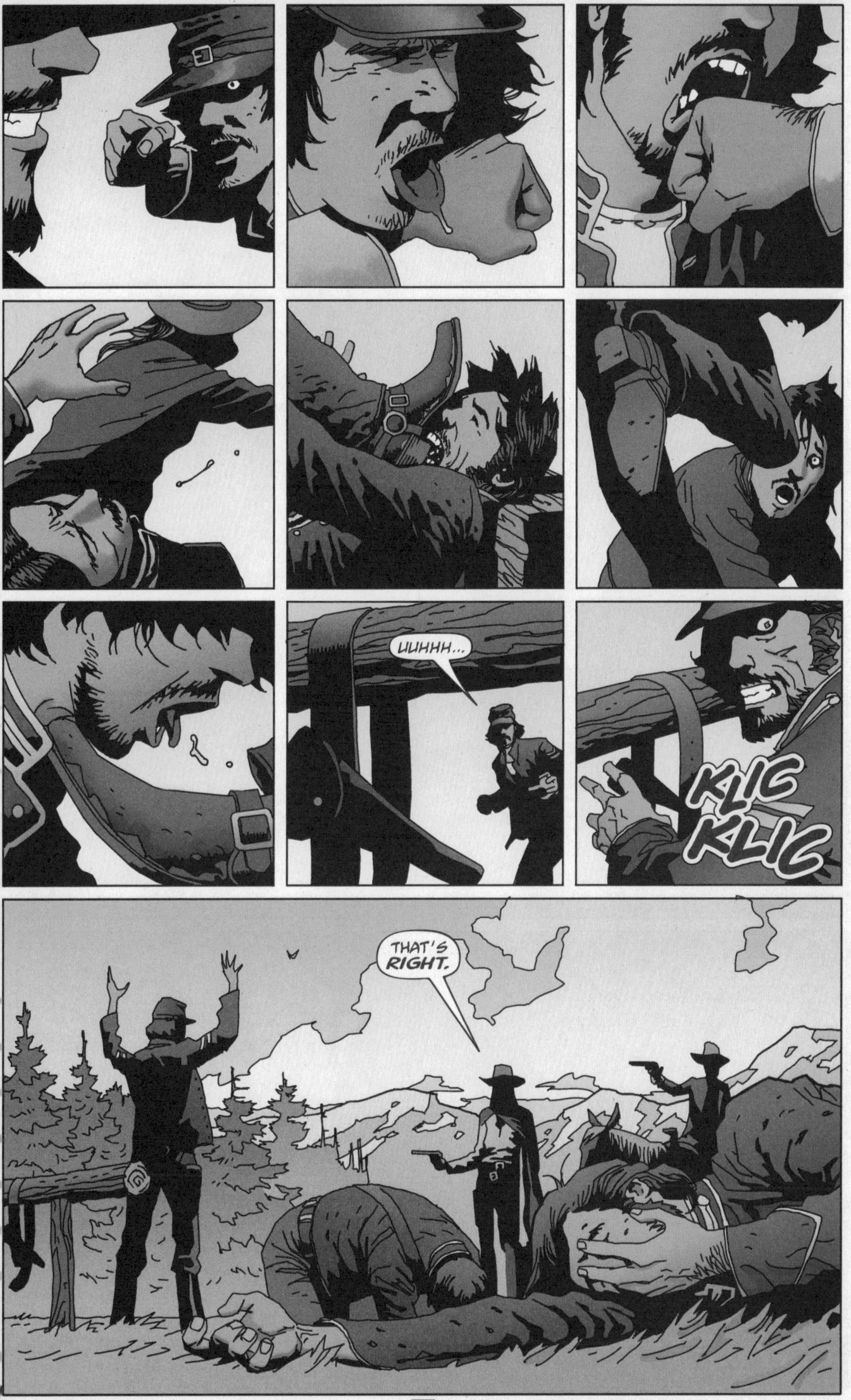
UUHHH...
KLIC
KLIC
THAT'S RIGHT.

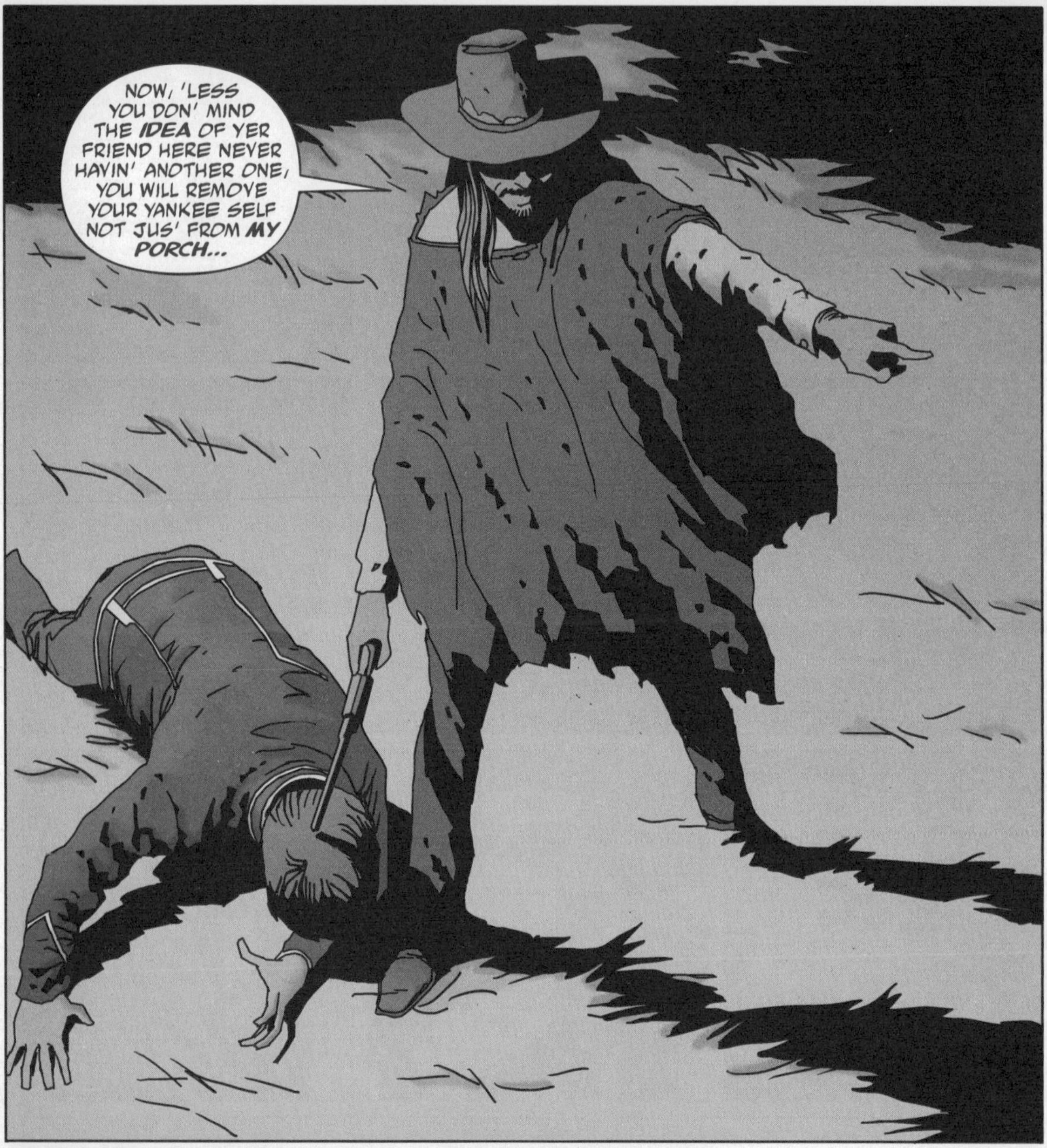
NOW, 'LESS YOU DON' MIND THE IDEA OF YER FRIEND HERE NEVER HAVIN' ANOTHER ONE, YOU WILL REMOVE YOUR YANKEE SELF NOT JUS' FROM MY PORCH...

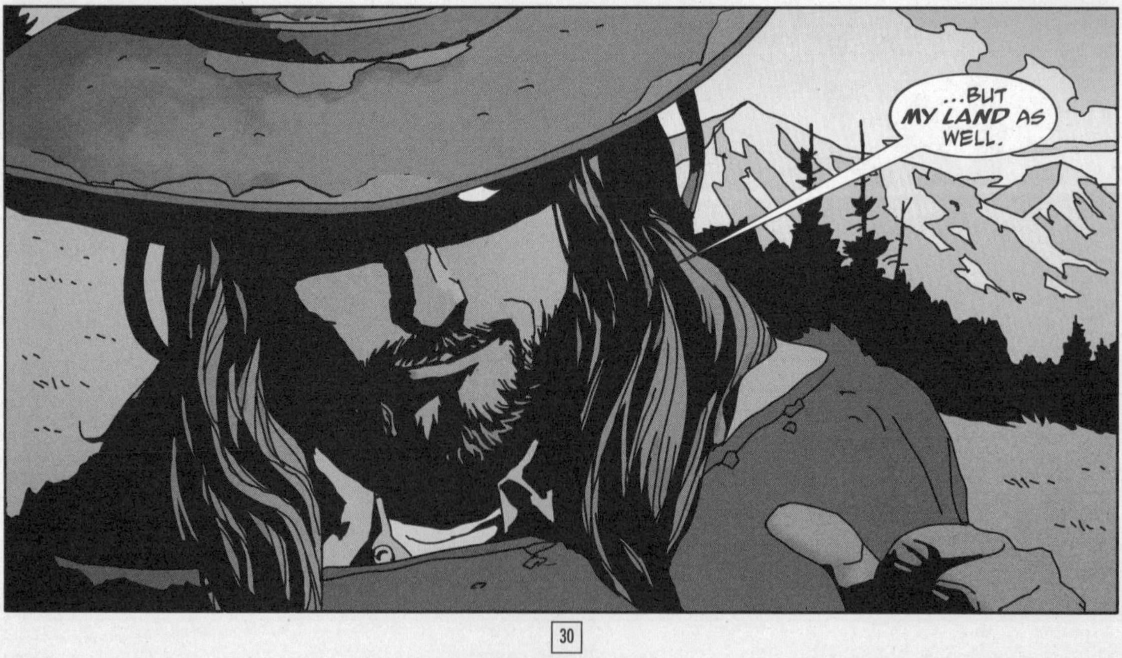
...BUT MY LAND AS WELL.

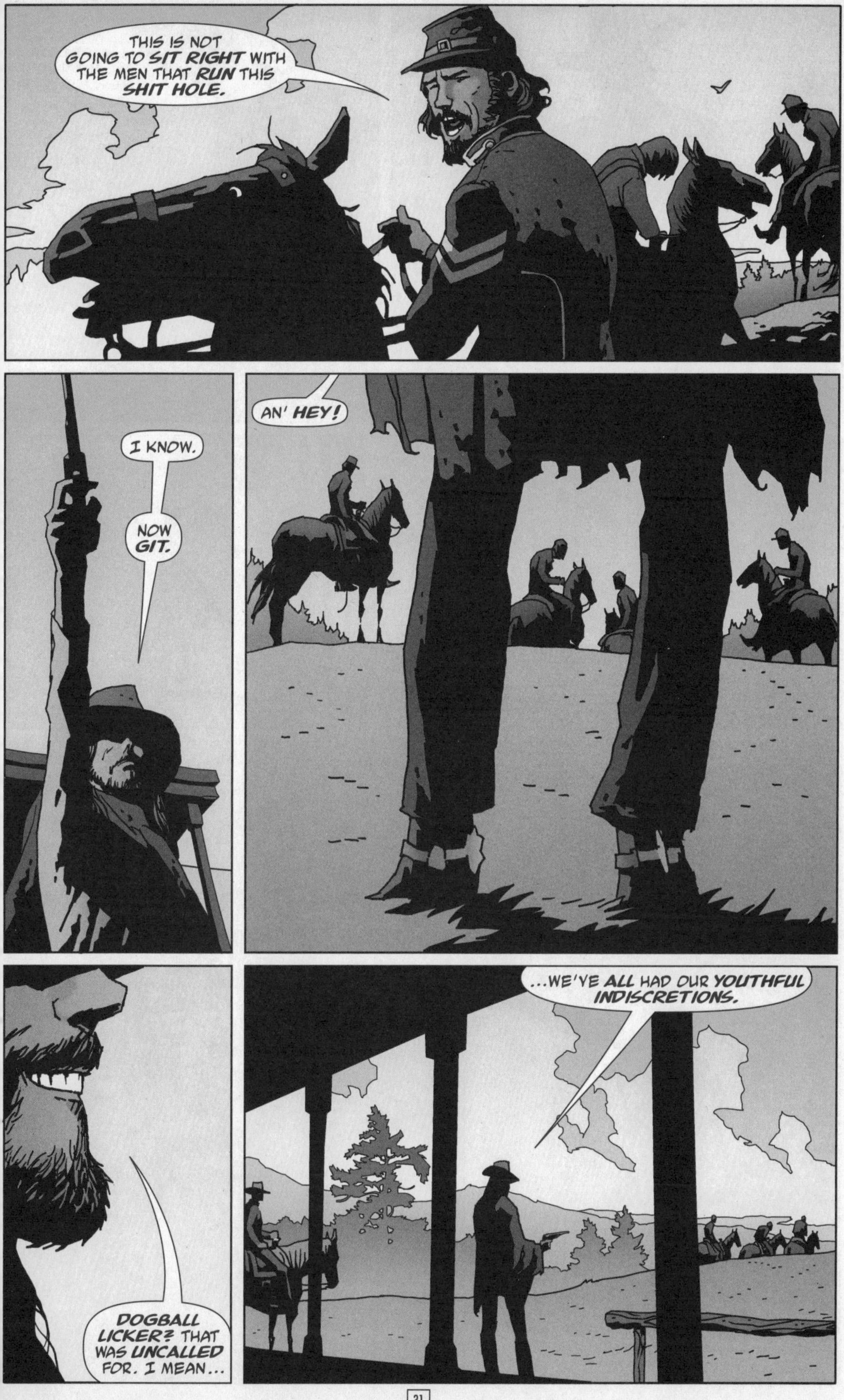
THIS IS NOT GOING TO SIT RIGHT WITH THE MEN THAT RUN THIS SHIT HOLE.
I KNOW.
NOW GIT.
AN' HEY!
DOGBALL LICKER? THAT WAS UNCALLED FOR. I MEAN...
...WE'VE ALL HAD OUR YOUTHFUL INDISCRETIONS.

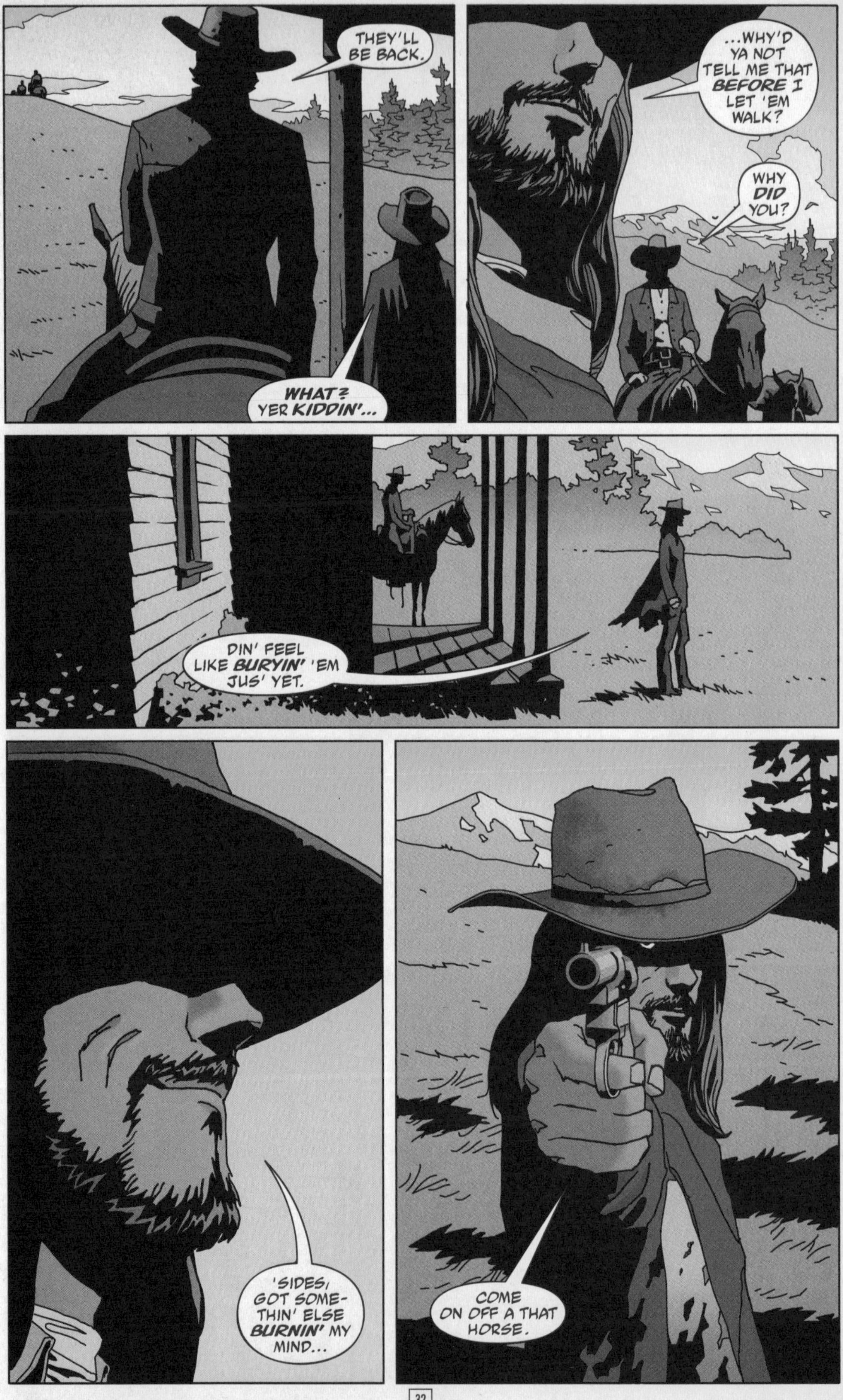
THEY'LL BE BACK.
WHAT? YER KIDDIN'...
...WHY'D YA NOT TELL ME THAT BEFORE I LET 'EM WALK?
WHY DID YOU?
DIN' FEEL LIKE BURYIN' 'EM JUS' YET.
'SIDES, GOT SOMETHIN' ELSE BURNIN' MY MIND...
COME ON OFF A THAT HORSE.

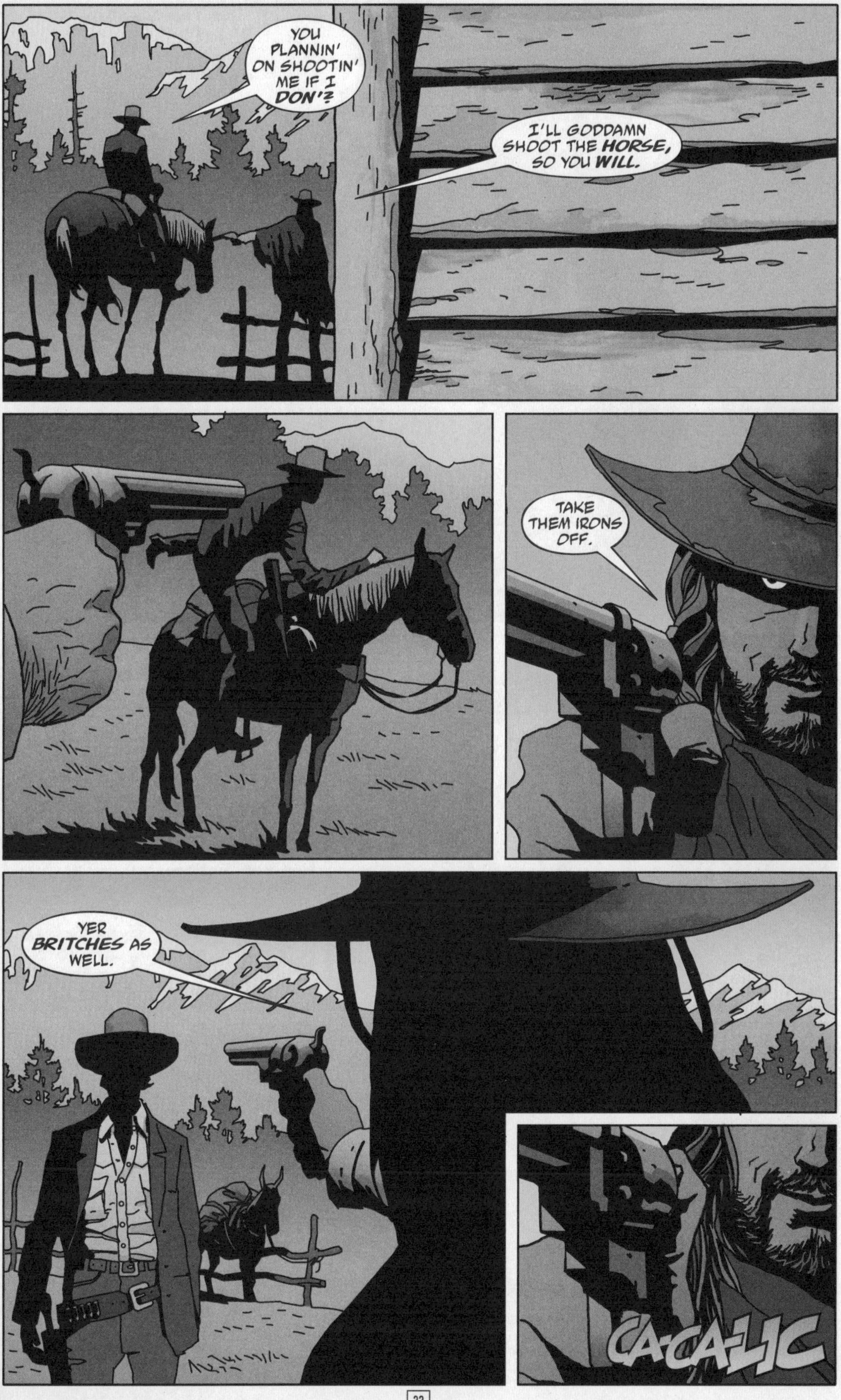
YOU PLANNIN' ON SHOOTIN' ME IF I DON'T?
I'LL GODDAMN SHOOT THE HORSE, SO YOU WILL.
TAKE THEM IRONS OFF.
YER BRITCHES AS WELL.
CA-CA-LIC

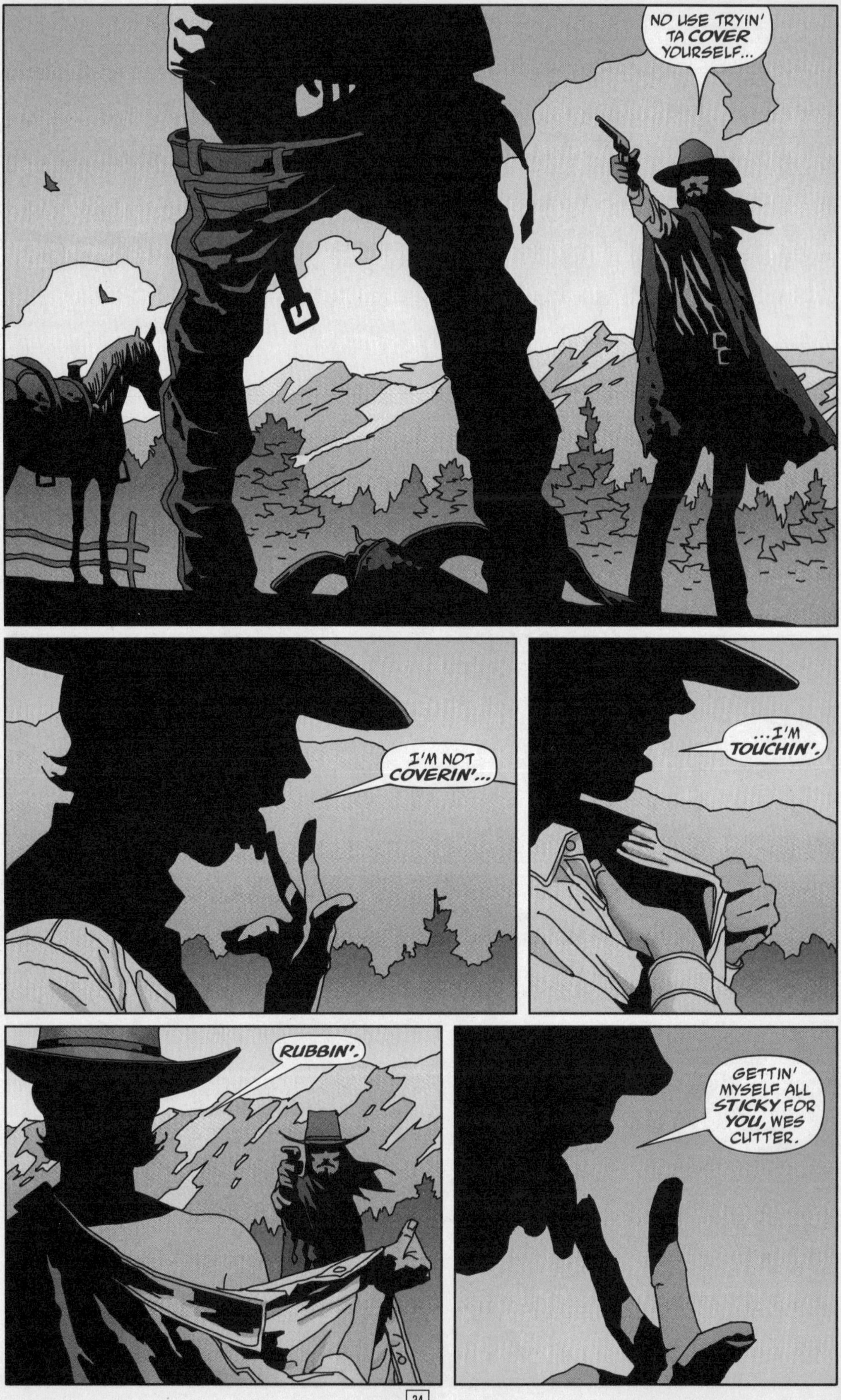
NO USE TRYIN' TA COVER YOURSELF...
I'M NOT COVERIN'...
...I'M TOUCHIN'.
RUBBIN'.
GETTIN' MYSELF ALL STICKY FOR YOU, WES CUTTER.

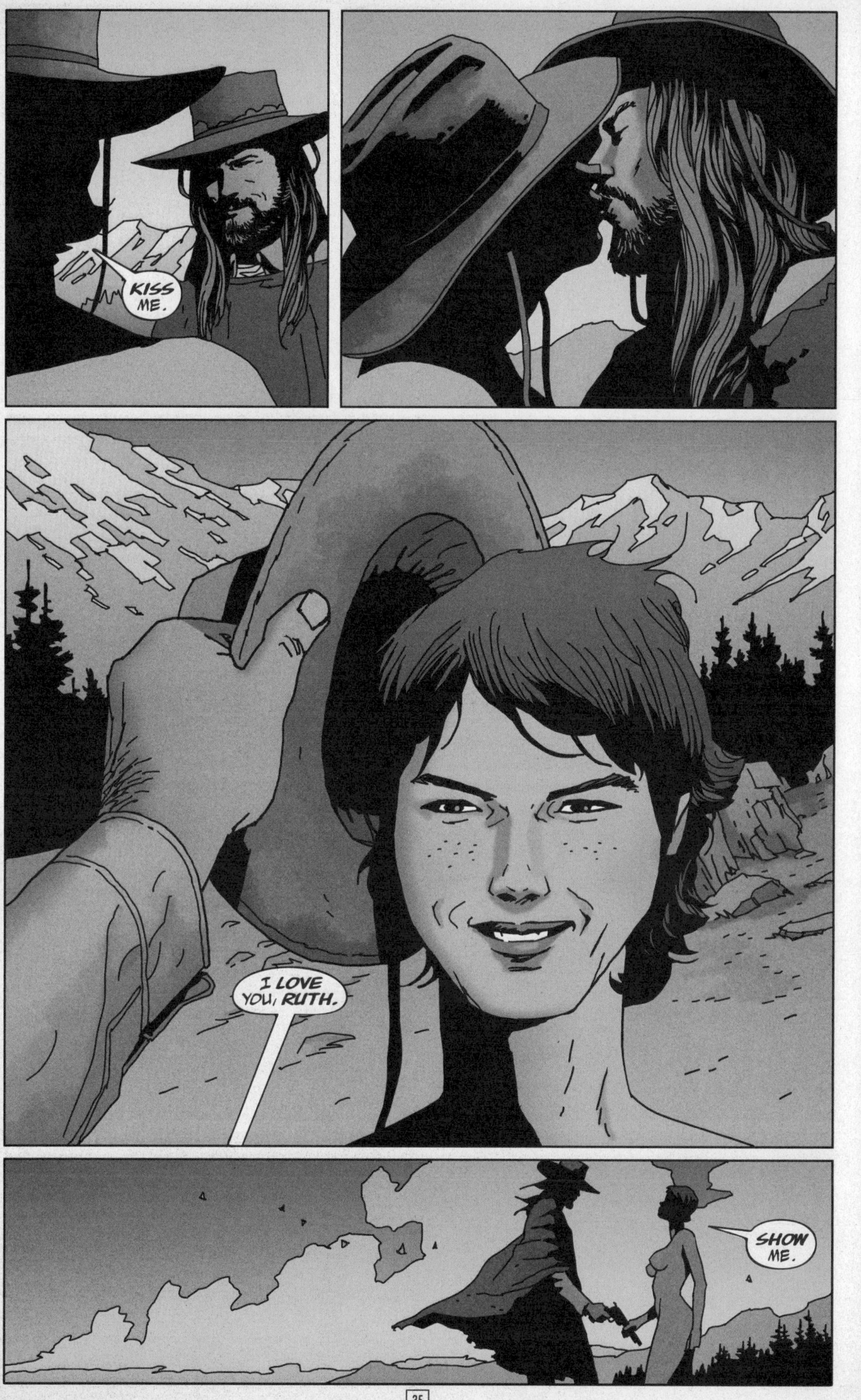
KISS ME.
I LOVE YOU, RUTH.
SHOW ME.

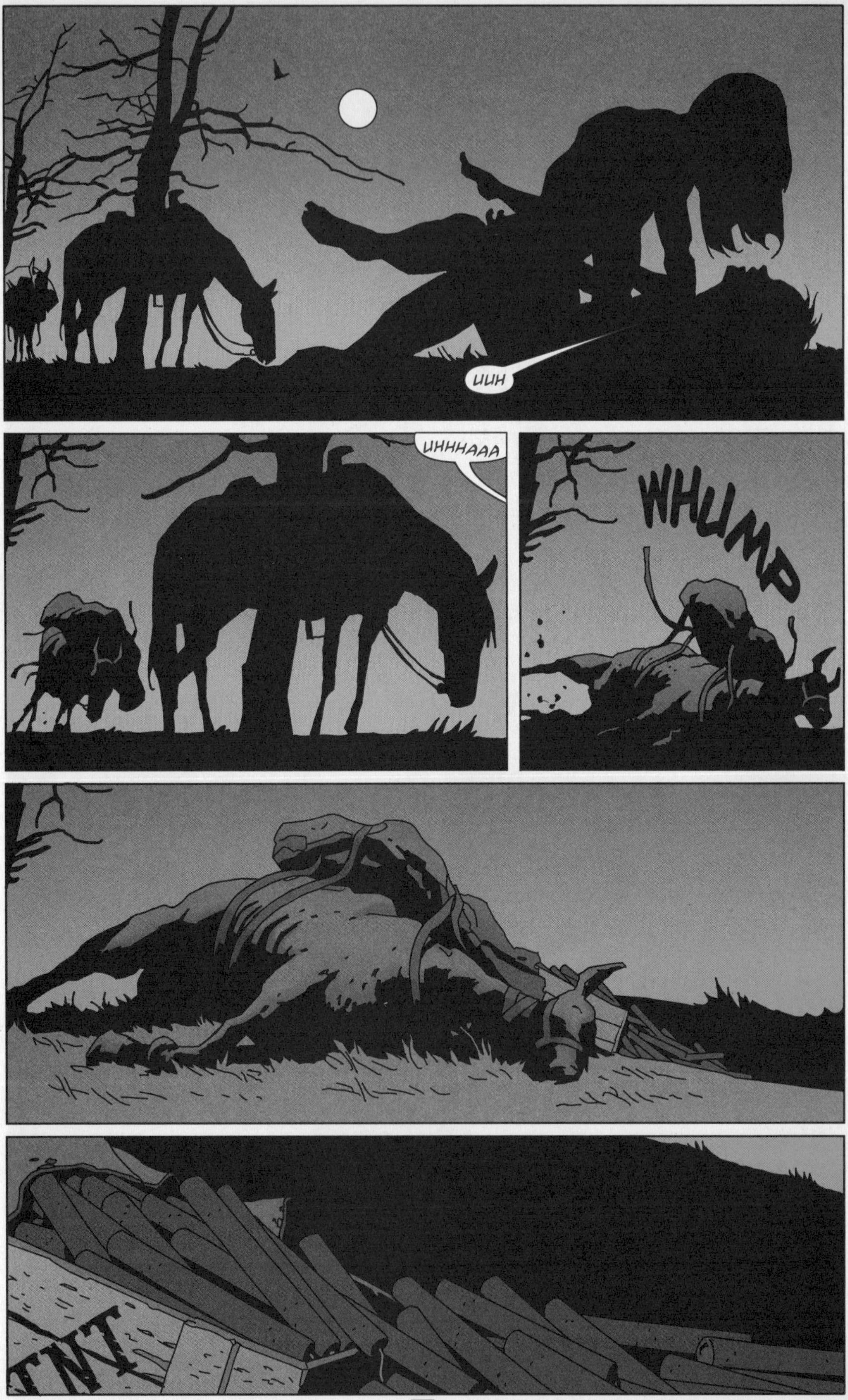
UUH
UHHHAAA
WHUMP
TNT

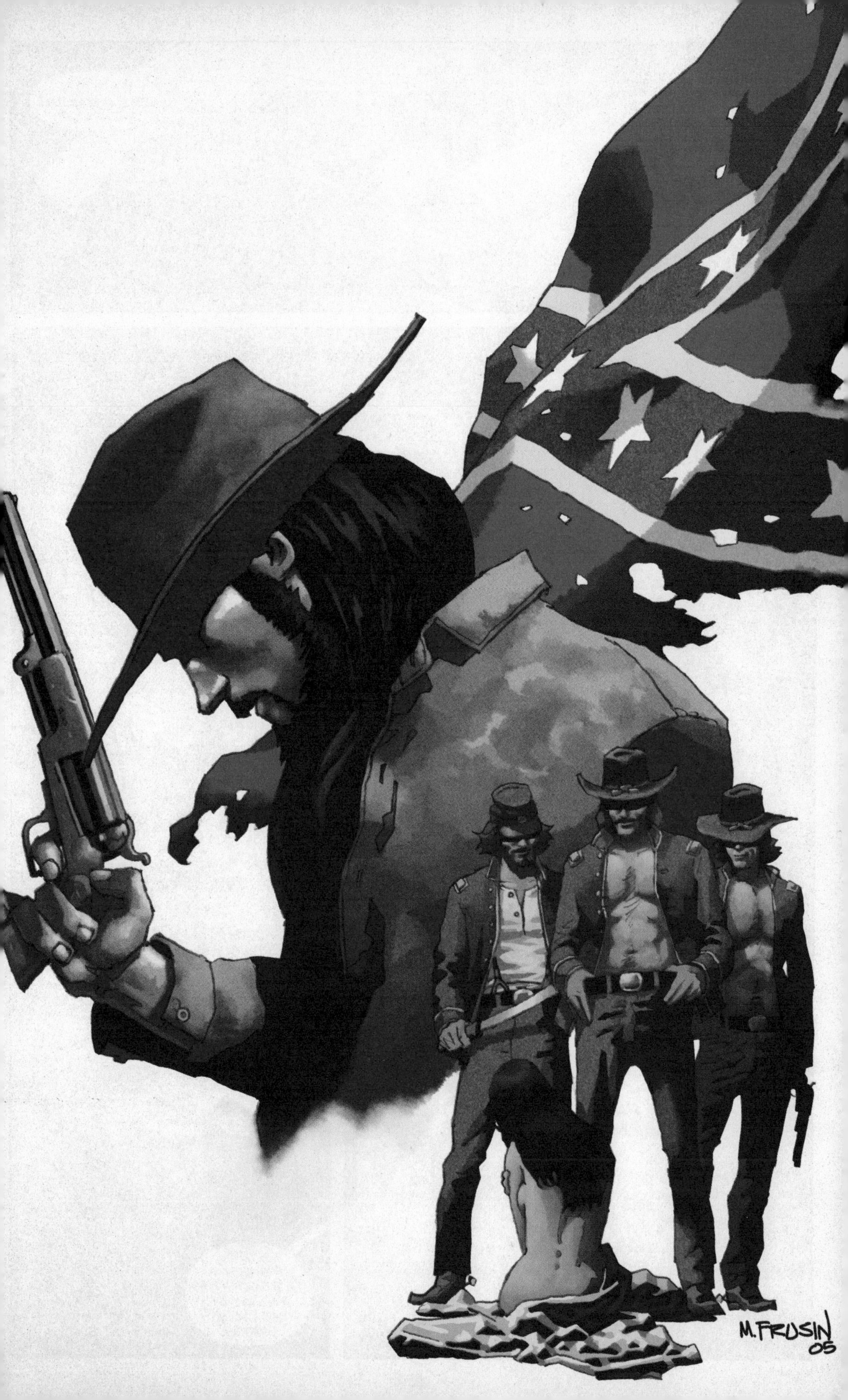
M. FRUSIN
05

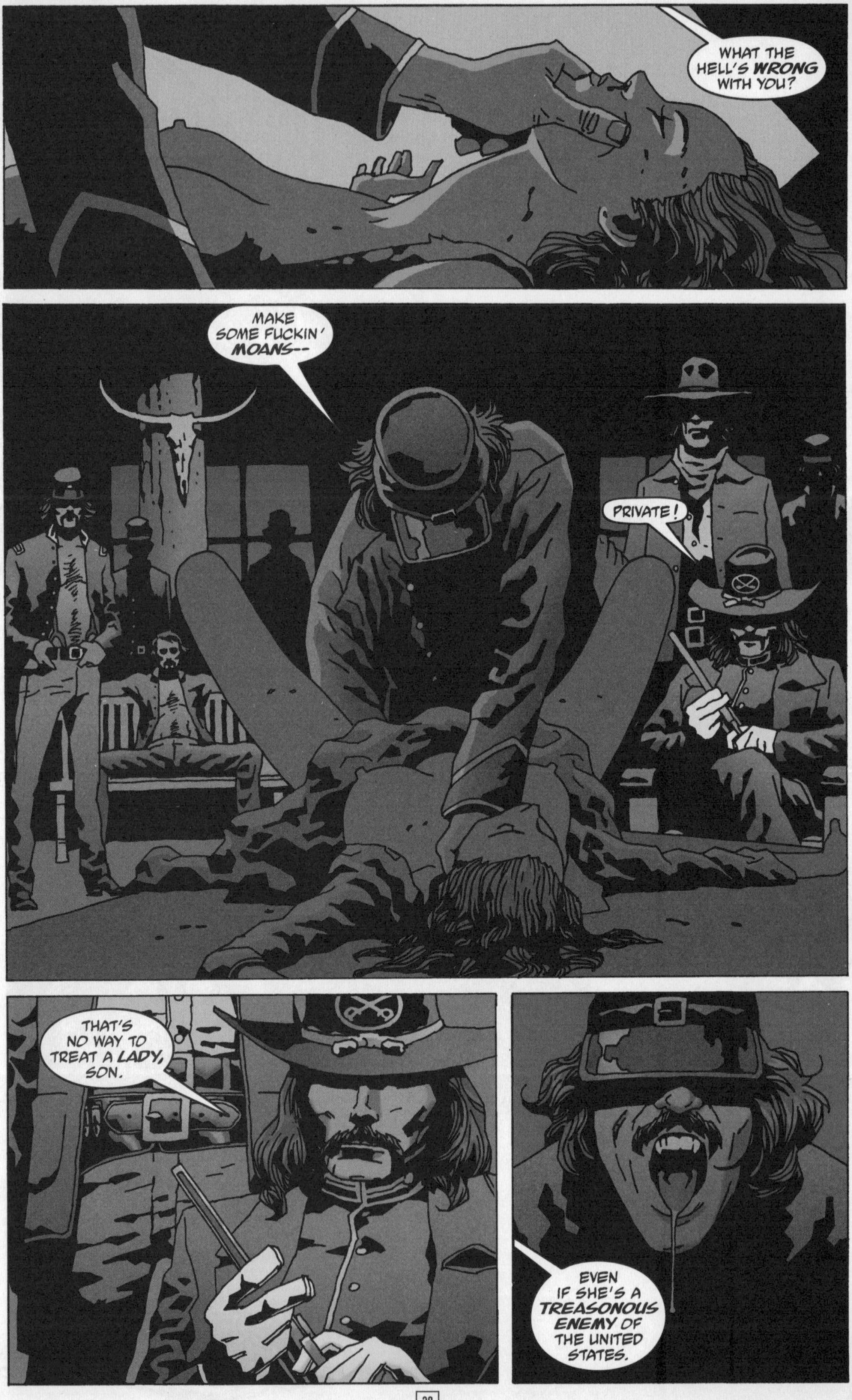
WHAT THE HELL'S **WRONG** WITH YOU?
MAKE SOME FUCKIN' **MOANS**--
PRIVATE!
THAT'S NO WAY TO TREAT A **LADY,** SON.
EVEN IF SHE'S A **TREASONOUS ENEMY** OF THE UNITED STATES.

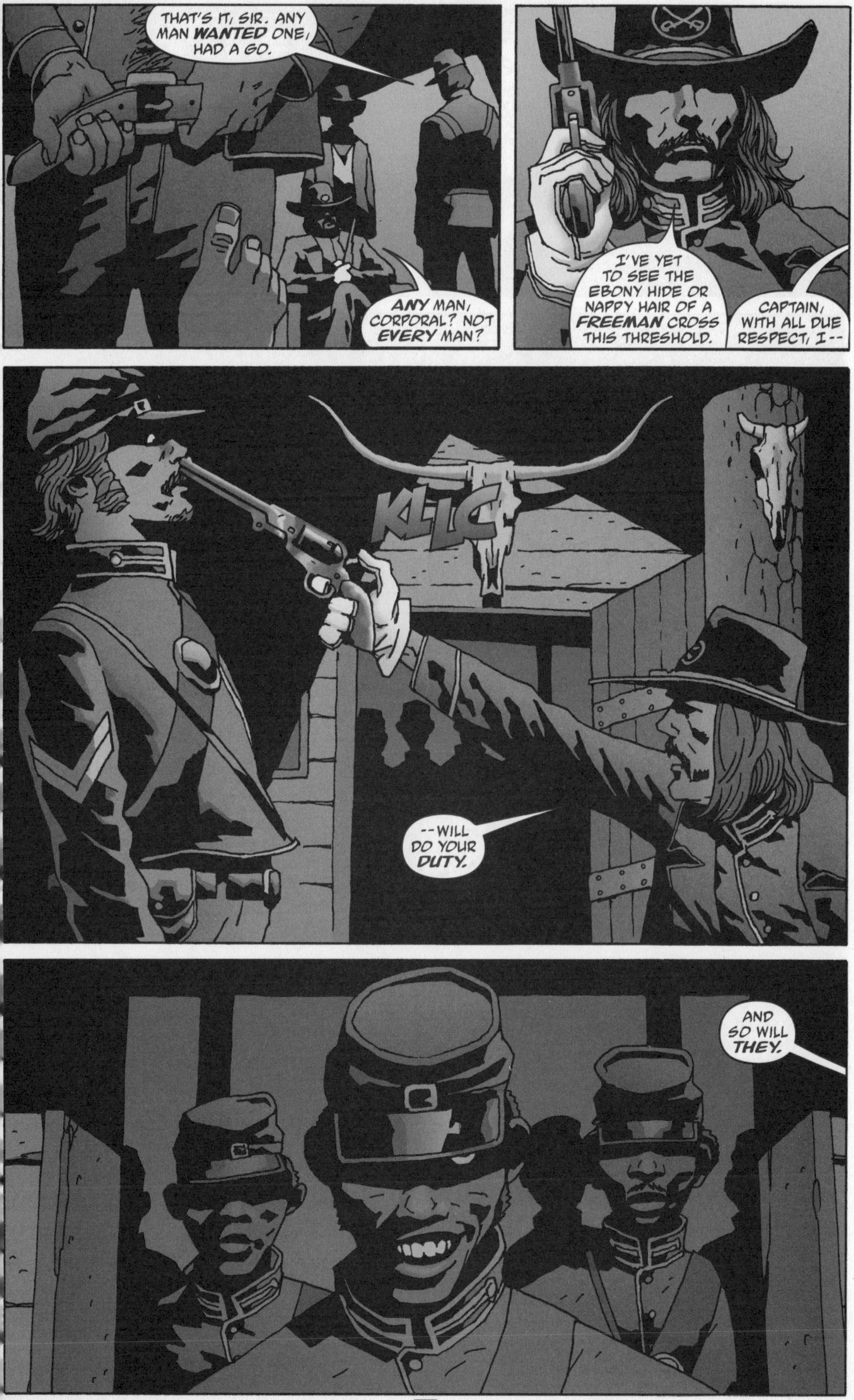
THAT'S IT, SIR. ANY MAN **WANTED** ONE, HAD A GO.
ANY MAN, CORPORAL? NOT **EVERY** MAN?
I'VE YET TO SEE THE EBONY HIDE OR NAPPY HAIR OF A **FREEMAN** CROSS THIS THRESHOLD.
CAPTAIN, WITH ALL DUE RESPECT, I--
KLIC
--WILL DO YOUR **DUTY.**
AND SO WILL **THEY.**

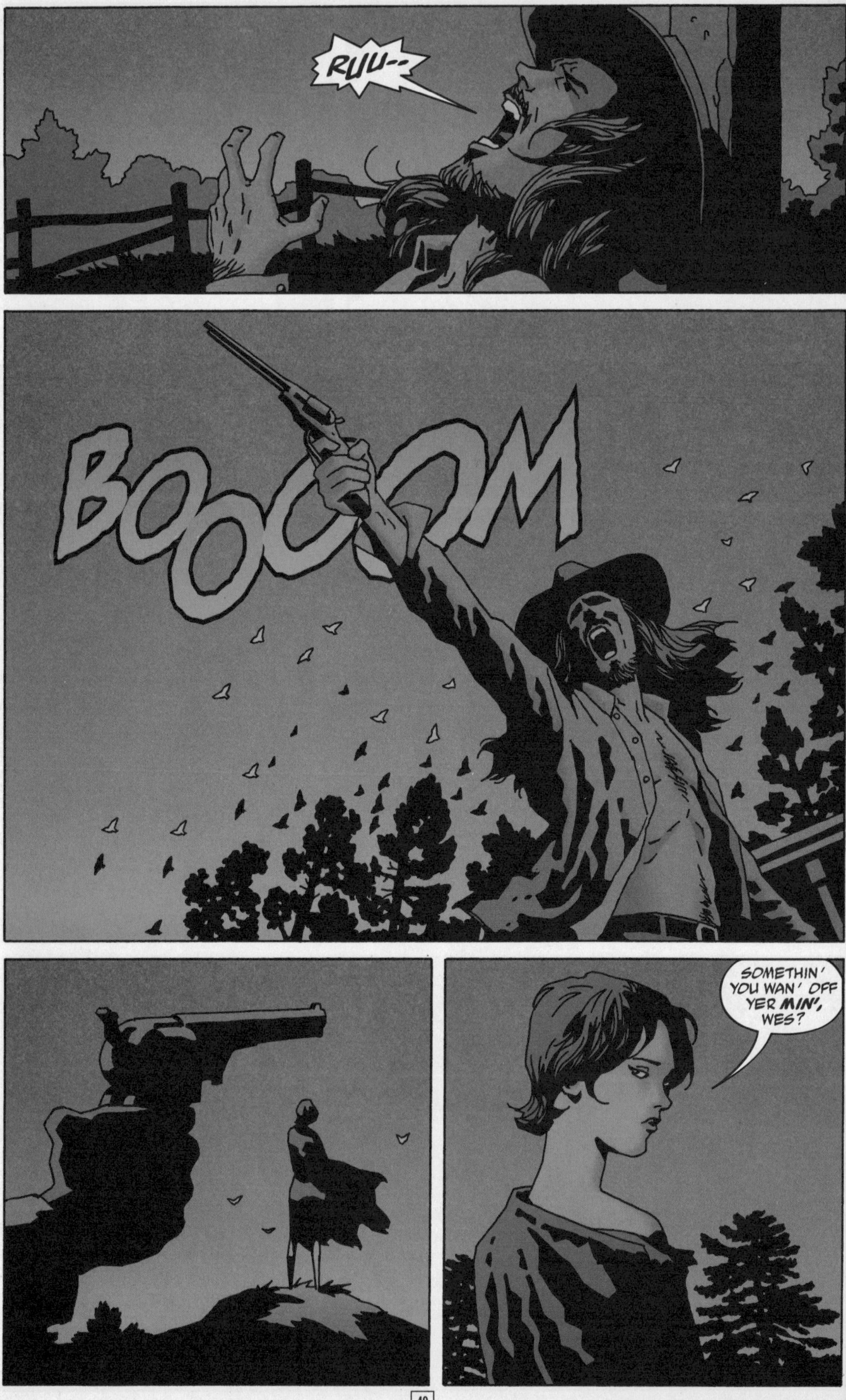
RUU--
BOOOOM
SOMETHIN' YOU WAN' OFF YER MIN', WES?

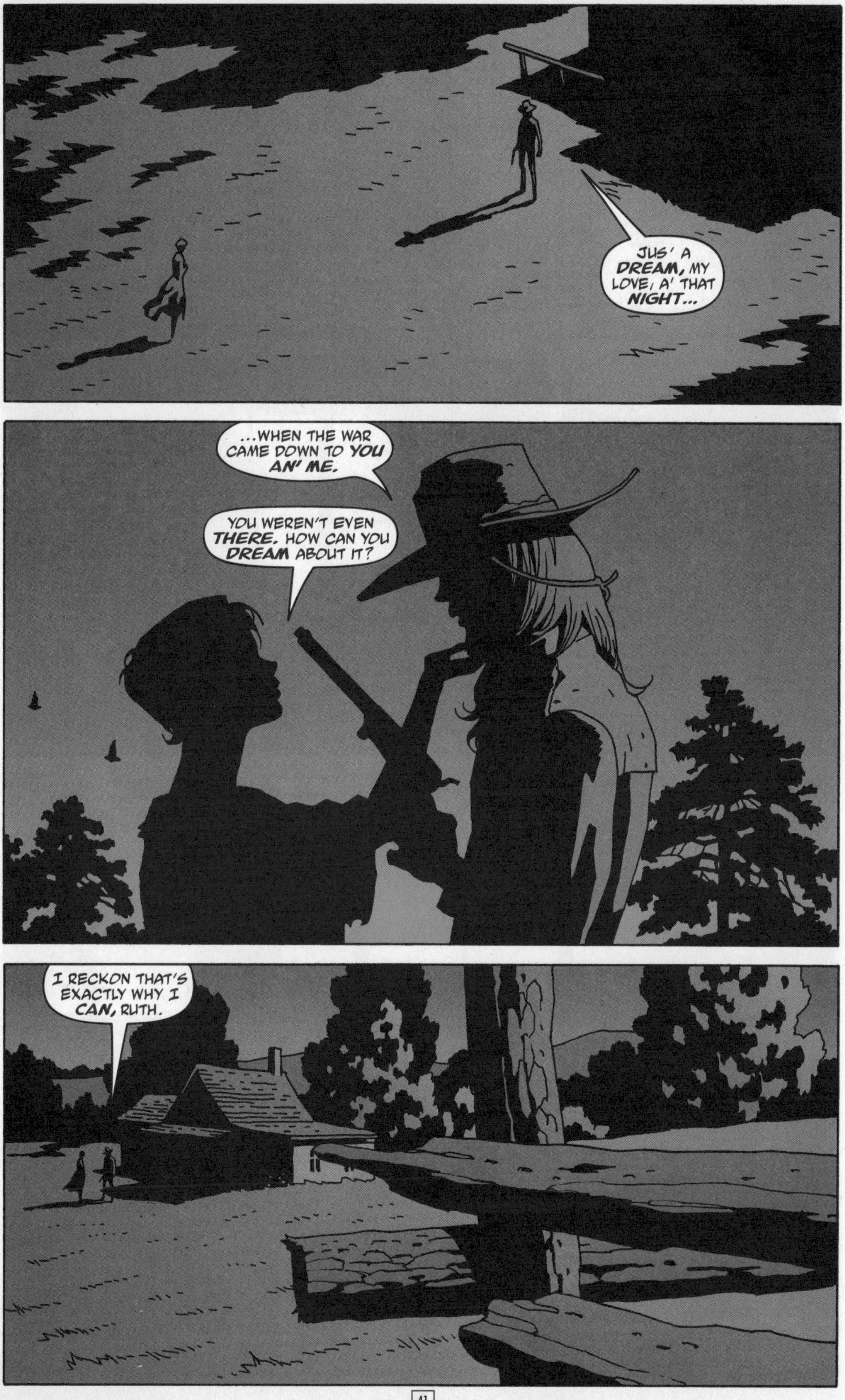
JUS' A DREAM, MY LOVE, A' THAT NIGHT...
...WHEN THE WAR CAME DOWN TO YOU AN' ME.
YOU WEREN'T EVEN THERE. HOW CAN YOU DREAM ABOUT IT?
I RECKON THAT'S EXACTLY WHY I CAN, RUTH.

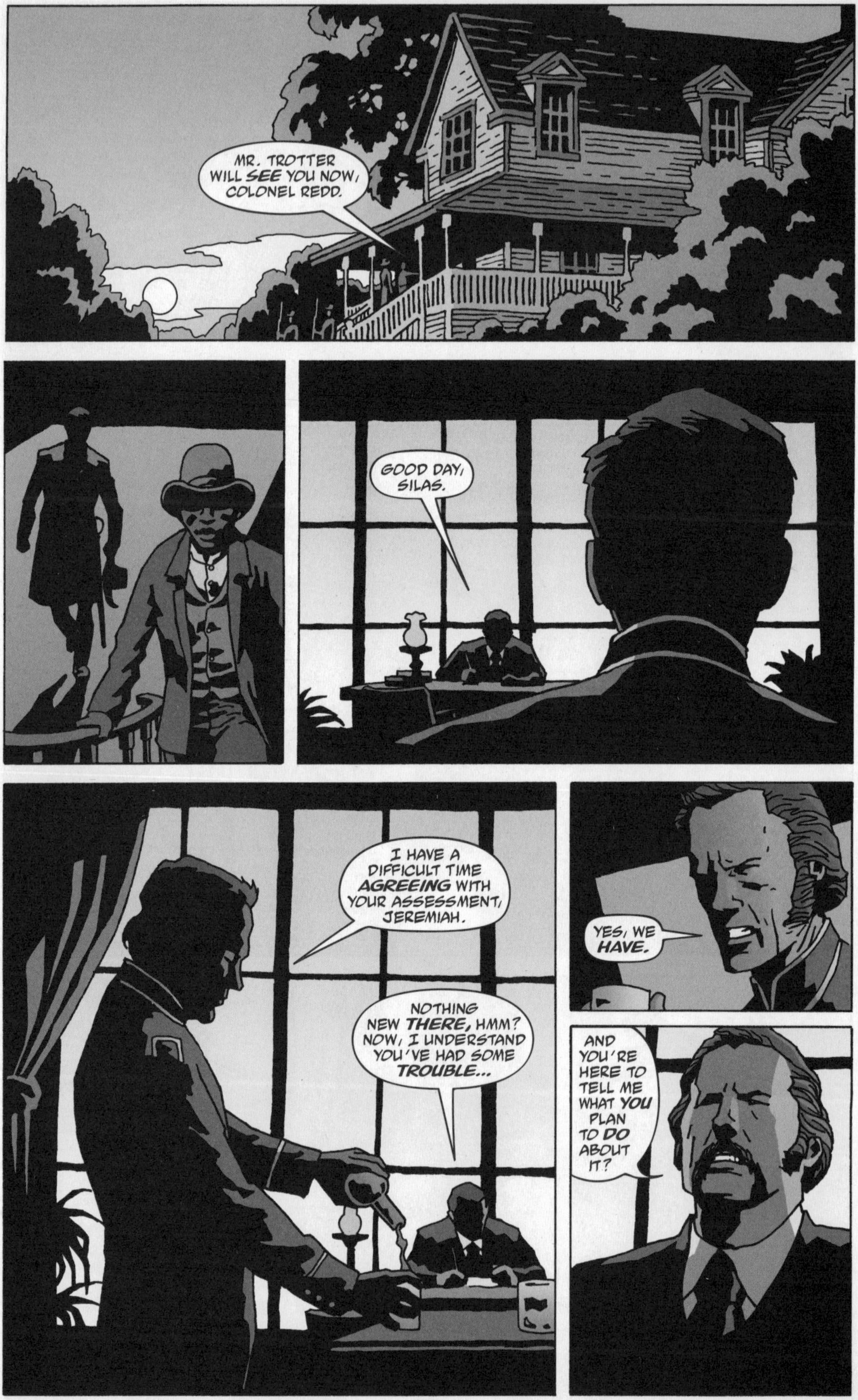
MR. TROTTER WILL SEE YOU NOW, COLONEL REDD.
GOOD DAY, SILAS.
I HAVE A DIFFICULT TIME AGREEING WITH YOUR ASSESSMENT, JEREMIAH.
NOTHING NEW THERE, HMM? NOW, I UNDERSTAND YOU'VE HAD SOME TROUBLE...
YES, WE HAVE.
AND YOU'RE HERE TO TELL ME WHAT YOU PLAN TO DO ABOUT IT?

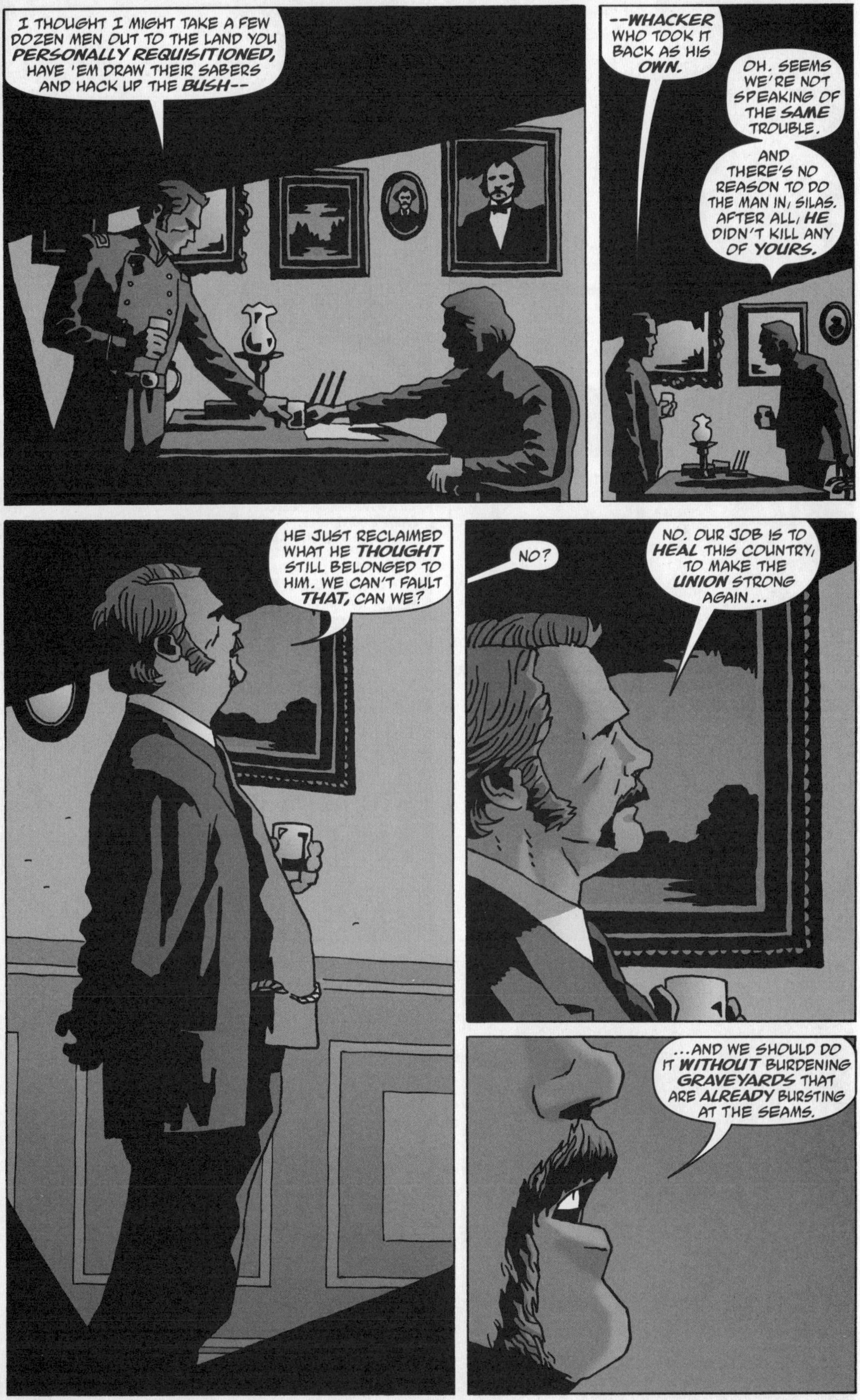
I THOUGHT I MIGHT TAKE A FEW DOZEN MEN OUT TO THE LAND YOU PERSONALLY REQUISITIONED, HAVE 'EM DRAW THEIR SABERS AND HACK UP THE BUSH--
--WHACKER WHO TOOK IT BACK AS HIS OWN.
OH. SEEMS WE'RE NOT SPEAKING OF THE SAME TROUBLE.
AND THERE'S NO REASON TO DO THE MAN IN, SILAS. AFTER ALL, HE DIDN'T KILL ANY OF YOURS.
HE JUST RECLAIMED WHAT HE THOUGHT STILL BELONGED TO HIM. WE CAN'T FAULT THAT, CAN WE?
NO?
NO. OUR JOB IS TO HEAL THIS COUNTRY, TO MAKE THE UNION STRONG AGAIN...
...AND WE SHOULD DO IT WITHOUT BURDENING GRAVEYARDS THAT ARE ALREADY BURSTING AT THE SEAMS.

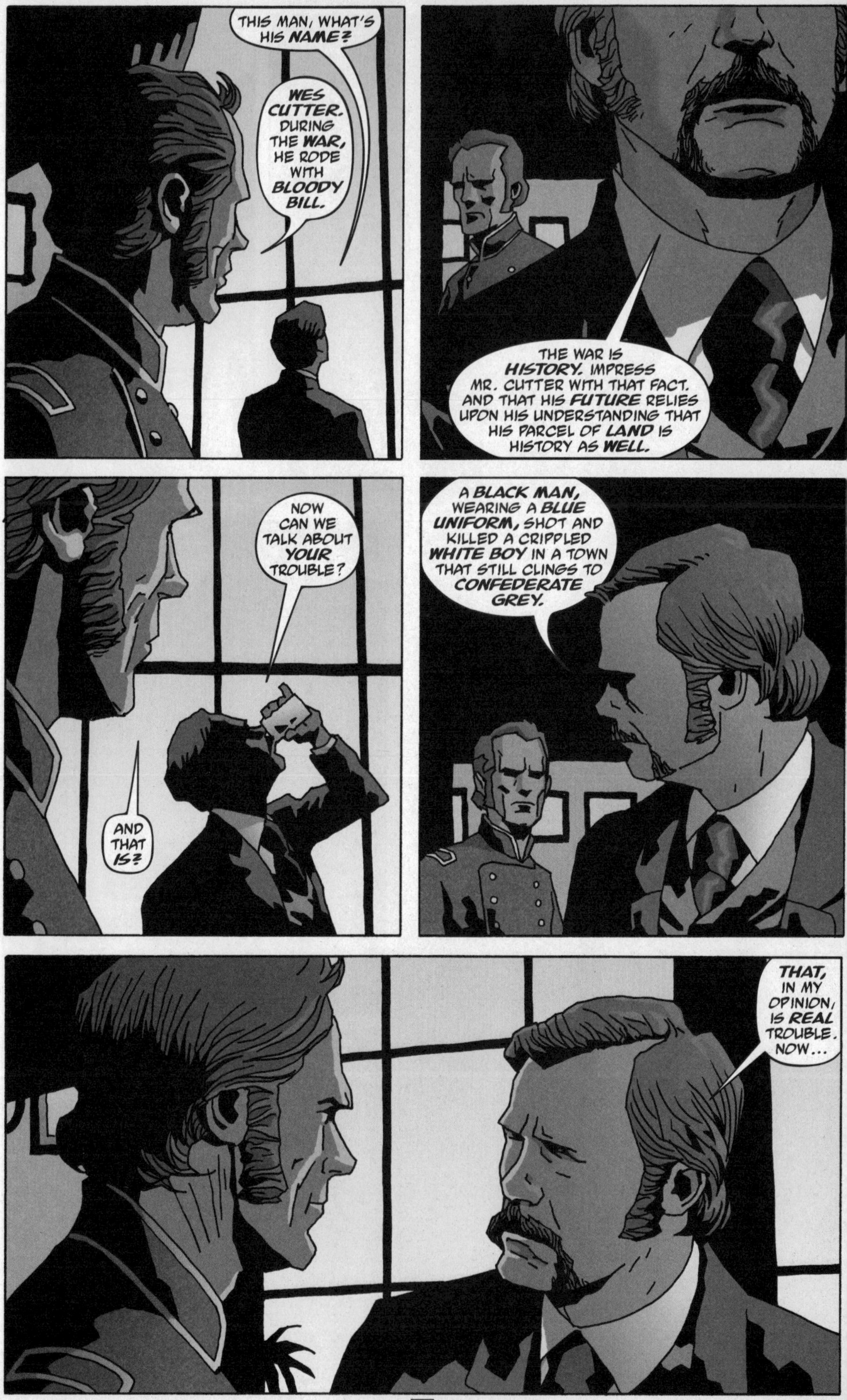
THIS MAN, WHAT'S HIS NAME?
WES CUTTER. DURING THE WAR, HE RODE WITH BLOODY BILL.
THE WAR IS HISTORY. IMPRESS MR. CUTTER WITH THAT FACT. AND THAT HIS FUTURE RELIES UPON HIS UNDERSTANDING THAT HIS PARCEL OF LAND IS HISTORY AS WELL.
NOW CAN WE TALK ABOUT YOUR TROUBLE?
AND THAT IS?
A BLACK MAN, WEARING A BLUE UNIFORM, SHOT AND KILLED A CRIPPLED WHITE BOY IN A TOWN THAT STILL CLINGS TO CONFEDERATE GREY.
THAT, IN MY OPINION, IS REAL TROUBLE. NOW...

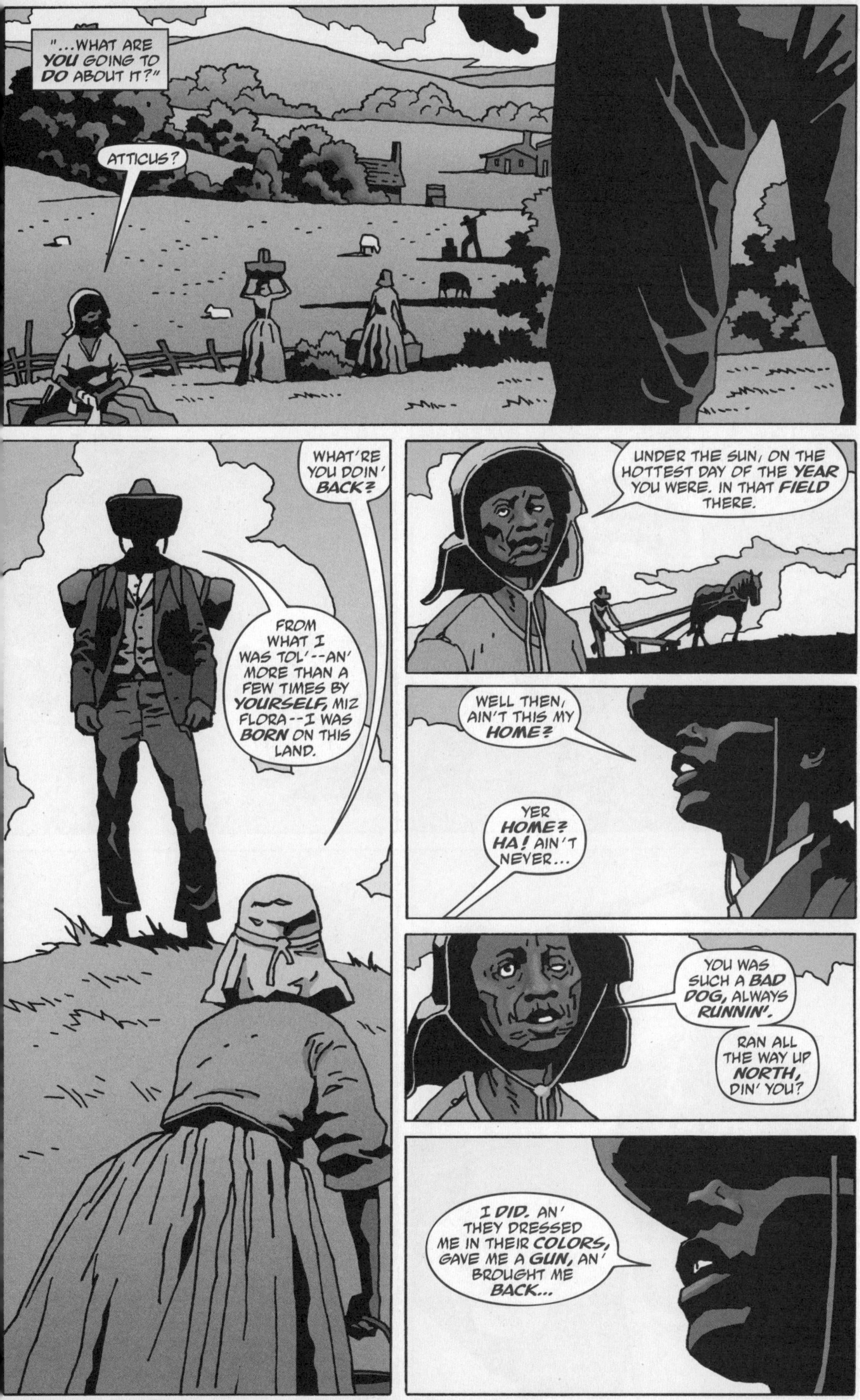
"...WHAT ARE YOU GOING TO DO ABOUT IT?"
ATTICUS?
WHAT'RE YOU DOIN' BACK?
FROM WHAT I WAS TOL'--AN' MORE THAN A FEW TIMES BY YOURSELF, MIZ FLORA--I WAS BORN ON THIS LAND.
UNDER THE SUN, ON THE HOTTEST DAY OF THE YEAR YOU WERE. IN THAT FIELD THERE.
WELL THEN, AIN'T THIS MY HOME?
YER HOME? HA! AIN'T NEVER...
YOU WAS SUCH A BAD DOG, ALWAYS RUNNIN'.
RAN ALL THE WAY UP NORTH, DIN' YOU?
I DID. AN' THEY DRESSED ME IN THEIR COLORS, GAVE ME A GUN, AN' BROUGHT ME BACK...

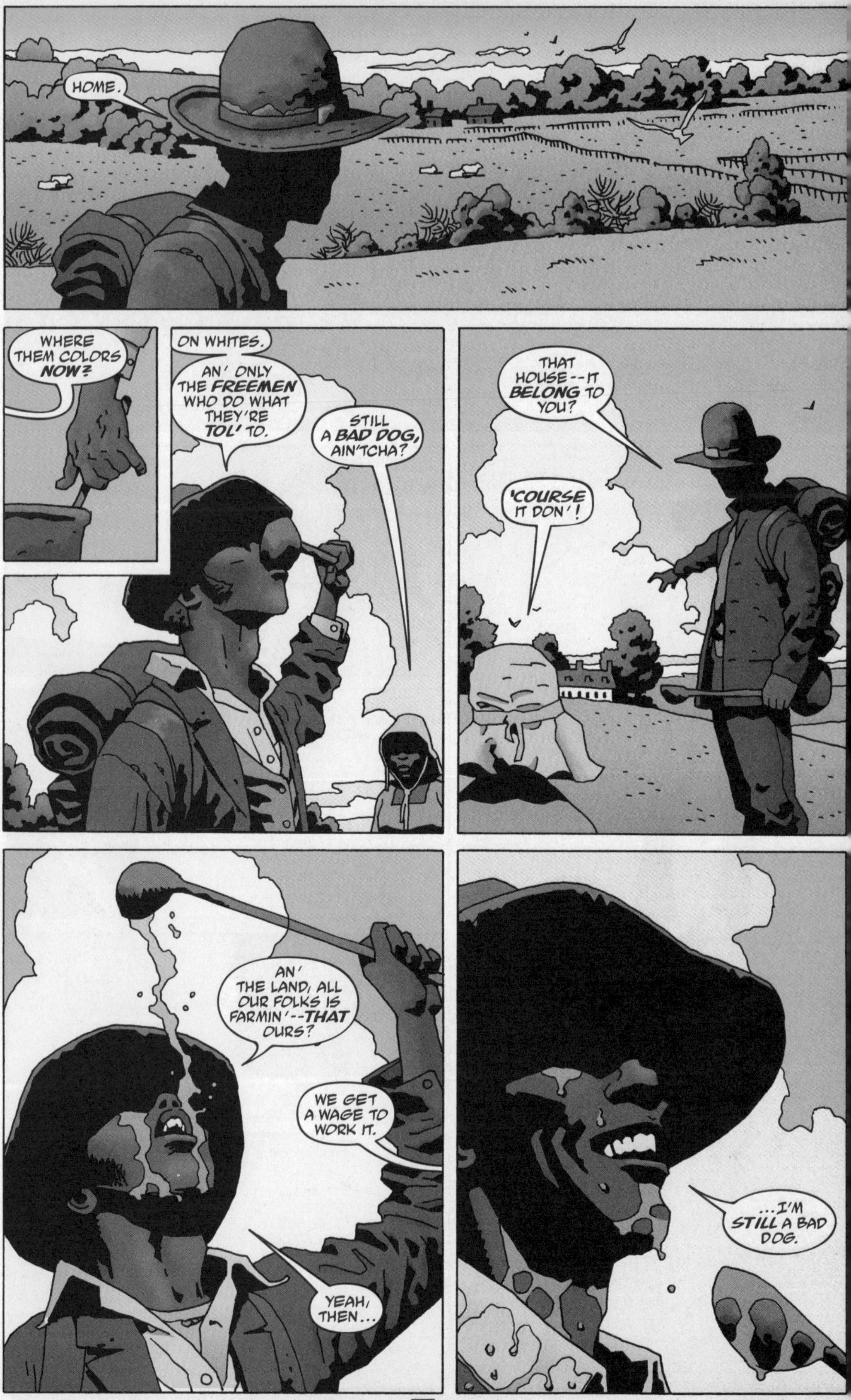
HOME.
WHERE THEM COLORS NOW?
ON WHITES.
AN' ONLY THE FREEMEN WHO DO WHAT THEY'RE TOL' TO.
STILL A BAD DOG, AIN'TCHA?
THAT HOUSE--IT BELONG TO YOU?
'COURSE IT DON'!
AN' THE LAND, ALL OUR FOLKS IS FARMIN'--THAT OURS?
WE GET A WAGE TO WORK IT.
YEAH, THEN...
...I'M STILL A BAD DOG.

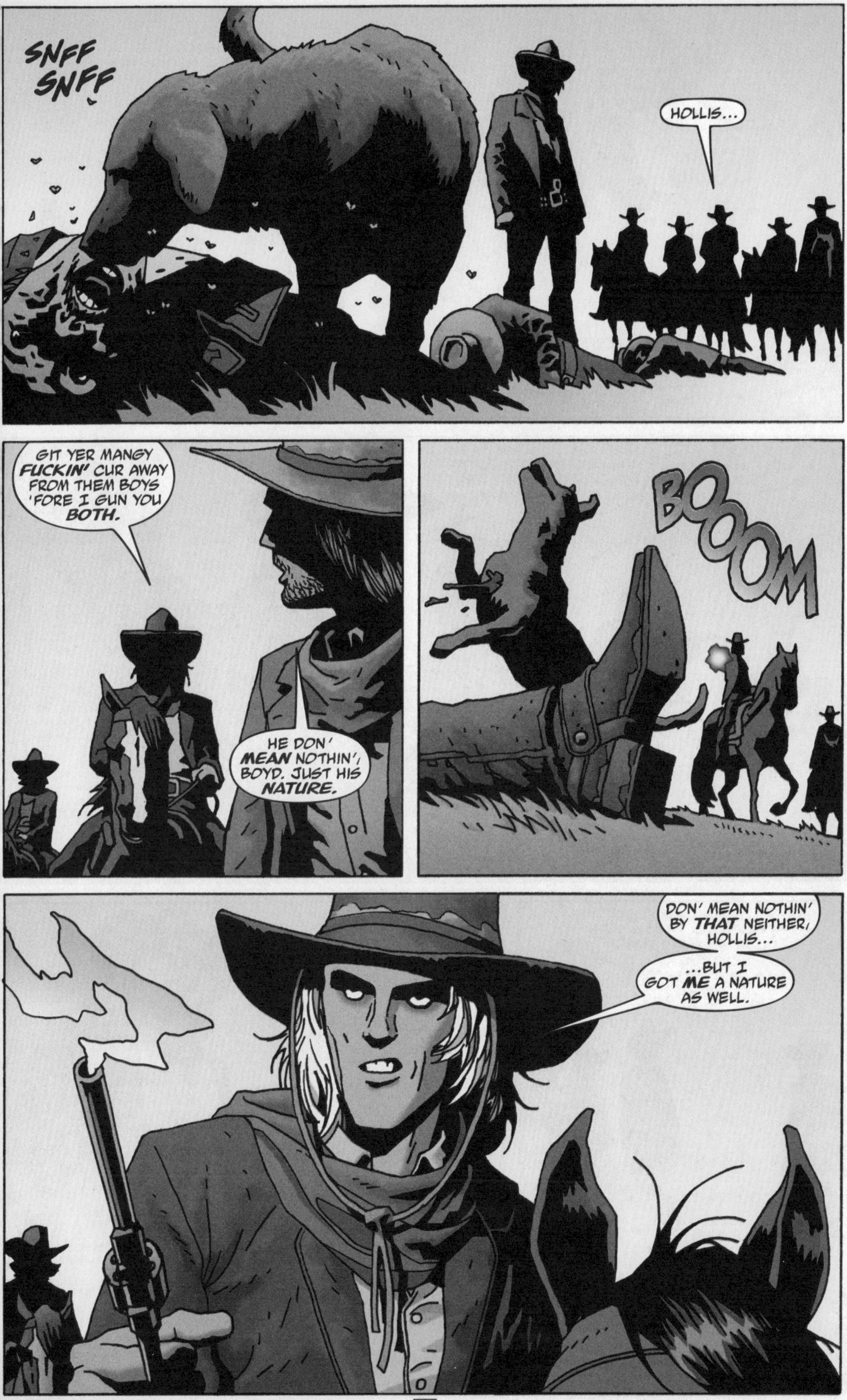
SNFF SNFF
HOLLIS...
GIT YER MANGY FUCKIN' CUR AWAY FROM THEM BOYS 'FORE I GUN YOU BOTH.
HE DON' MEAN NOTHIN', BOYD. JUST HIS NATURE.
BOOOOM
DON' MEAN NOTHIN' BY THAT NEITHER, HOLLIS...
...BUT I GOT ME A NATURE AS WELL.

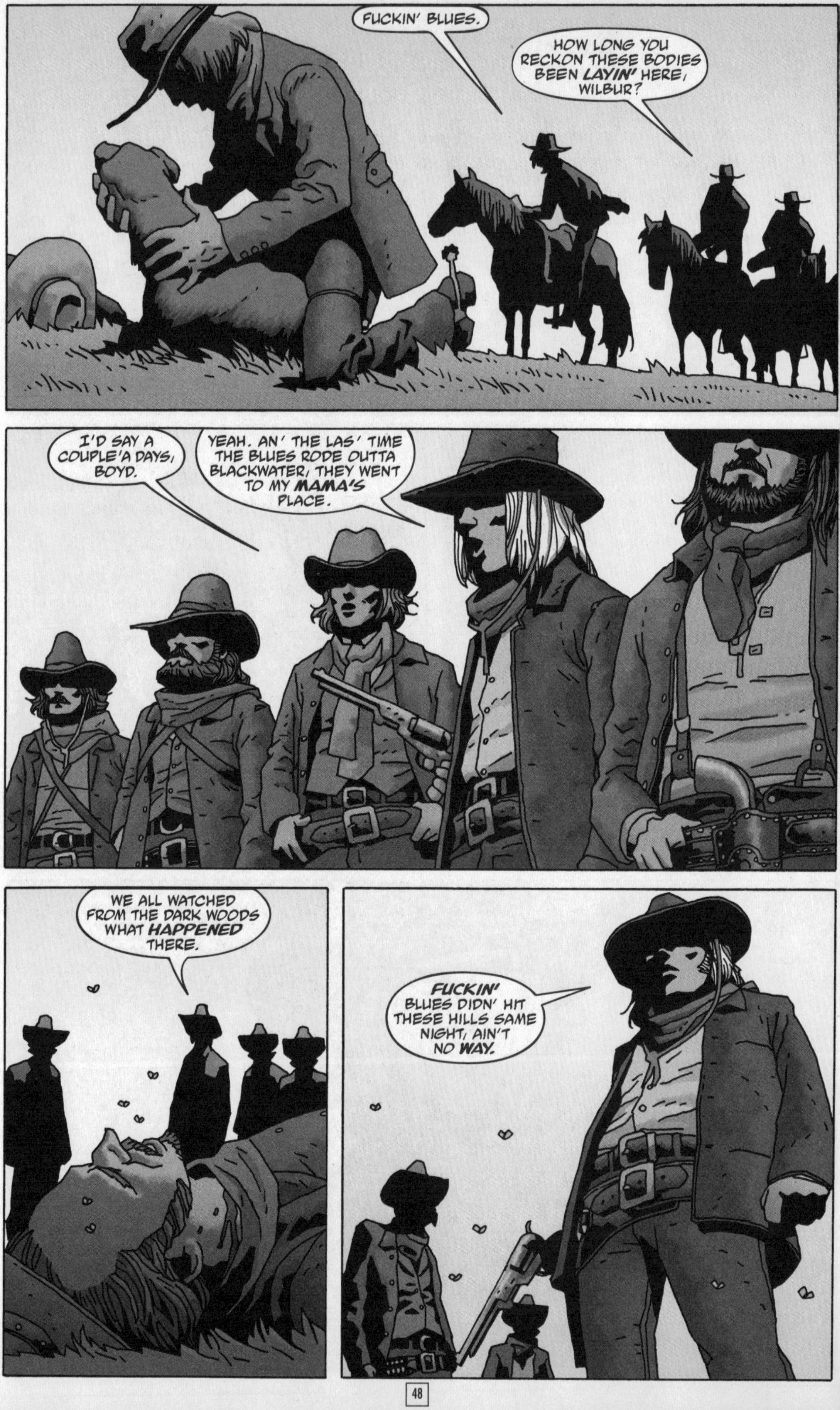
FUCKIN' BLUES.
HOW LONG YOU RECKON THESE BODIES BEEN LAYIN' HERE, WILBUR?
I'D SAY A COUPLE'A DAYS, BOYD.
YEAH. AN' THE LAS' TIME THE BLUES RODE OUTTA BLACKWATER, THEY WENT TO MY MAMA'S PLACE.
WE ALL WATCHED FROM THE DARK WOODS WHAT HAPPENED THERE.
FUCKIN' BLUES DIDN' HIT THESE HILLS SAME NIGHT, AIN'T NO WAY.

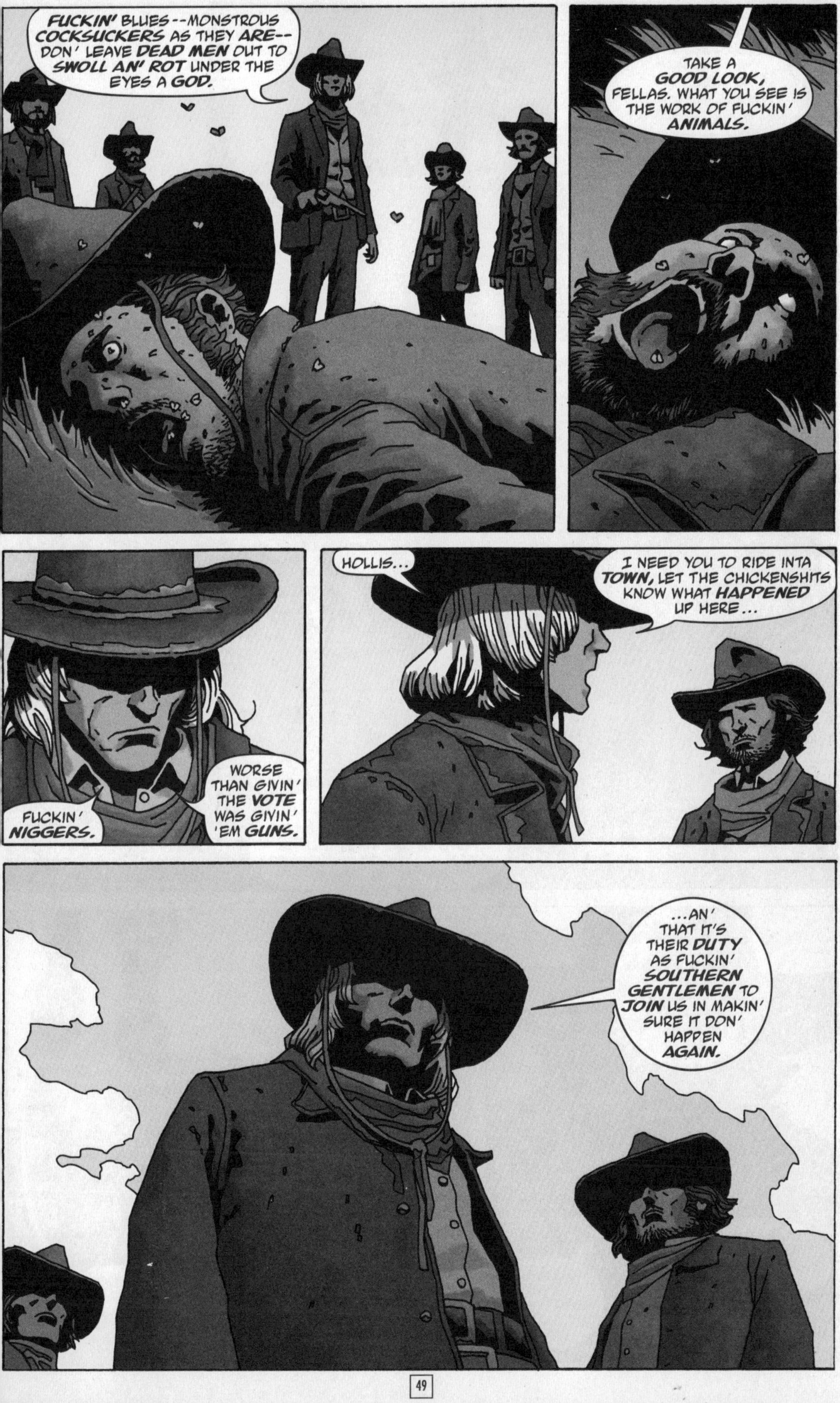
FUCKIN' BLUES--MONSTROUS COCKSUCKERS AS THEY ARE--DON' LEAVE DEAD MEN OUT TO SWOLL AN' ROT UNDER THE EYES A GOD.
TAKE A GOOD LOOK, FELLAS. WHAT YOU SEE IS THE WORK OF FUCKIN' ANIMALS.
FUCKIN' NIGGERS.
WORSE THAN GIVIN' THE VOTE WAS GIVIN' 'EM GUNS.
HOLLIS...
I NEED YOU TO RIDE INTA TOWN, LET THE CHICKENSHITS KNOW WHAT HAPPENED UP HERE...
...AN' THAT IT'S THEIR DUTY AS FUCKIN' SOUTHERN GENTLEMEN TO JOIN US IN MAKIN' SURE IT DON' HAPPEN AGAIN.

WHAT'S GOING TO **HAPPEN** WITH THIS MAN, GEORGE?

WHAT'RE YOU **DRIVIN'** AT, COLONEL?

MR. "KEEP THE PEACE, BECAUSE IF WE DON'T IT COSTS MONEY" TROTTER, PREFERS THAT THERE WILL BE **NO VIOLENCE.**

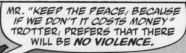

YOU'RE **FROM** THESE PARTS, SO I TAKE IT YOU **KNEW** CUTTER BEFORE THE WAR. WILL HE **COST** MR. "KEEP THE PEACE" ANY OF HIS MONEY?

THE MAN **I** KNEW HAD A GOOD HEAD ON HIS SHOULDERS.

THE WAR I KNEW TOOK A **LOT** OF THOSE **OFF.**

INDEED IT **DID.**

50

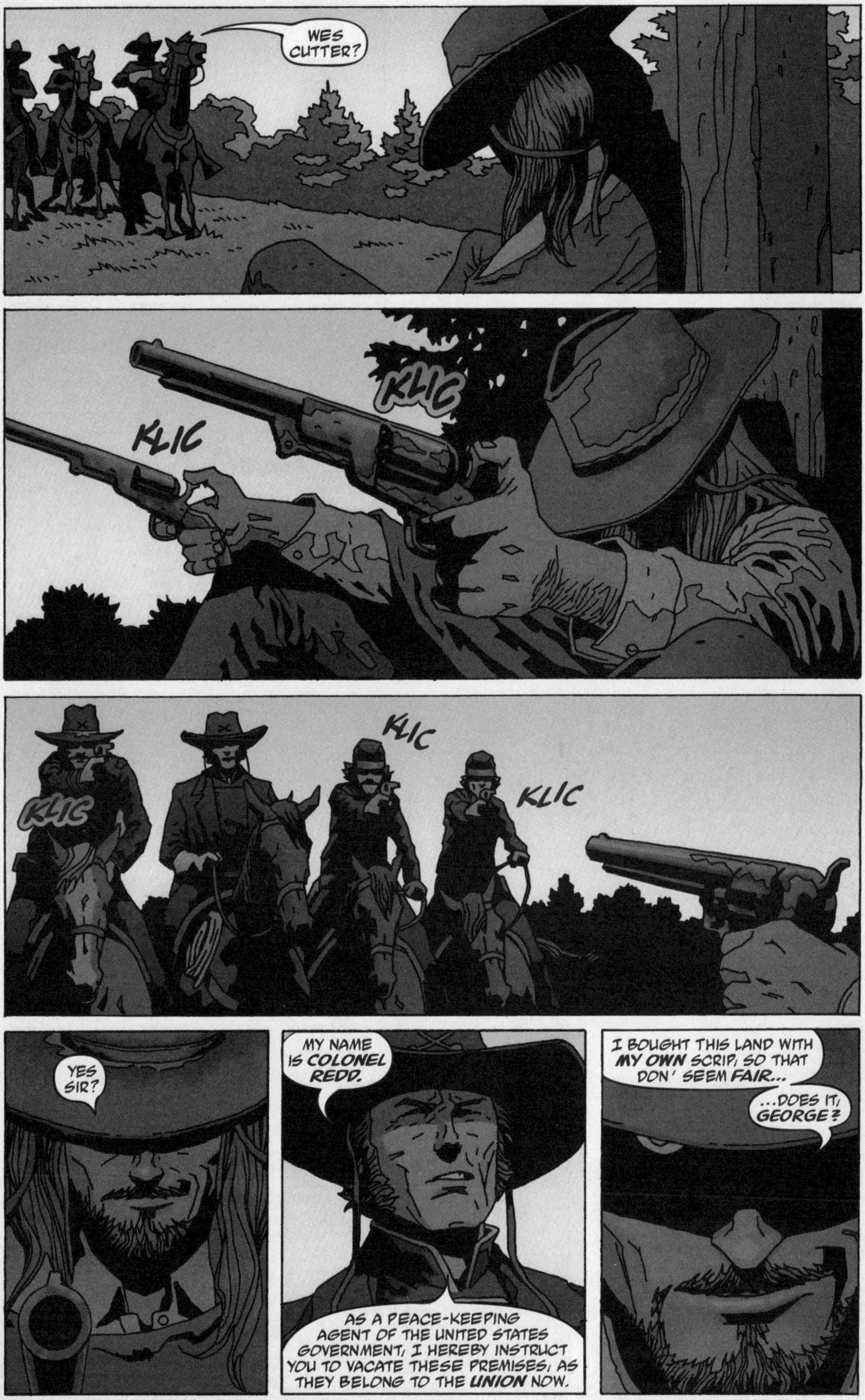
WES CUTTER?
KLIC
KLIC
KLIC
KLIC
KLIC
YES SIR?
MY NAME IS COLONEL REDD.
AS A PEACE-KEEPING AGENT OF THE UNITED STATES GOVERNMENT, I HEREBY INSTRUCT YOU TO VACATE THESE PREMISES, AS THEY BELONG TO THE UNION NOW.
I BOUGHT THIS LAND WITH MY OWN SCRIP, SO THAT DON' SEEM FAIR...
...DOES IT, GEORGE?

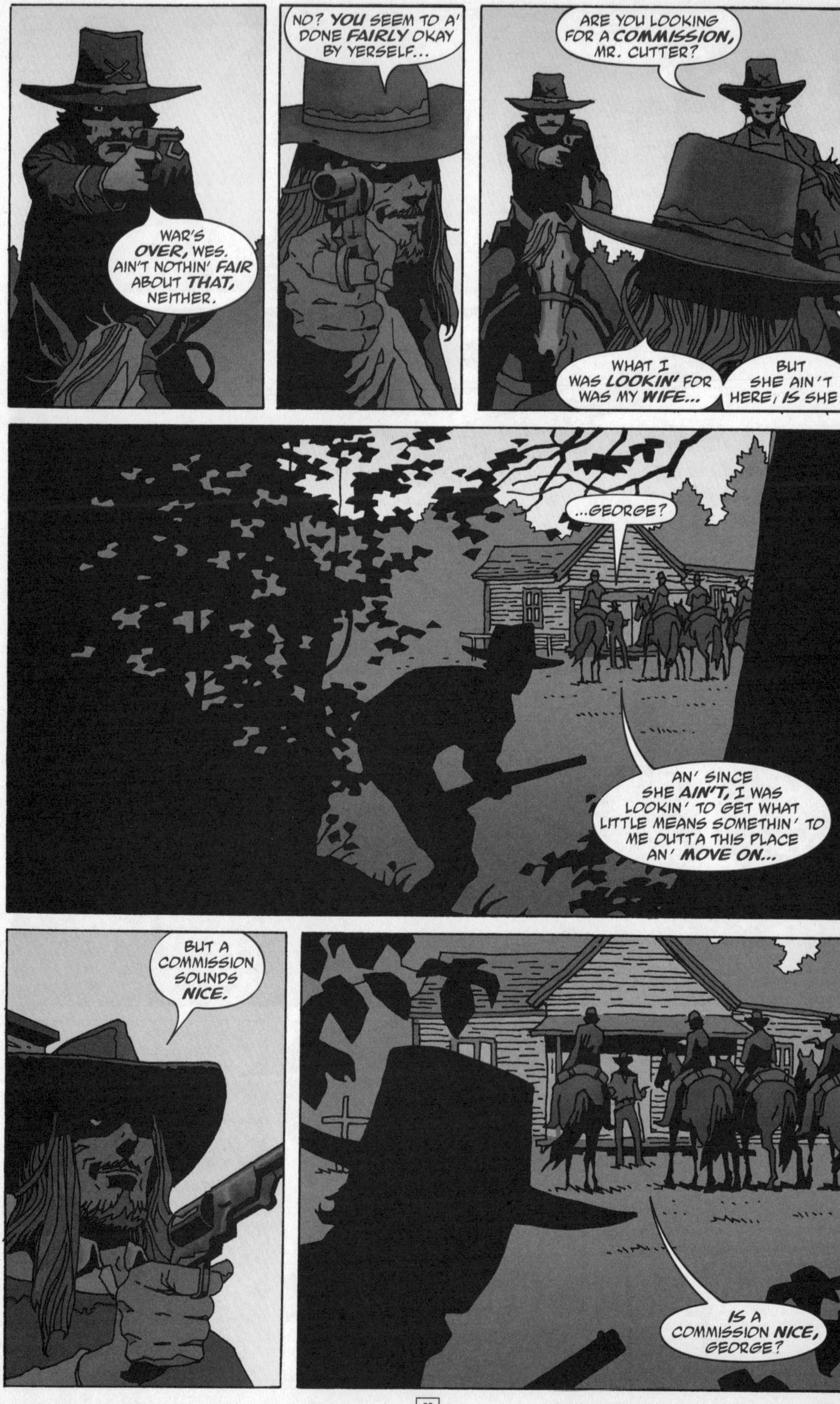

WAR'S OVER, WES. AIN'T NOTHIN' FAIR ABOUT THAT, NEITHER.
NO? YOU SEEM TO A' DONE FAIRLY OKAY BY YERSELF...
ARE YOU LOOKING FOR A COMMISSION, MR. CUTTER?
WHAT I WAS LOOKIN' FOR WAS MY WIFE...
BUT SHE AIN'T HERE, IS SHE...
...GEORGE?
AN' SINCE SHE AIN'T, I WAS LOOKIN' TO GET WHAT LITTLE MEANS SOMETHIN' TO ME OUTTA THIS PLACE AN' MOVE ON...
BUT A COMMISSION SOUNDS NICE.
IS A COMMISSION NICE, GEORGE?

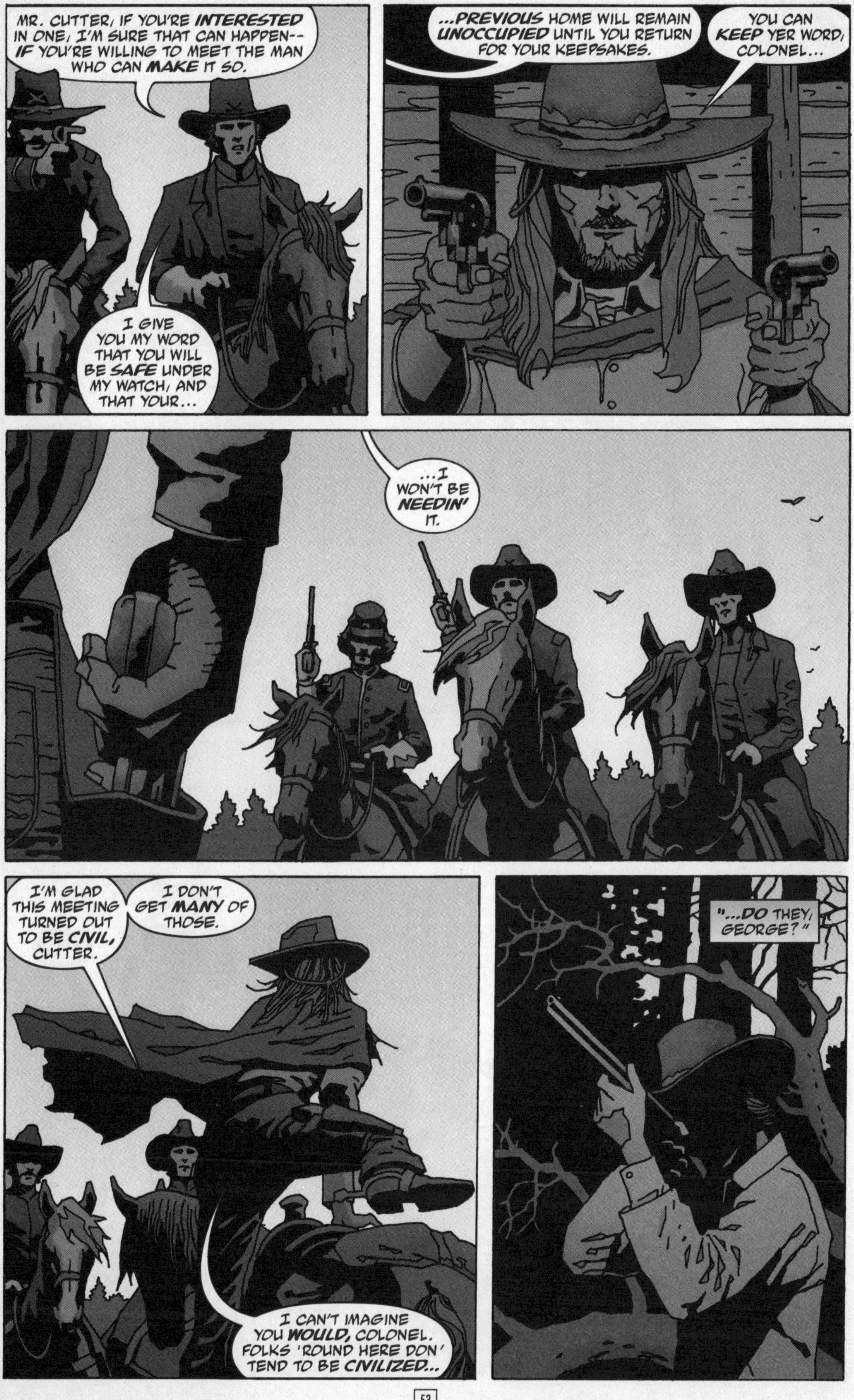
MR. CUTTER, IF YOU'RE INTERESTED IN ONE, I'M SURE THAT CAN HAPPEN-- IF YOU'RE WILLING TO MEET THE MAN WHO CAN MAKE IT SO.
I GIVE YOU MY WORD THAT YOU WILL BE SAFE UNDER MY WATCH, AND THAT YOUR...
...PREVIOUS HOME WILL REMAIN UNOCCUPIED UNTIL YOU RETURN FOR YOUR KEEPSAKES.
YOU CAN KEEP YER WORD, COLONEL...
...I WON'T BE NEEDIN' IT.
I'M GLAD THIS MEETING TURNED OUT TO BE CIVIL, CUTTER.
I DON'T GET MANY OF THOSE.
I CAN'T IMAGINE YOU WOULD, COLONEL. FOLKS 'ROUND HERE DON' TEND TO BE CIVILIZED...
"...DO THEY, GEORGE?"

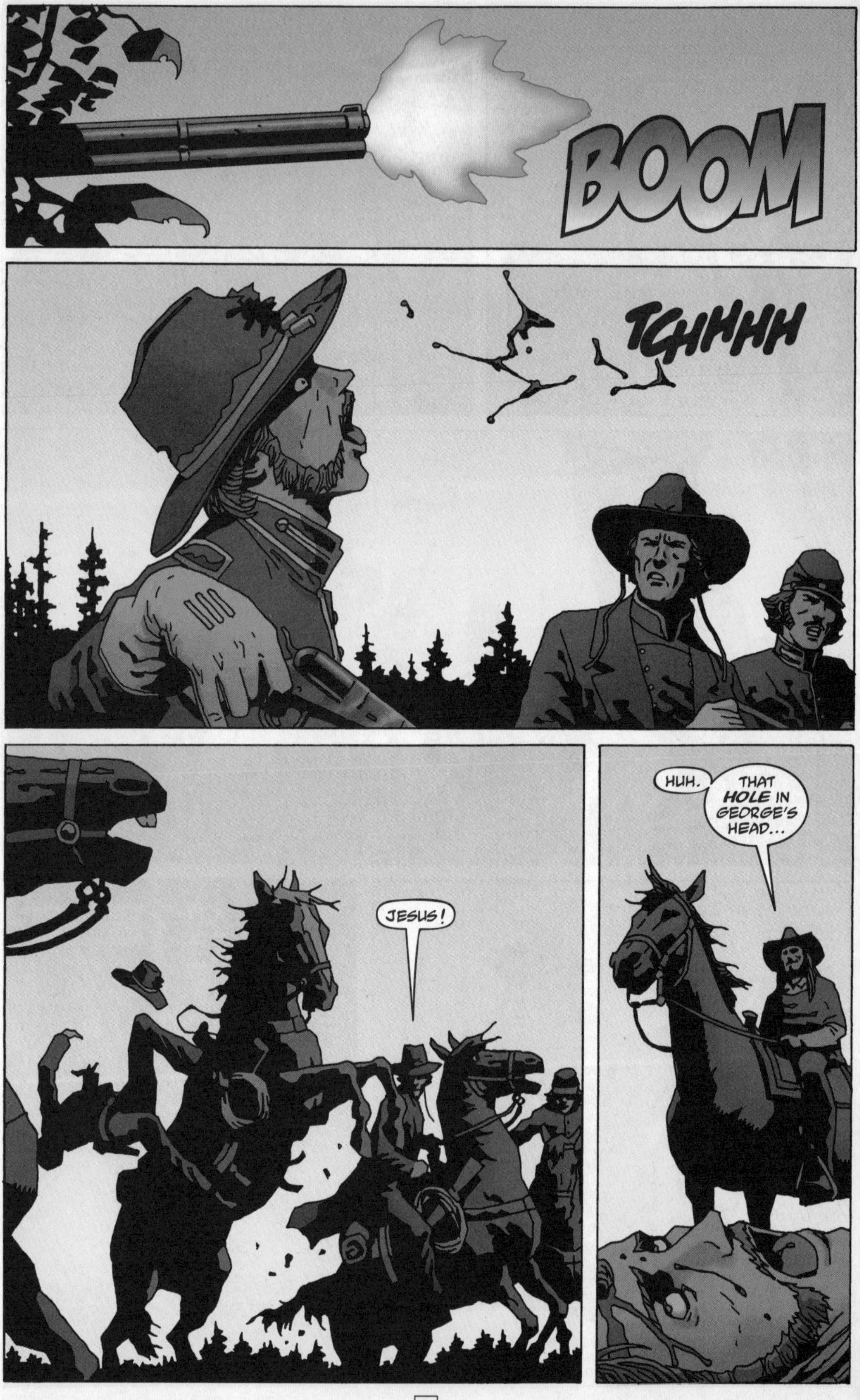
BOOM
TCHHHH
JESUS!
HUH.
THAT HOLE IN GEORGE'S HEAD...

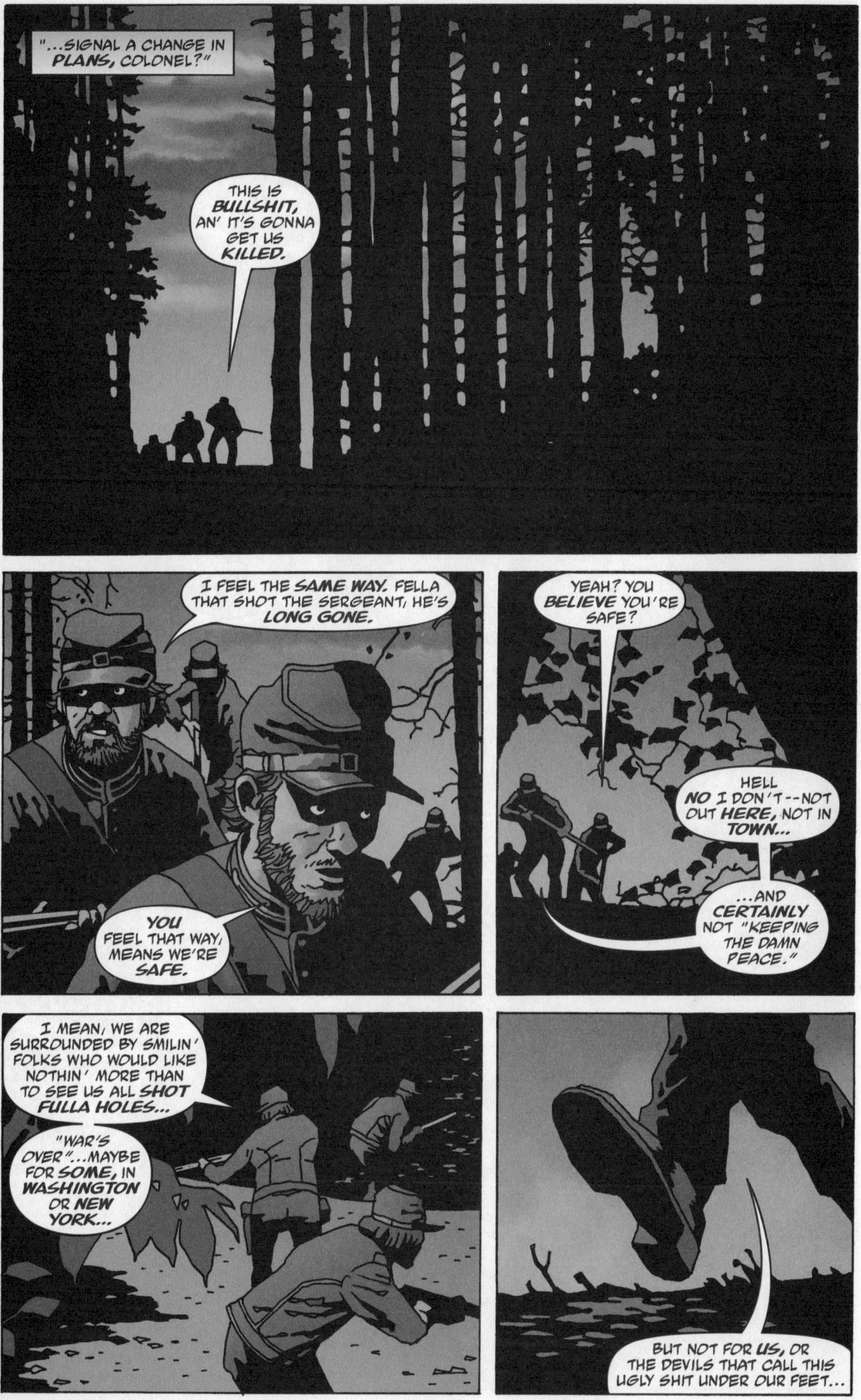
"...SIGNAL A CHANGE IN PLANS, COLONEL?"
THIS IS BULLSHIT, AN' IT'S GONNA GET US KILLED.
I FEEL THE SAME WAY. FELLA THAT SHOT THE SERGEANT, HE'S LONG GONE.
YOU FEEL THAT WAY, MEANS WE'RE SAFE.
YEAH? YOU BELIEVE YOU'RE SAFE?
HELL NO I DON'T--NOT OUT HERE, NOT IN TOWN...
...AND CERTAINLY NOT "KEEPING THE DAMN PEACE."
I MEAN, WE ARE SURROUNDED BY SMILIN' FOLKS WHO WOULD LIKE NOTHIN' MORE THAN TO SEE US ALL SHOT FULLA HOLES...
"WAR'S OVER"...MAYBE FOR SOME, IN WASHINGTON OR NEW YORK...
BUT NOT FOR US, OR THE DEVILS THAT CALL THIS UGLY SHIT UNDER OUR FEET...

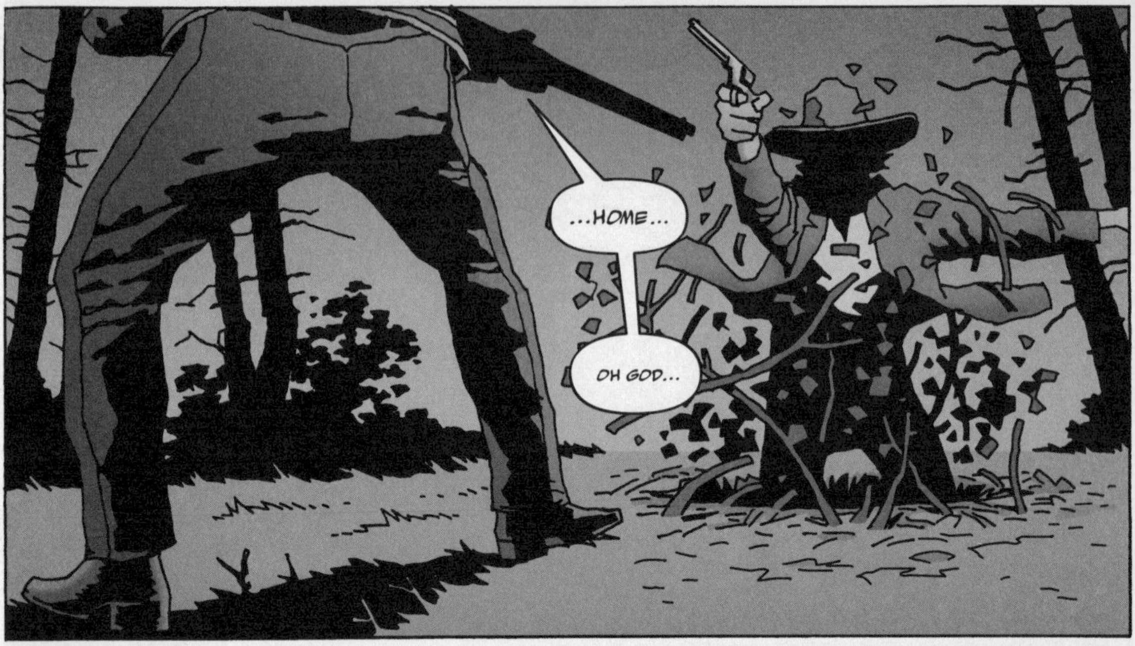
...HOME...
OH GOD...

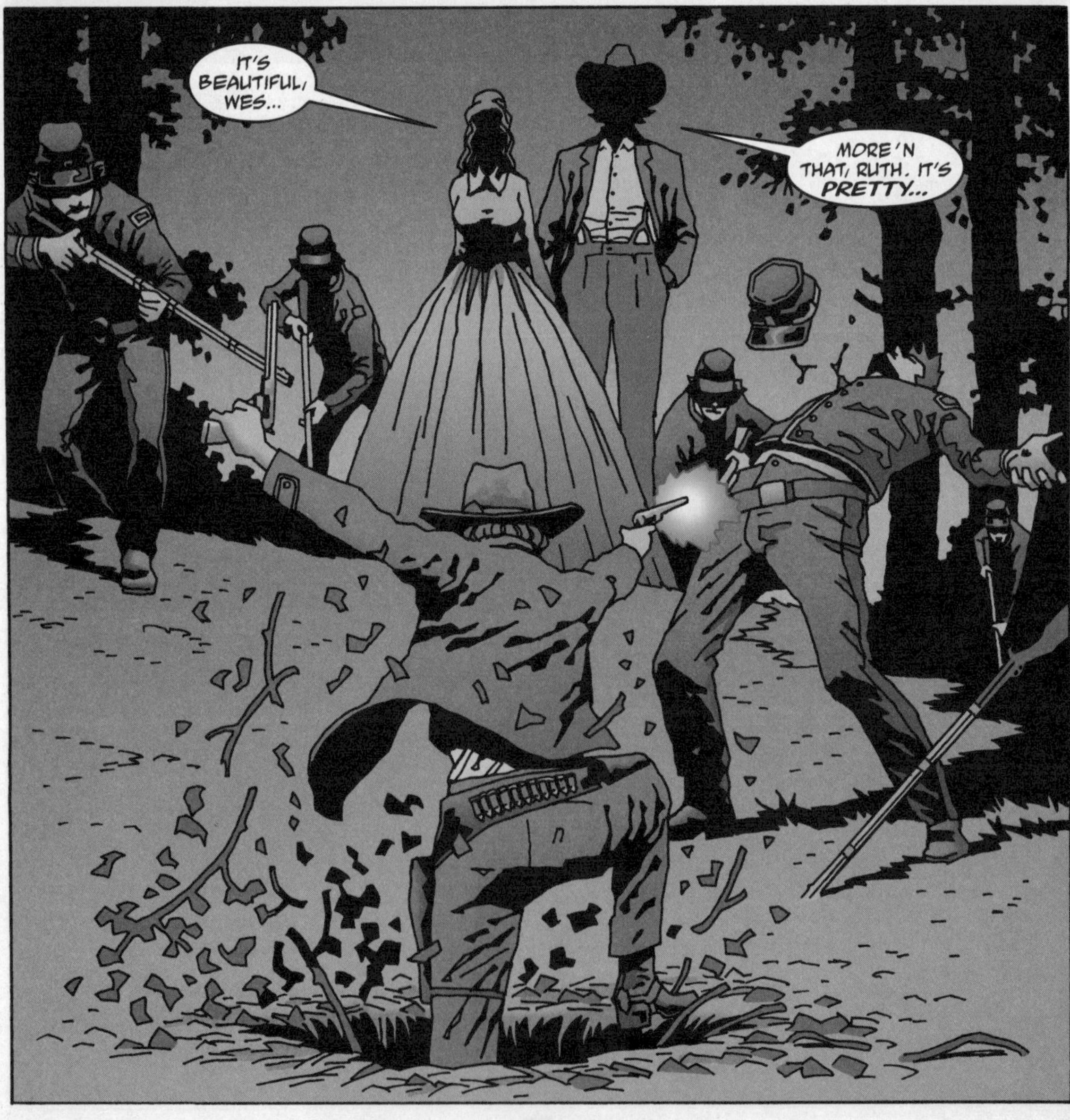
IT'S BEAUTIFUL, WES...
MORE'N THAT, RUTH. IT'S PRETTY...

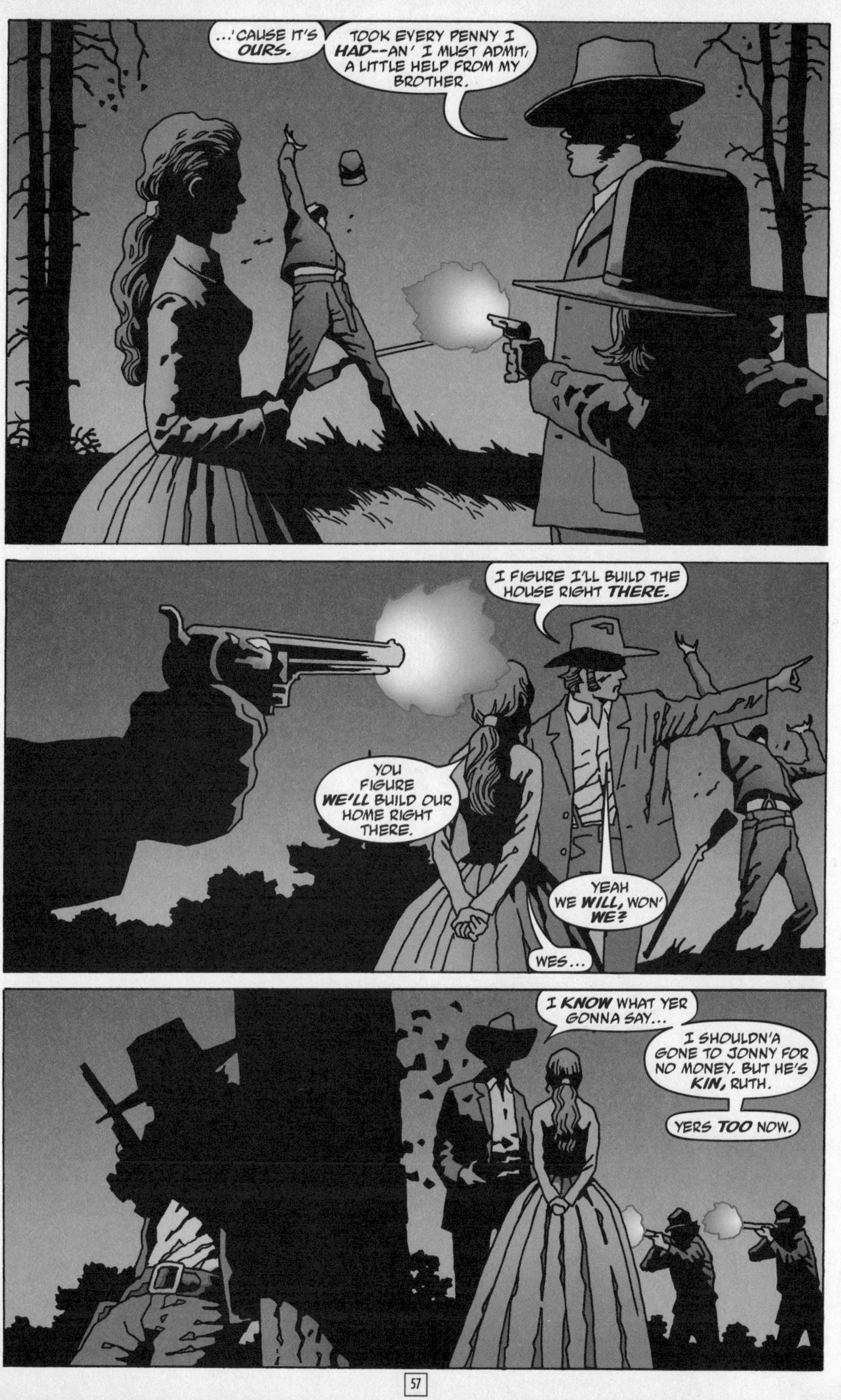
...'CAUSE IT'S **OURS.**
TOOK EVERY PENNY I **HAD**--AN' I MUST ADMIT, A LITTLE HELP FROM MY BROTHER.
I FIGURE I'LL BUILD THE HOUSE RIGHT **THERE.**
YOU FIGURE **WE'LL** BUILD OUR HOME RIGHT THERE.
YEAH WE **WILL,** WON' **WE?**
WES...
I **KNOW** WHAT YER GONNA SAY...
I SHOULDN'A GONE TO JONNY FOR NO MONEY. BUT HE'S **KIN,** RUTH.
YERS **TOO** NOW.

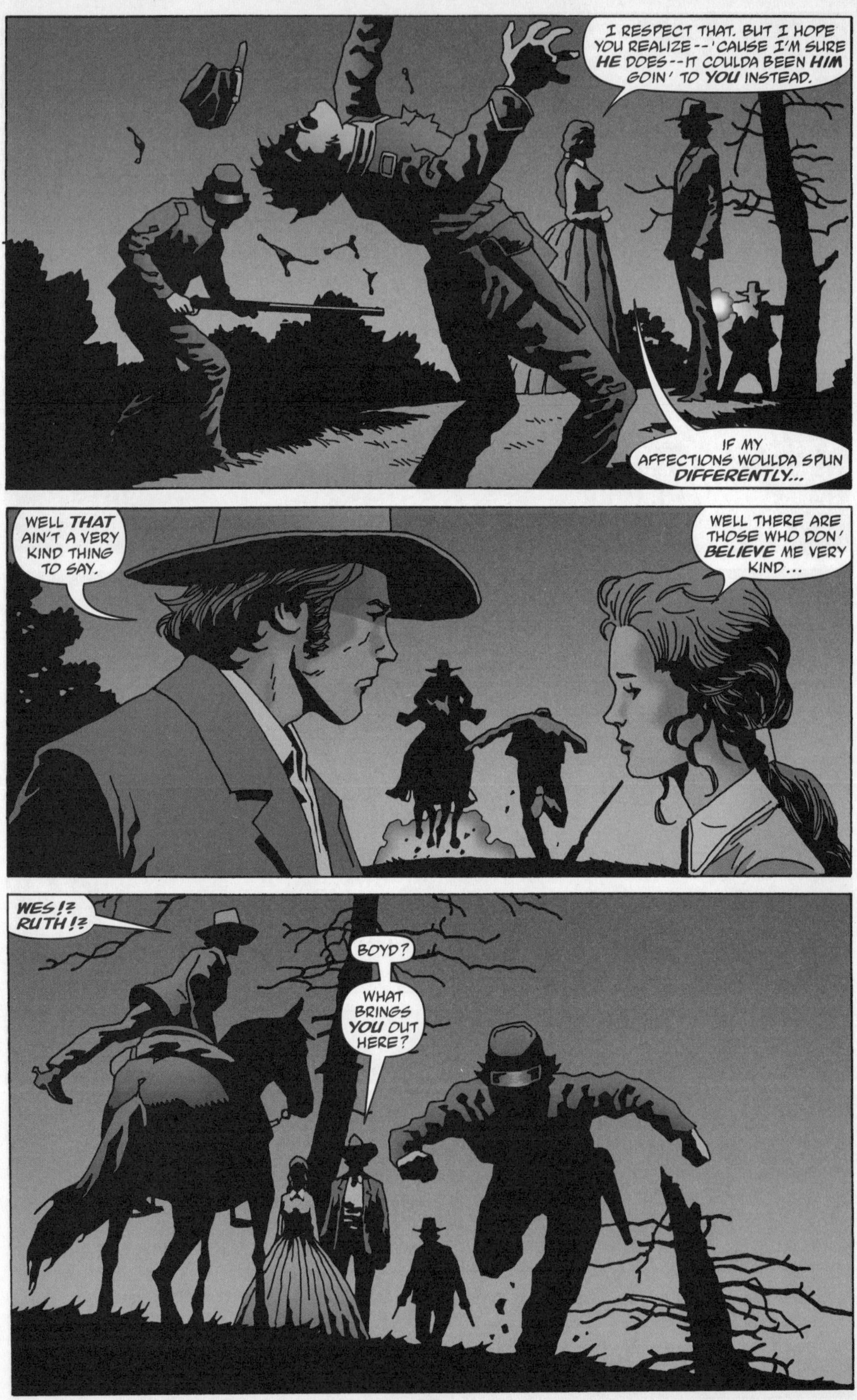
I RESPECT THAT. BUT I HOPE YOU REALIZE--'CAUSE I'M SURE HE DOES--IT COULDA BEEN HIM GOIN' TO YOU INSTEAD.
IF MY AFFECTIONS WOULDA SPUN DIFFERENTLY...
WELL THAT AIN'T A VERY KIND THING TO SAY.
WELL THERE ARE THOSE WHO DON' BELIEVE ME VERY KIND...
WES!? RUTH!?
BOYD?
WHAT BRINGS YOU OUT HERE?

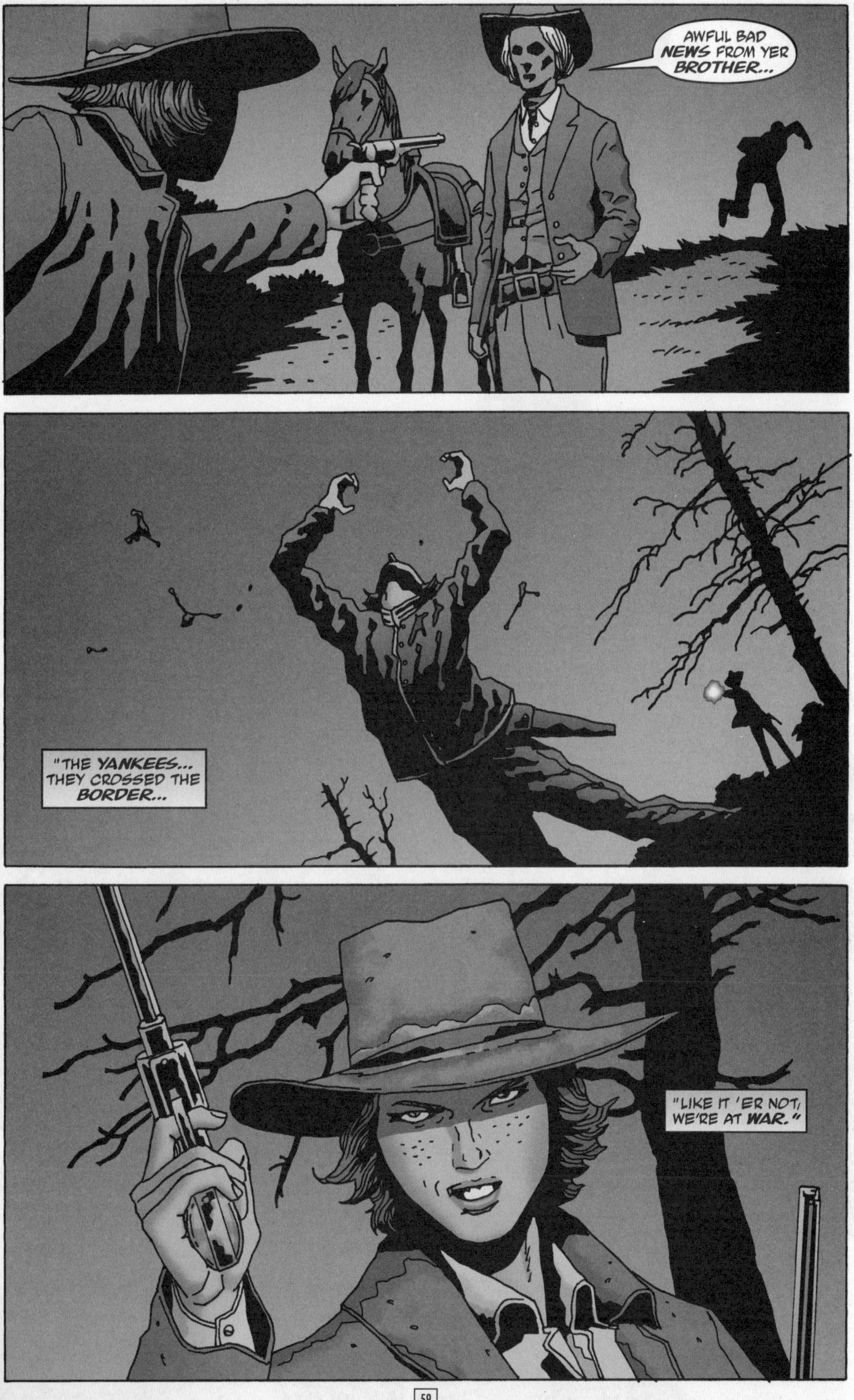
AWFUL BAD NEWS FROM YER BROTHER...
"THE YANKEES... THEY CROSSED THE BORDER...
"LIKE IT 'ER NOT, WE'RE AT WAR."

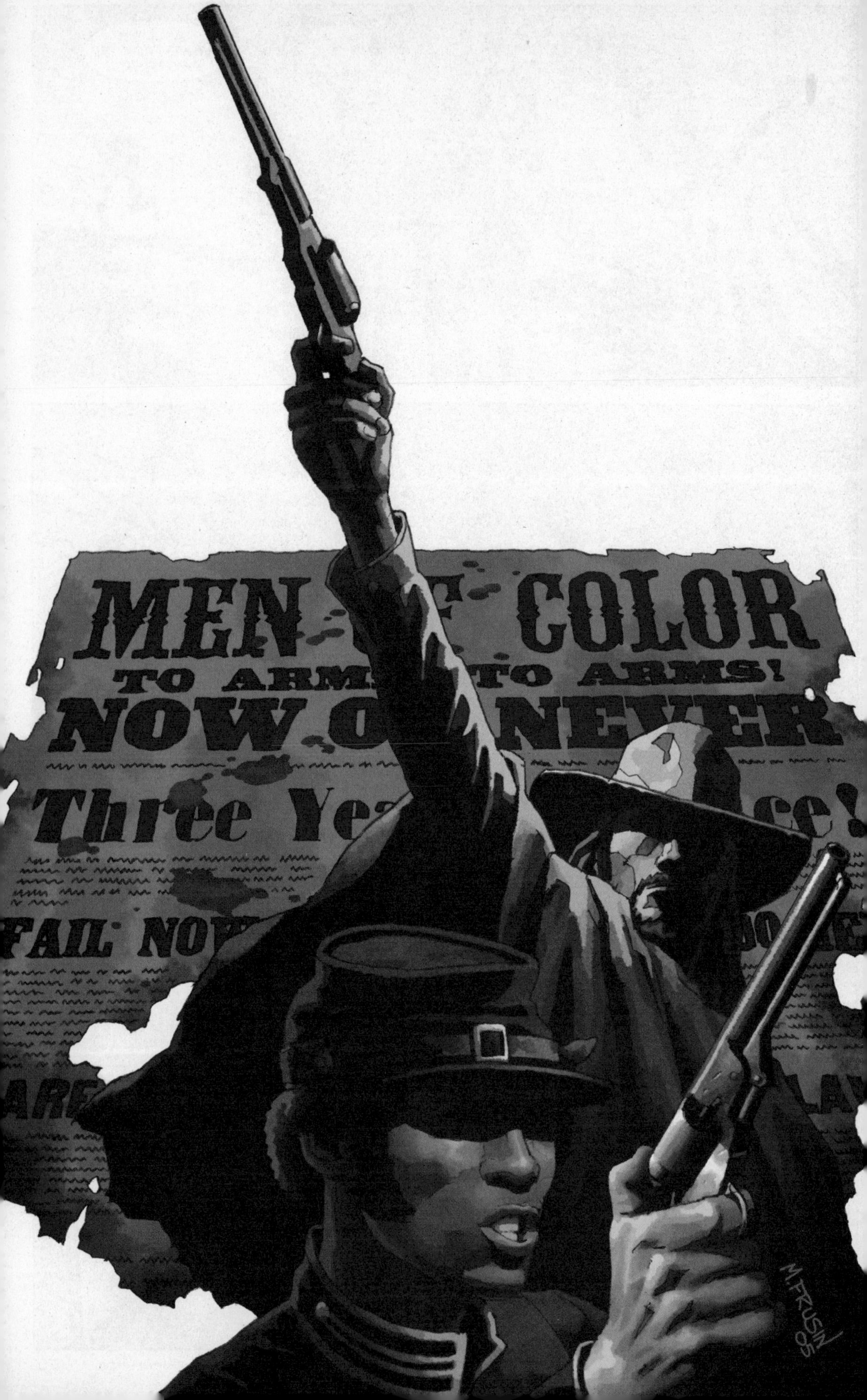
MEN COLOR
TO ARMS!
NEVER
Three
M. FRUSIN 05

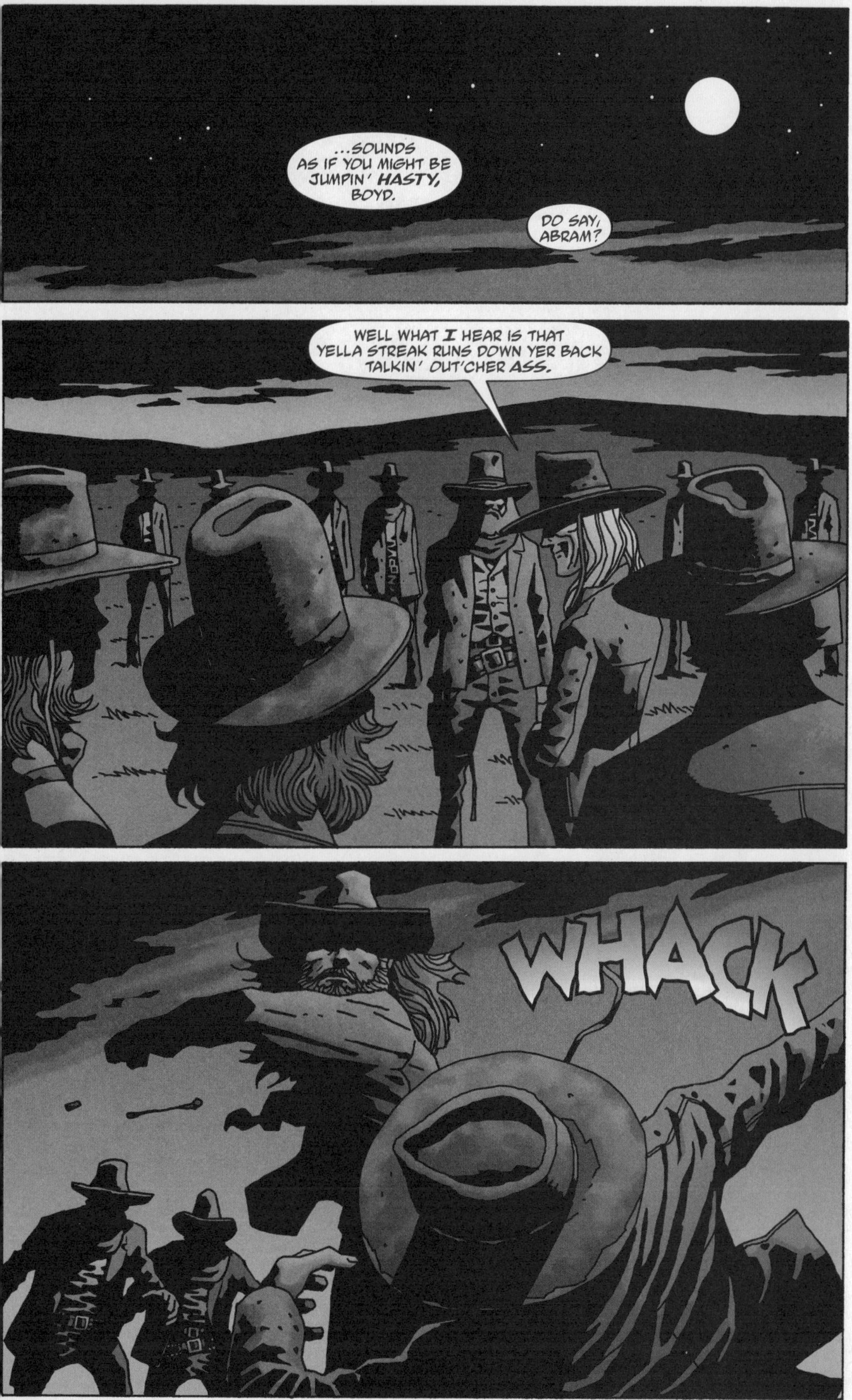
...SOUNDS AS IF YOU MIGHT BE JUMPIN' HASTY, BOYD.
DO SAY, ABRAM?
WELL WHAT I HEAR IS THAT YELLA STREAK RUNS DOWN YER BACK TALKIN' OUT'CHER ASS.
WHACK

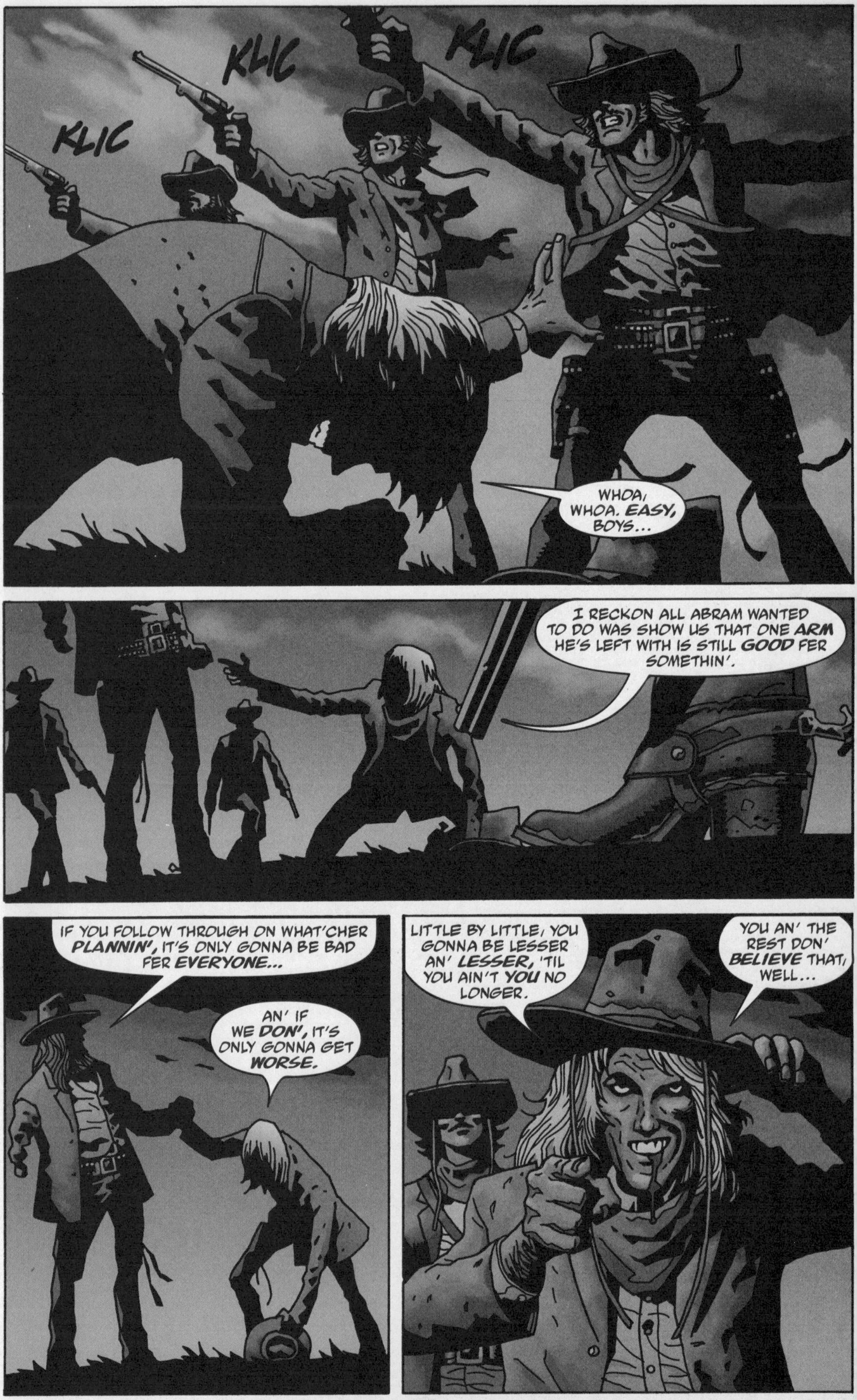
KLIC
KLIC
KLIC
WHOA, WHOA. EASY, BOYS...
I RECKON ALL ABRAM WANTED TO DO WAS SHOW US THAT ONE ARM HE'S LEFT WITH IS STILL GOOD FER SOMETHIN'.
IF YOU FOLLOW THROUGH ON WHAT'CHER PLANNIN', IT'S ONLY GONNA BE BAD FER EVERYONE...
AN' IF WE DON', IT'S ONLY GONNA GET WORSE.
LITTLE BY LITTLE, YOU GONNA BE LESSER AN' LESSER, 'TIL YOU AIN'T YOU NO LONGER.
YOU AN' THE REST DON' BELIEVE THAT, WELL...

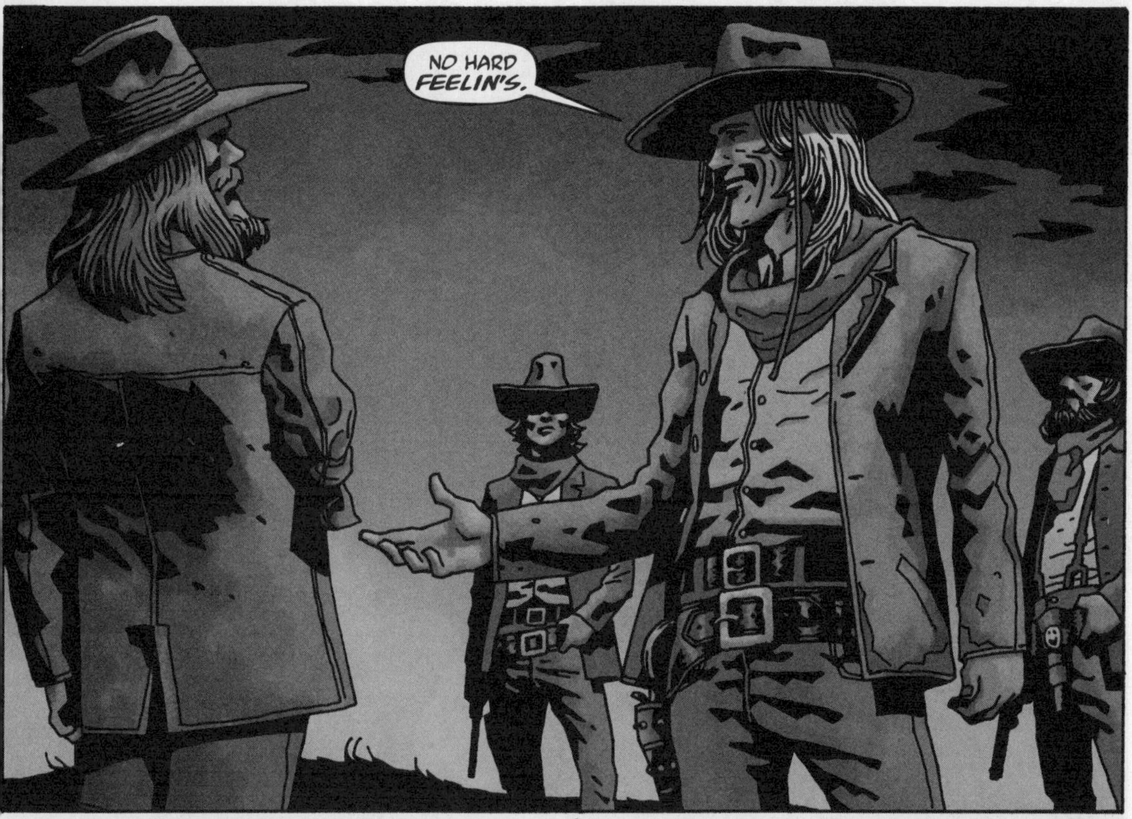
NO HARD
FEELIN'S.

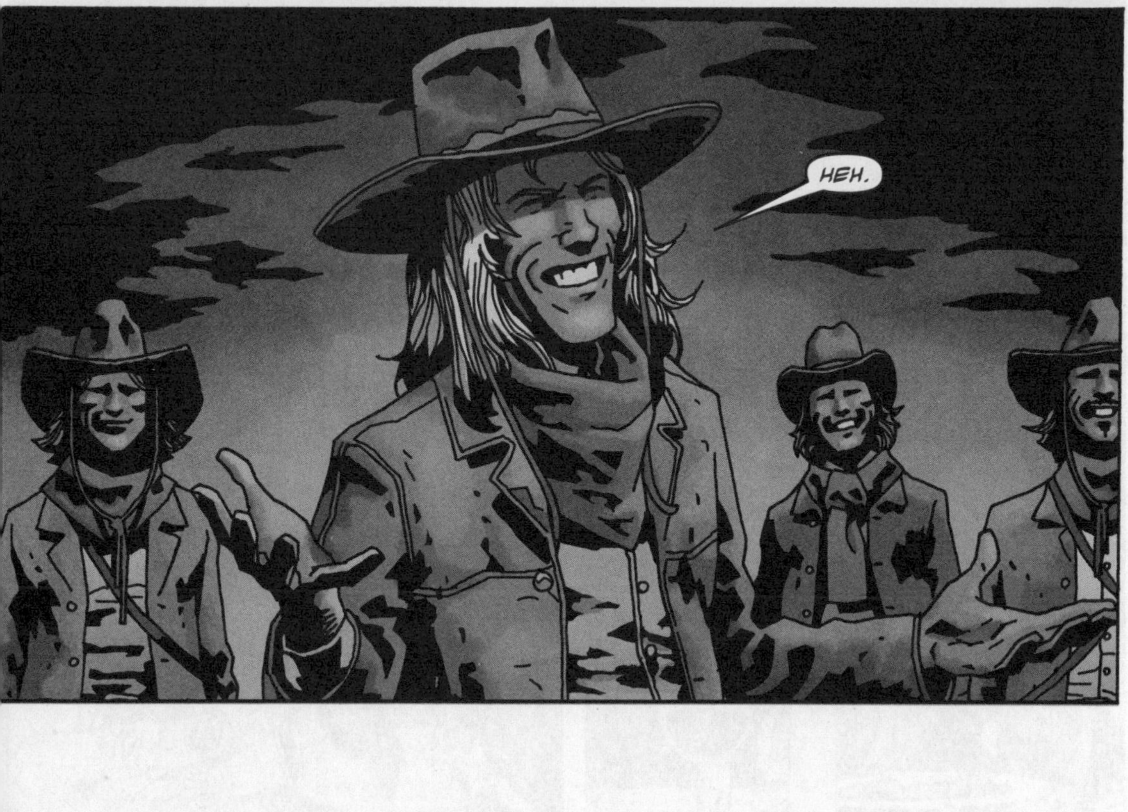
HEH.

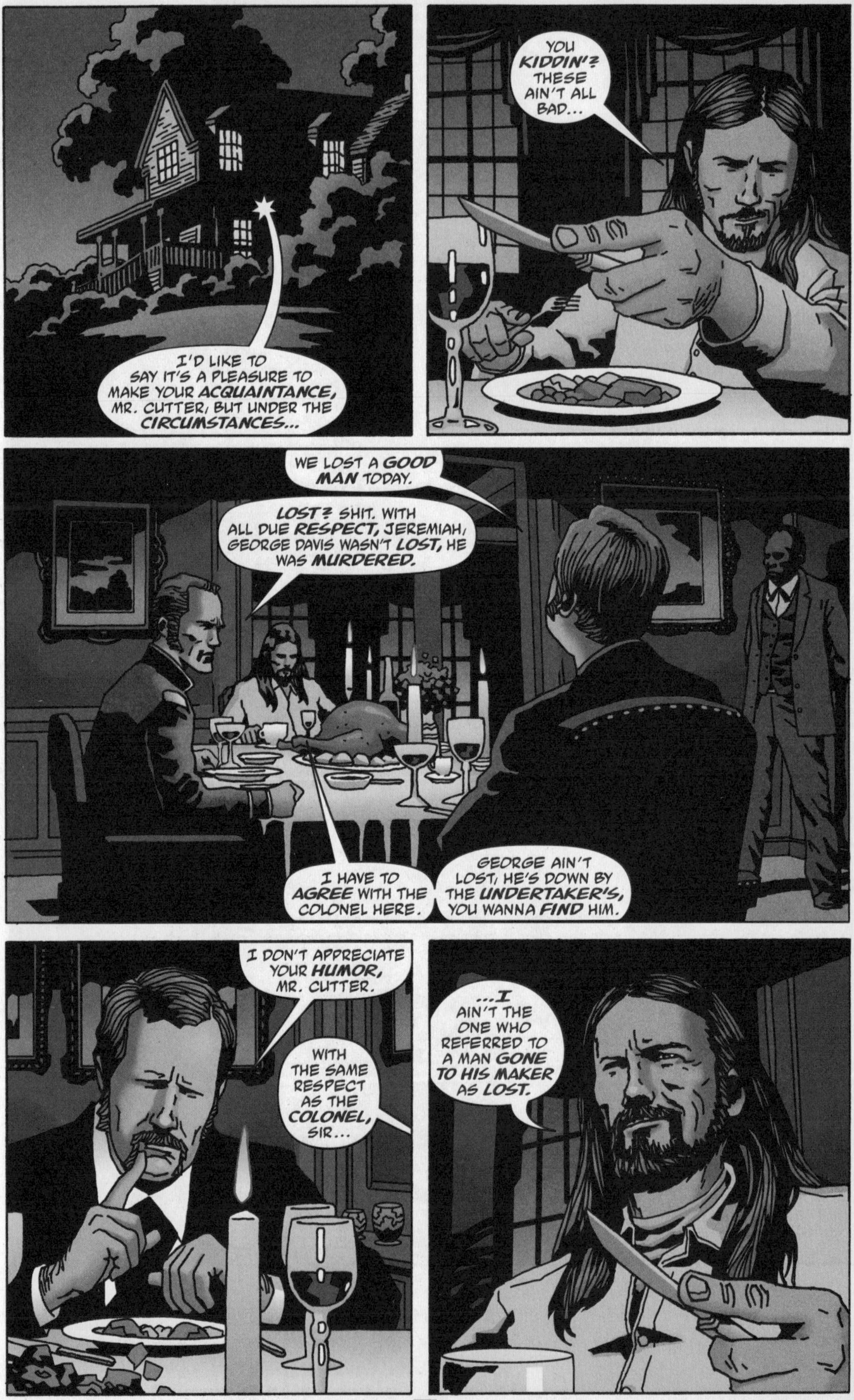
I'D LIKE TO SAY IT'S A PLEASURE TO MAKE YOUR ACQUAINTANCE, MR. CUTTER, BUT UNDER THE CIRCUMSTANCES...
YOU KIDDIN'? THESE AIN'T ALL BAD...
WE LOST A GOOD MAN TODAY.
LOST? SHIT. WITH ALL DUE RESPECT, JEREMIAH, GEORGE DAVIS WASN'T LOST, HE WAS MURDERED.
I HAVE TO AGREE WITH THE COLONEL HERE.
GEORGE AIN'T LOST, HE'S DOWN BY THE UNDERTAKER'S, YOU WANNA FIND HIM.
I DON'T APPRECIATE YOUR HUMOR, MR. CUTTER.
WITH THE SAME RESPECT AS THE COLONEL, SIR...
...I AIN'T THE ONE WHO REFERRED TO A MAN GONE TO HIS MAKER AS LOST.

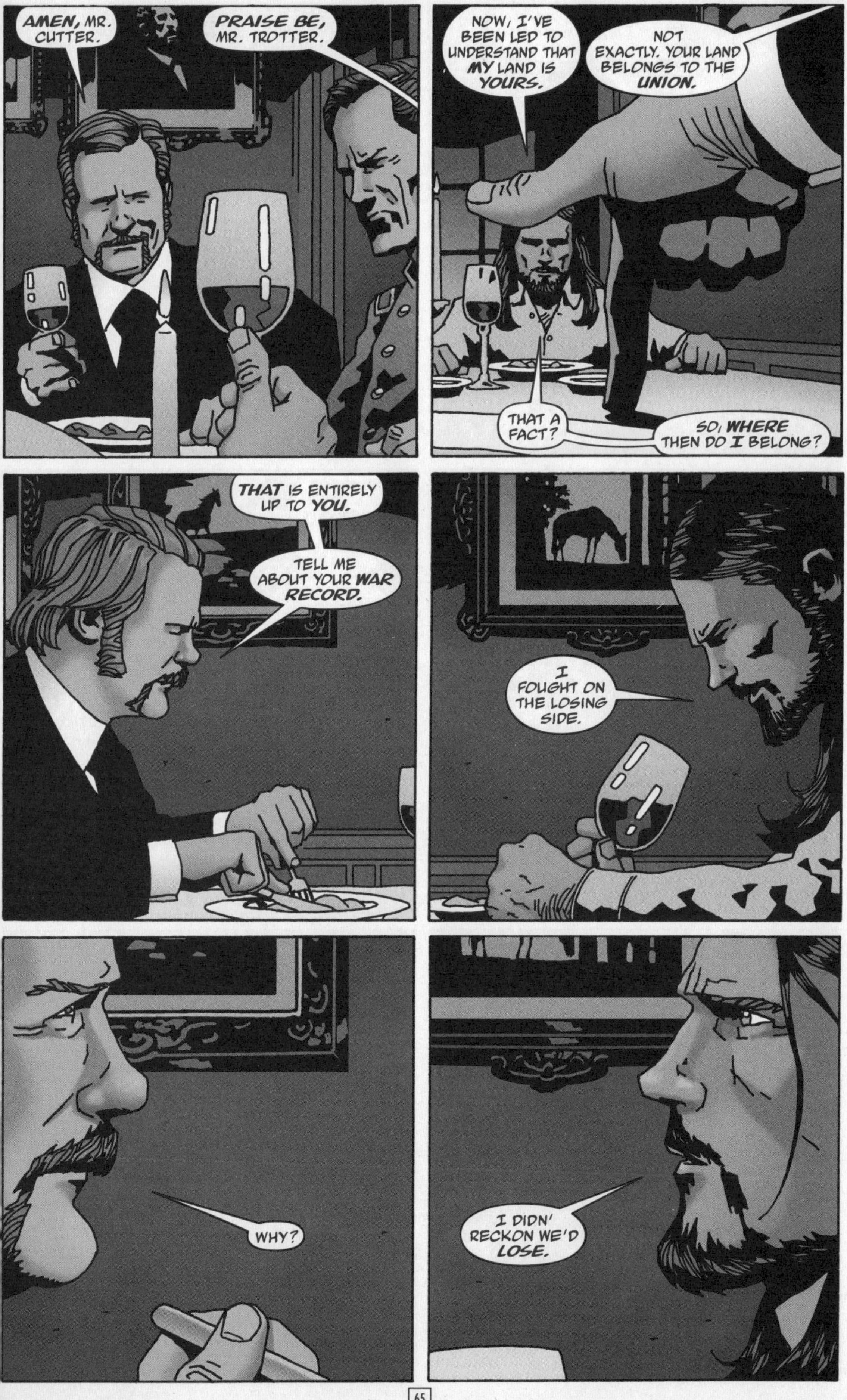
AMEN, MR. CUTTER.
PRAISE BE, MR. TROTTER.
NOW, I'VE BEEN LED TO UNDERSTAND THAT MY LAND IS YOURS.
NOT EXACTLY. YOUR LAND BELONGS TO THE UNION.
THAT A FACT?
SO, WHERE THEN DO I BELONG?
THAT IS ENTIRELY UP TO YOU.
TELL ME ABOUT YOUR WAR RECORD.
I FOUGHT ON THE LOSING SIDE.
WHY?
I DIDN' RECKON WE'D LOSE.

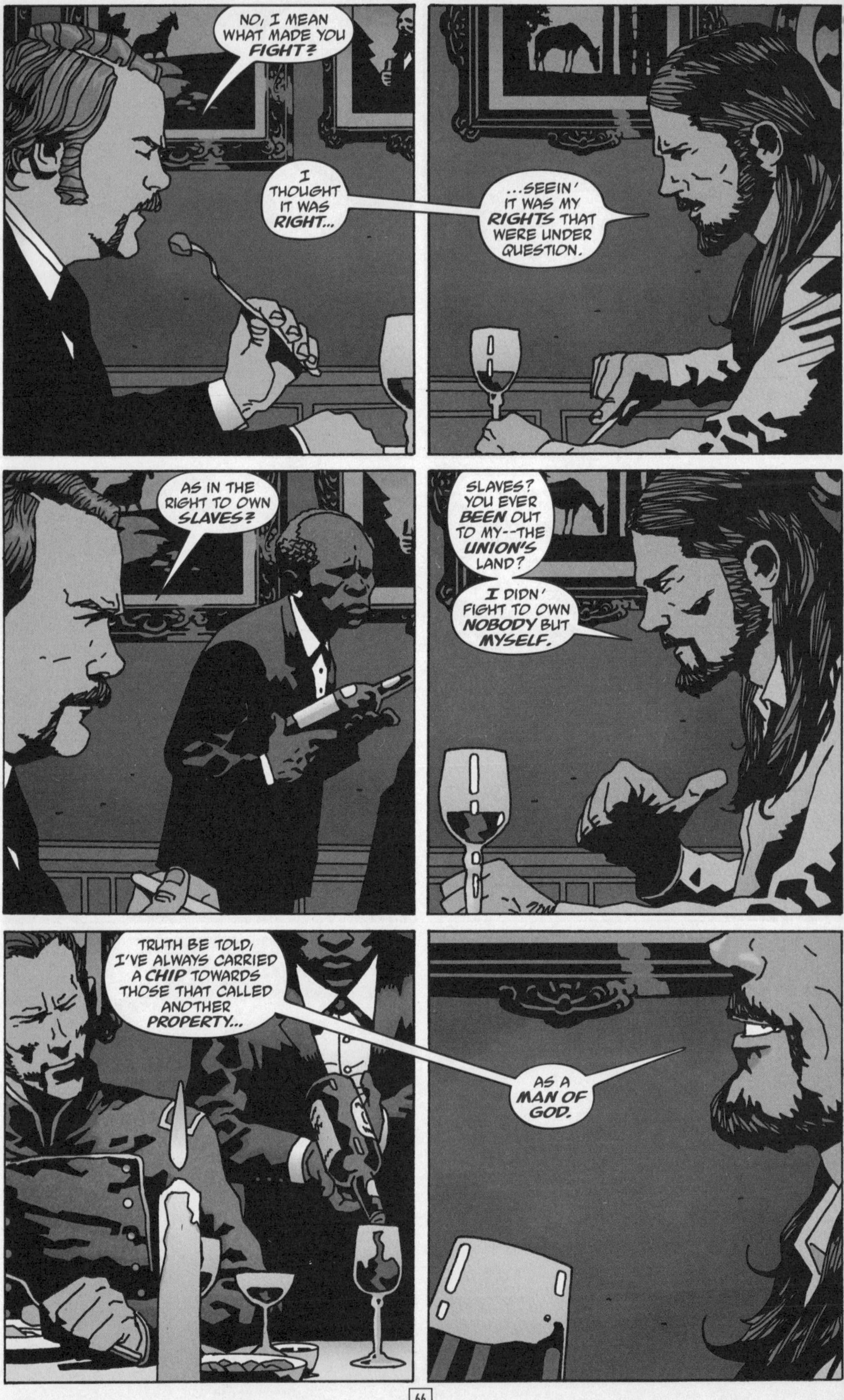
NO, I MEAN WHAT MADE YOU FIGHT?
I THOUGHT IT WAS RIGHT...
...SEEIN' IT WAS MY RIGHTS THAT WERE UNDER QUESTION.
AS IN THE RIGHT TO OWN SLAVES?
SLAVES? YOU EVER BEEN OUT TO MY--THE UNION'S LAND?
I DIDN' FIGHT TO OWN NOBODY BUT MYSELF.
TRUTH BE TOLD, I'VE ALWAYS CARRIED A CHIP TOWARDS THOSE THAT CALLED ANOTHER PROPERTY...
AS A MAN OF GOD.

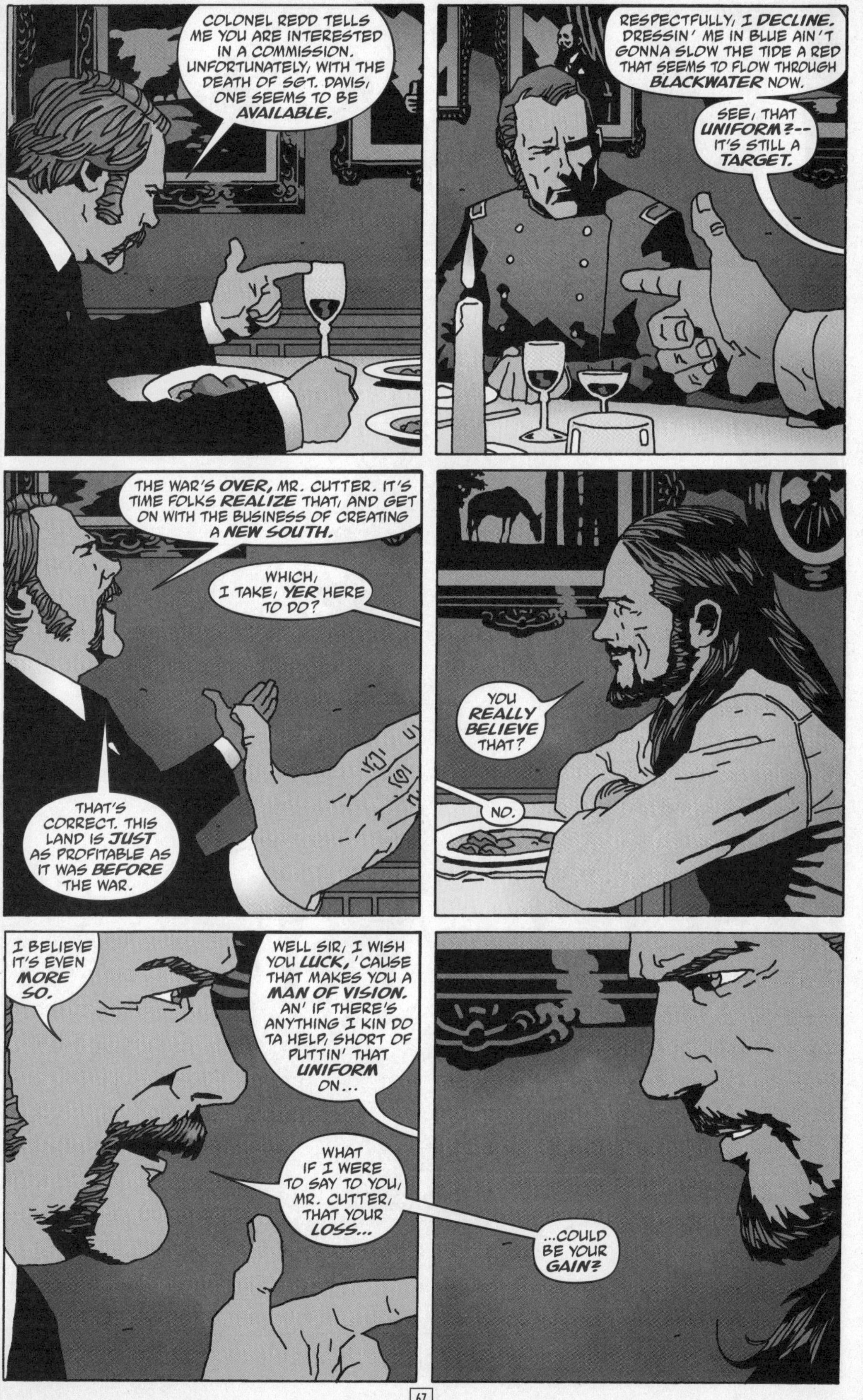
COLONEL REDD TELLS ME YOU ARE INTERESTED IN A COMMISSION. UNFORTUNATELY, WITH THE DEATH OF SGT. DAVIS, ONE SEEMS TO BE AVAILABLE.
RESPECTFULLY, I DECLINE. DRESSIN' ME IN BLUE AIN'T GONNA SLOW THE TIDE A RED THAT SEEMS TO FLOW THROUGH BLACKWATER NOW.
SEE, THAT UNIFORM?-- IT'S STILL A TARGET.
THE WAR'S OVER, MR. CUTTER. IT'S TIME FOLKS REALIZE THAT, AND GET ON WITH THE BUSINESS OF CREATING A NEW SOUTH.
WHICH, I TAKE, YER HERE TO DO?
THAT'S CORRECT. THIS LAND IS JUST AS PROFITABLE AS IT WAS BEFORE THE WAR.
YOU REALLY BELIEVE THAT?
NO.
I BELIEVE IT'S EVEN MORE SO.
WELL SIR, I WISH YOU LUCK, 'CAUSE THAT MAKES YOU A MAN OF VISION. AN' IF THERE'S ANYTHING I KIN DO TA HELP, SHORT OF PUTTIN' THAT UNIFORM ON...
WHAT IF I WERE TO SAY TO YOU, MR. CUTTER, THAT YOUR LOSS...
...COULD BE YOUR GAIN?

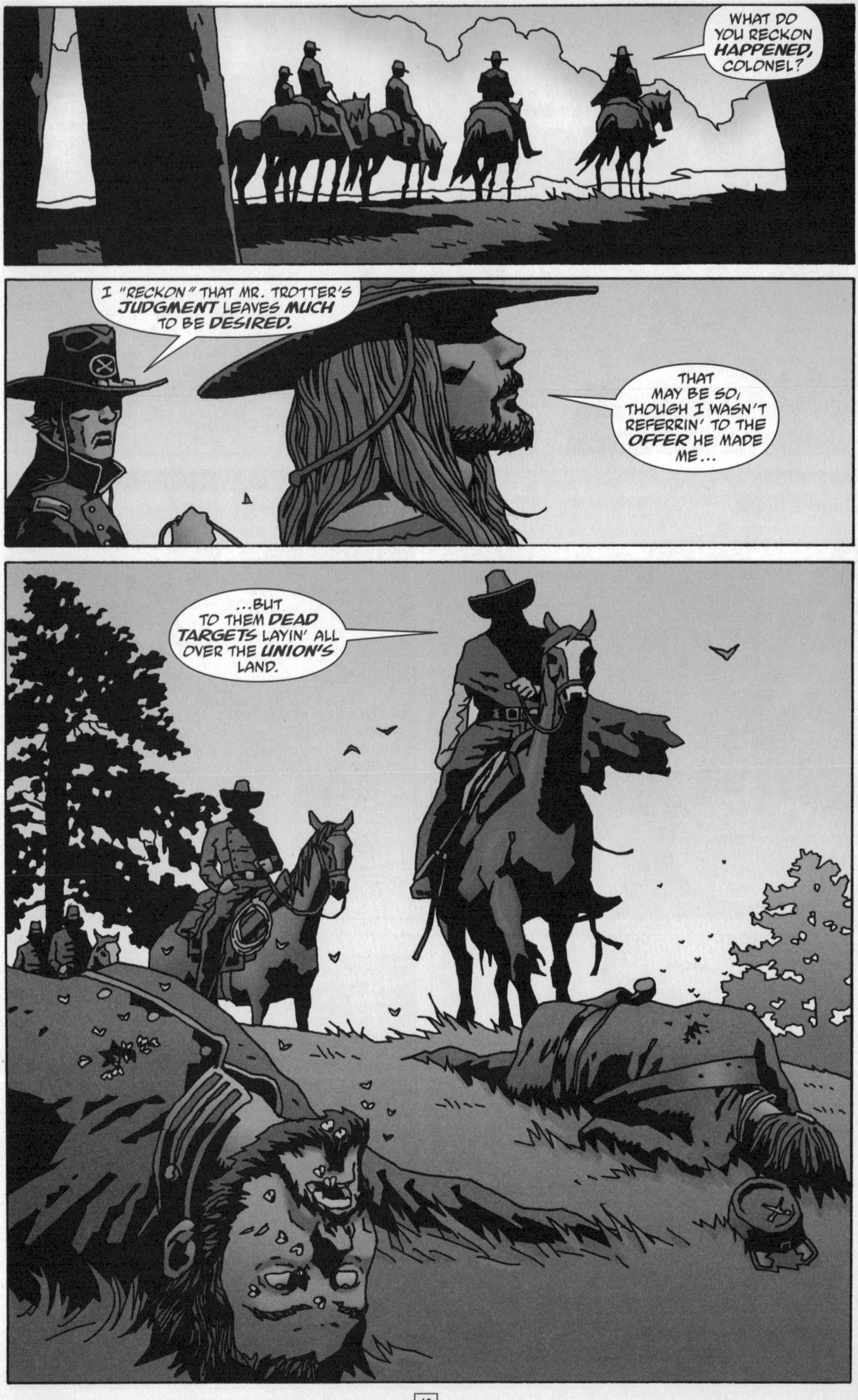
WHAT DO YOU RECKON HAPPENED, COLONEL?
I "RECKON" THAT MR. TROTTER'S JUDGMENT LEAVES MUCH TO BE DESIRED.
THAT MAY BE SO, THOUGH I WASN'T REFERRIN' TO THE OFFER HE MADE ME...
...BUT TO THEM DEAD TARGETS LAYIN' ALL OVER THE UNION'S LAND.

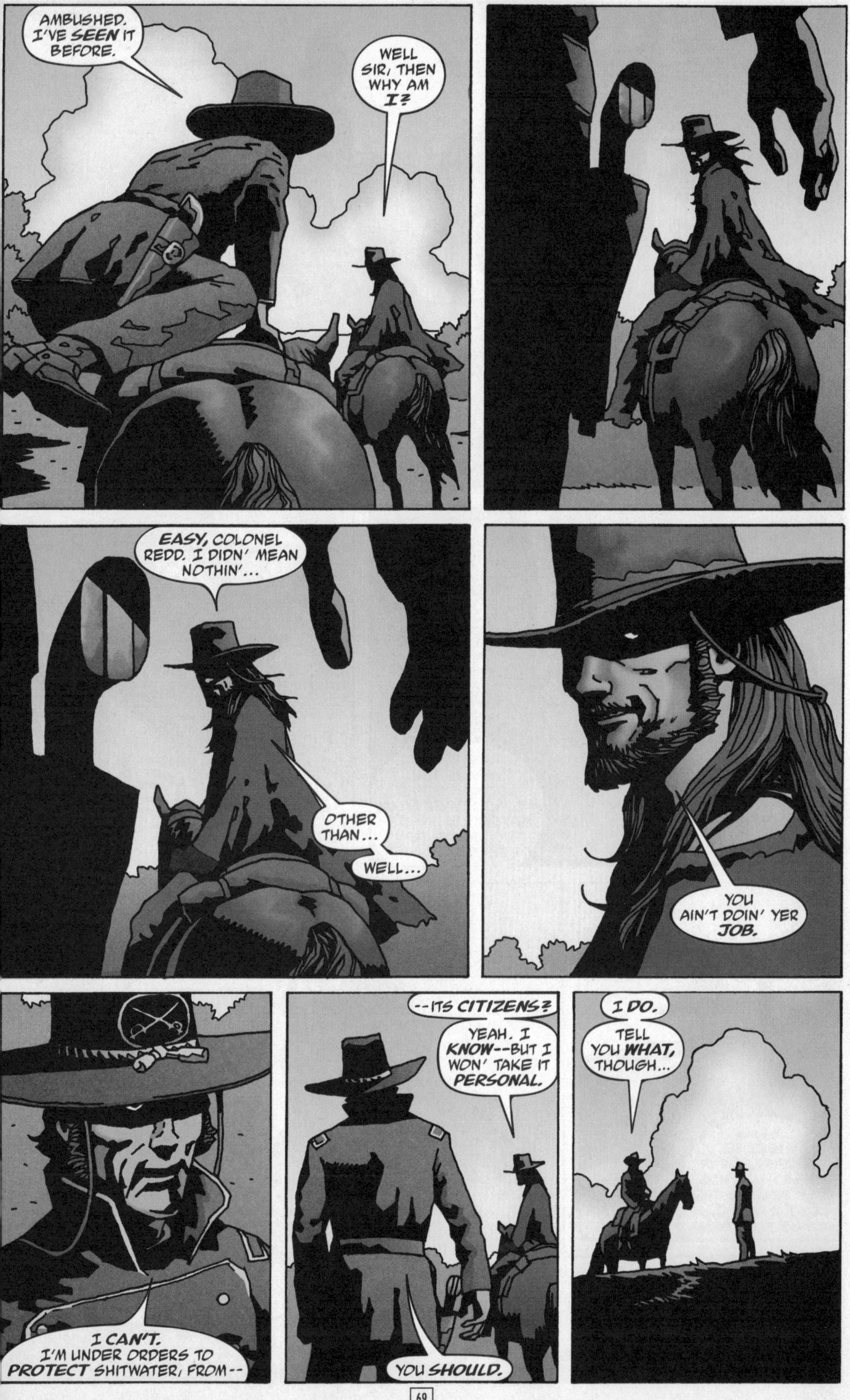
AMBUSHED. I'VE SEEN IT BEFORE.
WELL SIR, THEN WHY AM I?
EASY, COLONEL REDD. I DIDN' MEAN NOTHIN'...
OTHER THAN...
WELL...
YOU AIN'T DOIN' YER JOB.
I CAN'T. I'M UNDER ORDERS TO PROTECT SHITWATER, FROM--
--ITS CITIZENS?
YEAH. I KNOW--BUT I WON' TAKE IT PERSONAL.
YOU SHOULD.
I DO.
TELL YOU WHAT, THOUGH...

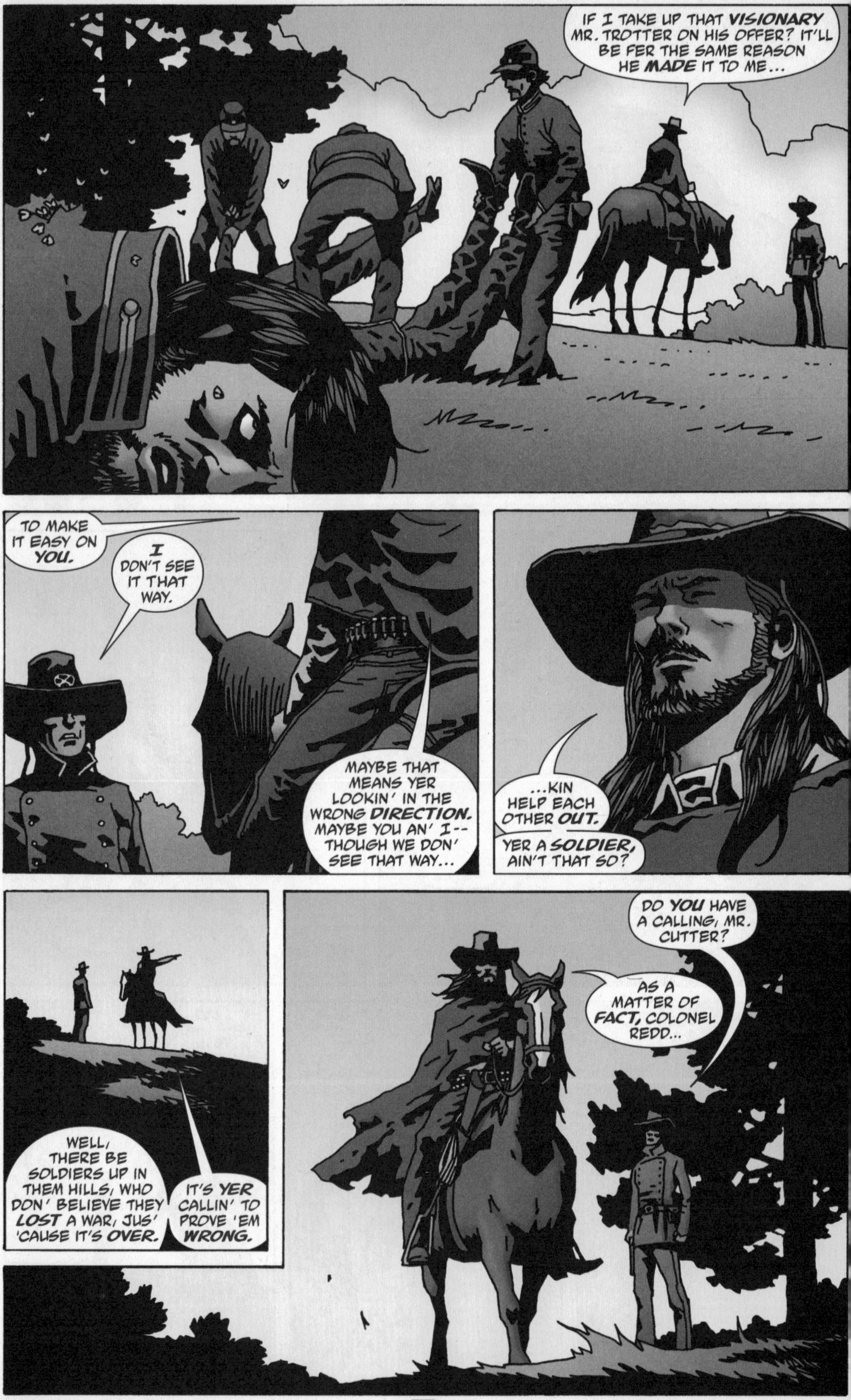

IF I TAKE UP THAT VISIONARY MR. TROTTER ON HIS OFFER? IT'LL BE FER THE SAME REASON HE MADE IT TO ME...
TO MAKE IT EASY ON YOU.
I DON'T SEE IT THAT WAY.
MAYBE THAT MEANS YER LOOKIN' IN THE WRONG DIRECTION. MAYBE YOU AN' I-- THOUGH WE DON' SEE THAT WAY...
...KIN HELP EACH OTHER OUT.
YER A SOLDIER, AIN'T THAT SO?
WELL, THERE BE SOLDIERS UP IN THEM HILLS, WHO DON' BELIEVE THEY LOST A WAR, JUS' 'CAUSE IT'S OVER.
IT'S YER CALLIN' TO PROVE 'EM WRONG.
DO YOU HAVE A CALLING, MR. CUTTER?
AS A MATTER OF FACT, COLONEL REDD...

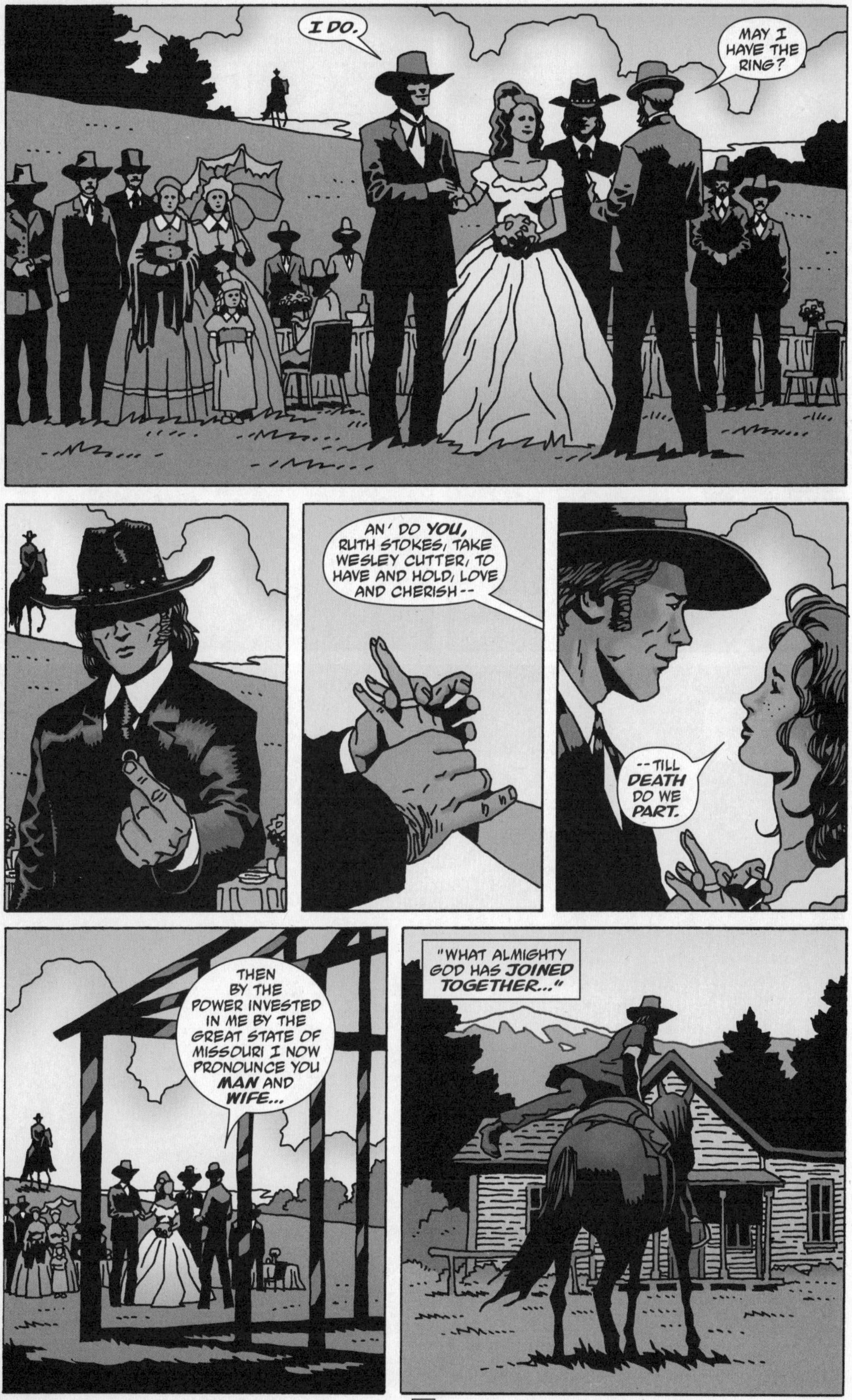
I DO.
MAY I HAVE THE RING?
AN' DO YOU, RUTH STOKES, TAKE WESLEY CUTTER, TO HAVE AND HOLD, LOVE AND CHERISH--
--TILL DEATH DO WE PART.
THEN BY THE POWER INVESTED IN ME BY THE GREAT STATE OF MISSOURI I NOW PRONOUNCE YOU MAN AND WIFE...
"WHAT ALMIGHTY GOD HAS JOINED TOGETHER..."

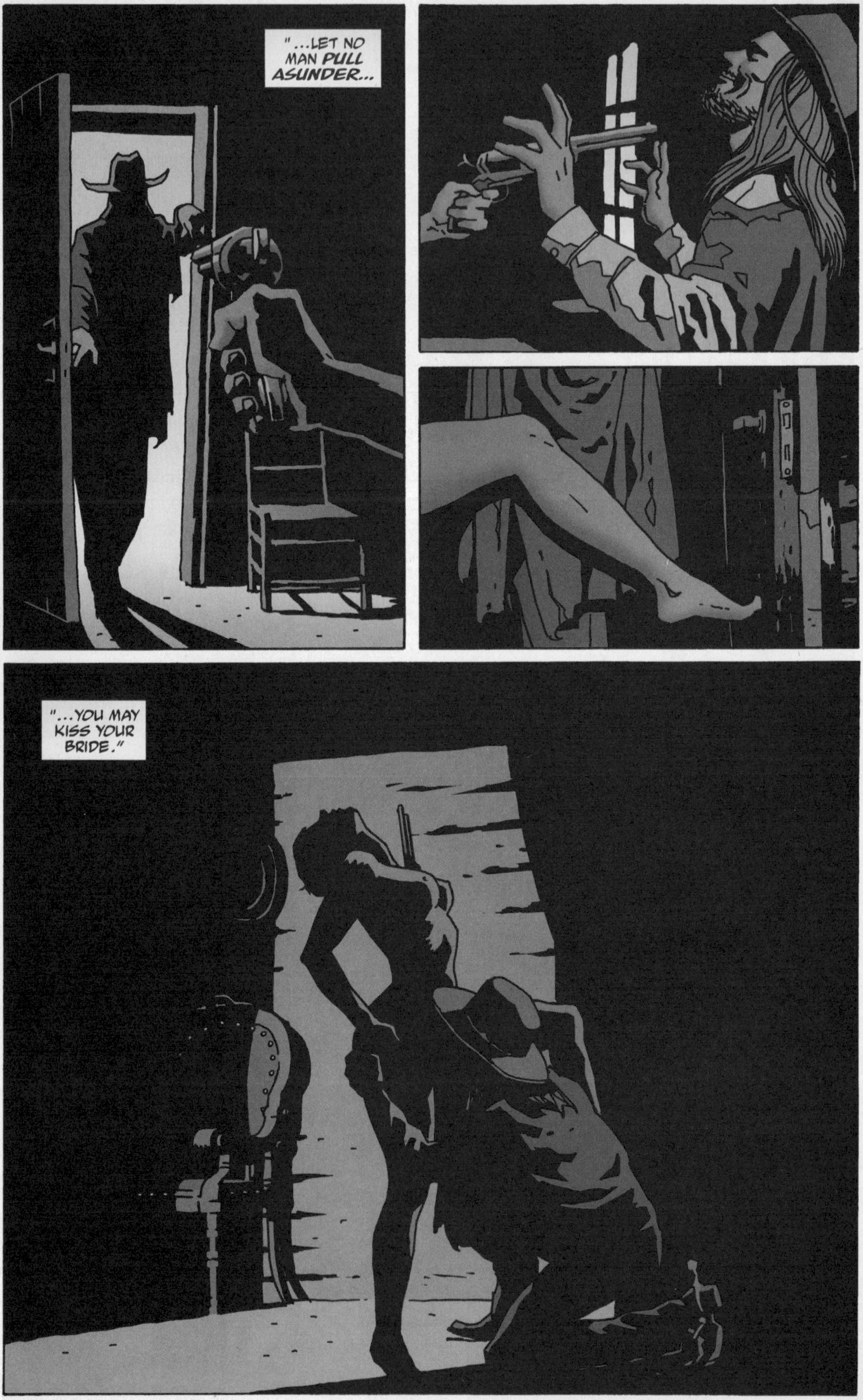
"...LET NO MAN PULL ASUNDER...
"...YOU MAY KISS YOUR BRIDE."

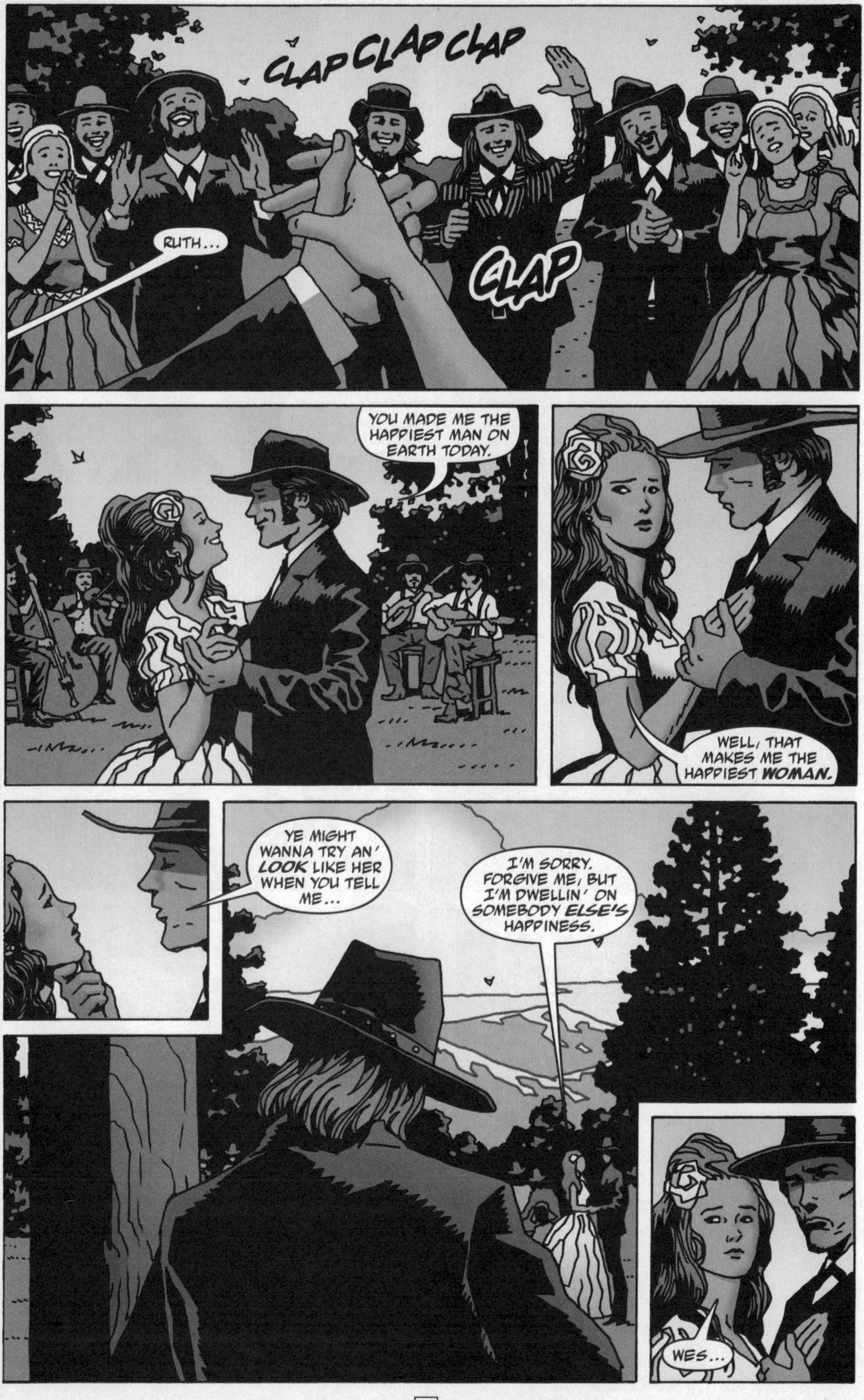
CLAP CLAP CLAP
RUTH...
CLAP
YOU MADE ME THE HAPPIEST MAN ON EARTH TODAY.
WELL, THAT MAKES ME THE HAPPIEST WOMAN.
YE MIGHT WANNA TRY AN' LOOK LIKE HER WHEN YOU TELL ME...
I'M SORRY. FORGIVE ME, BUT I'M DWELLIN' ON SOMEBODY ELSE'S HAPPINESS.
WES...

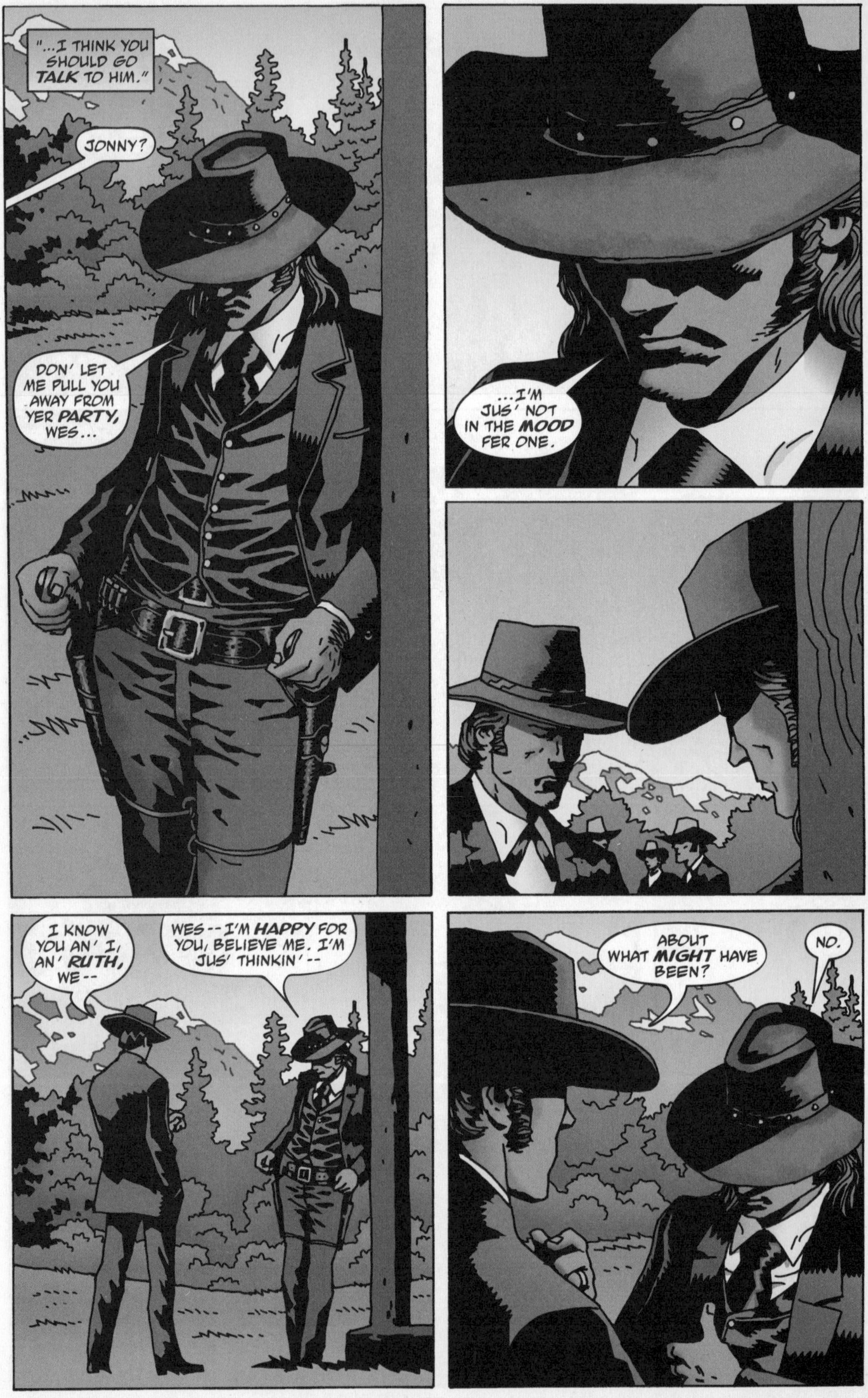
"...I THINK YOU SHOULD GO TALK TO HIM."
JONNY?
DON' LET ME PULL YOU AWAY FROM YER PARTY, WES...
...I'M JUS' NOT IN THE MOOD FER ONE.
I KNOW YOU AN' I, AN' RUTH, WE--
WES--I'M HAPPY FOR YOU, BELIEVE ME. I'M JUS' THINKIN'--
ABOUT WHAT MIGHT HAVE BEEN?
NO.

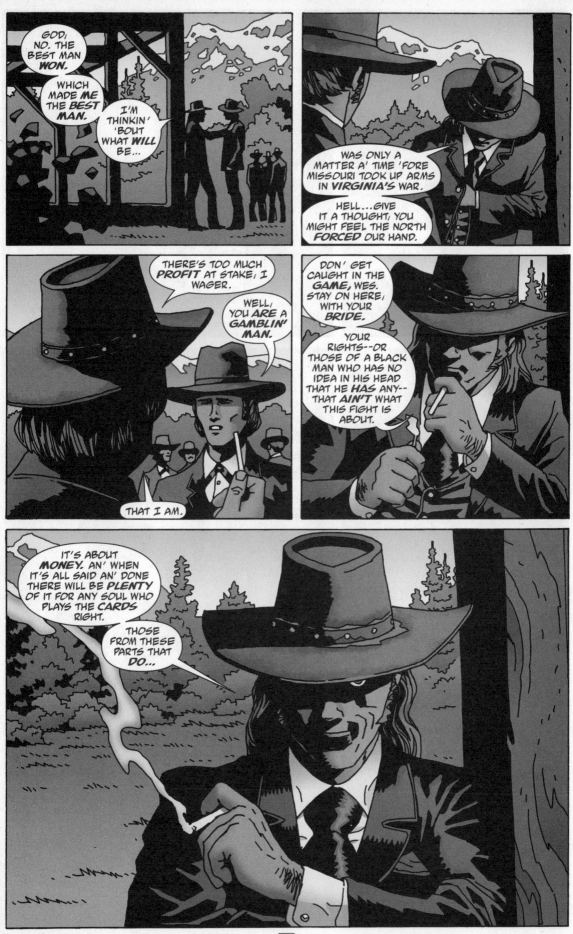

GOD, NO. THE BEST MAN **WON**.

WHICH MADE **ME** THE **BEST MAN**.

I'M THINKIN' 'BOUT WHAT **WILL** BE...

WAS ONLY A MATTER A' TIME 'FORE MISSOURI TOOK UP ARMS IN **VIRGINIA'S** WAR.

HELL...GIVE IT A THOUGHT, YOU MIGHT FEEL THE NORTH **FORCED** OUR HAND.

THERE'S TOO MUCH **PROFIT** AT STAKE, I WAGER.

WELL, YOU **ARE** A **GAMBLIN'** MAN.

THAT I AM.

DON' GET CAUGHT IN THE **GAME**, WES. STAY ON HERE, WITH YOUR **BRIDE**.

YOUR RIGHTS--OR THOSE OF A BLACK MAN WHO HAS NO IDEA IN HIS HEAD THAT HE **HAS** ANY-- THAT **AIN'T** WHAT THIS FIGHT IS ABOUT.

IT'S ABOUT **MONEY**. AN' WHEN IT'S ALL SAID AN' DONE THERE WILL BE **PLENTY** OF IT FOR ANY SOUL WHO PLAYS THE **CARDS** RIGHT.

THOSE FROM THESE PARTS THAT **DO**...

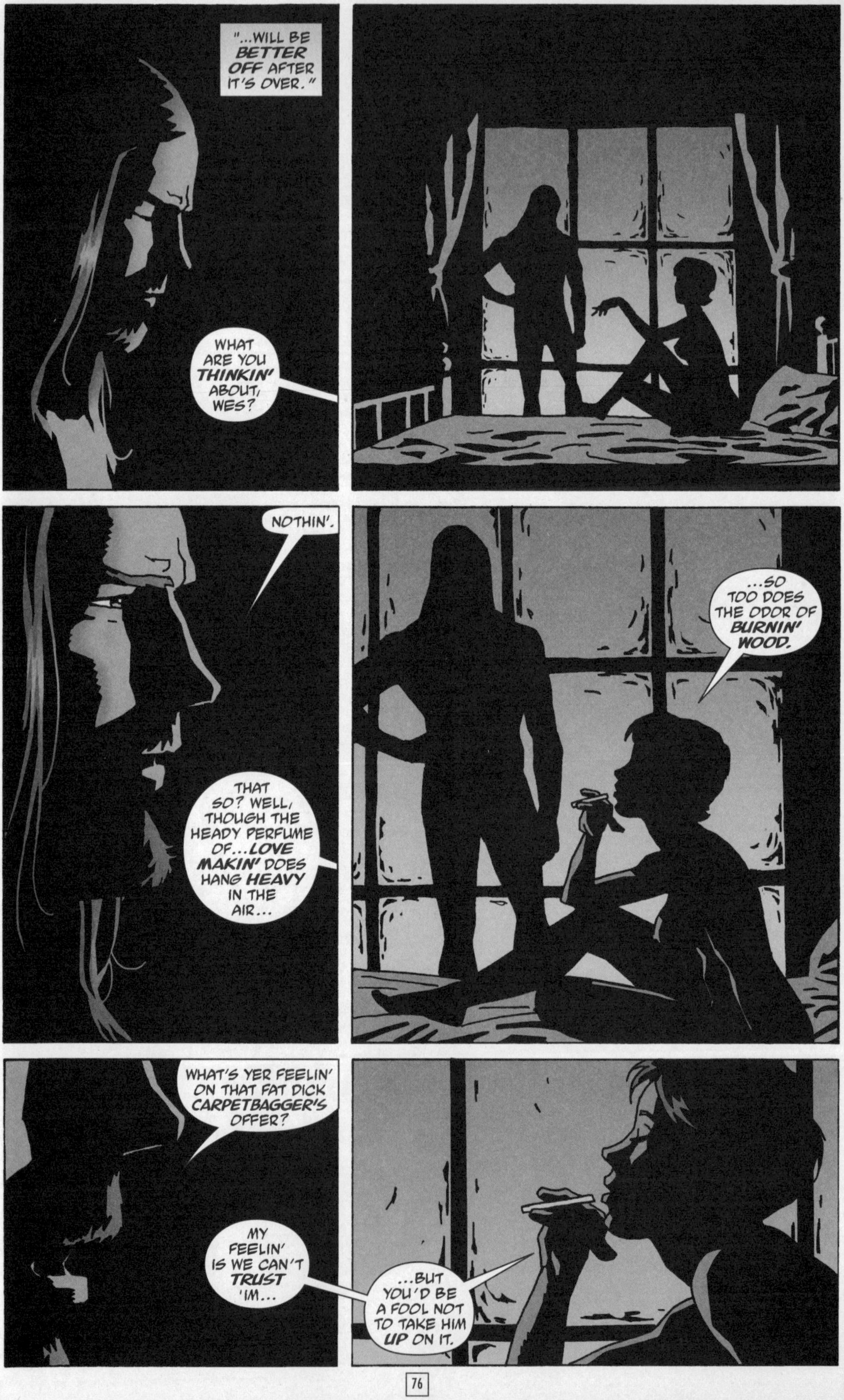
"...WILL BE BETTER OFF AFTER IT'S OVER."
WHAT ARE YOU THINKIN' ABOUT, WES?
NOTHIN'.
THAT SO? WELL, THOUGH THE HEADY PERFUME OF...LOVE MAKIN' DOES HANG HEAVY IN THE AIR...
...SO TOO DOES THE ODOR OF BURNIN' WOOD.
WHAT'S YER FEELIN' ON THAT FAT DICK CARPETBAGGER'S OFFER?
MY FEELIN' IS WE CAN'T TRUST 'IM...
...BUT YOU'D BE A FOOL NOT TO TAKE HIM UP ON IT.

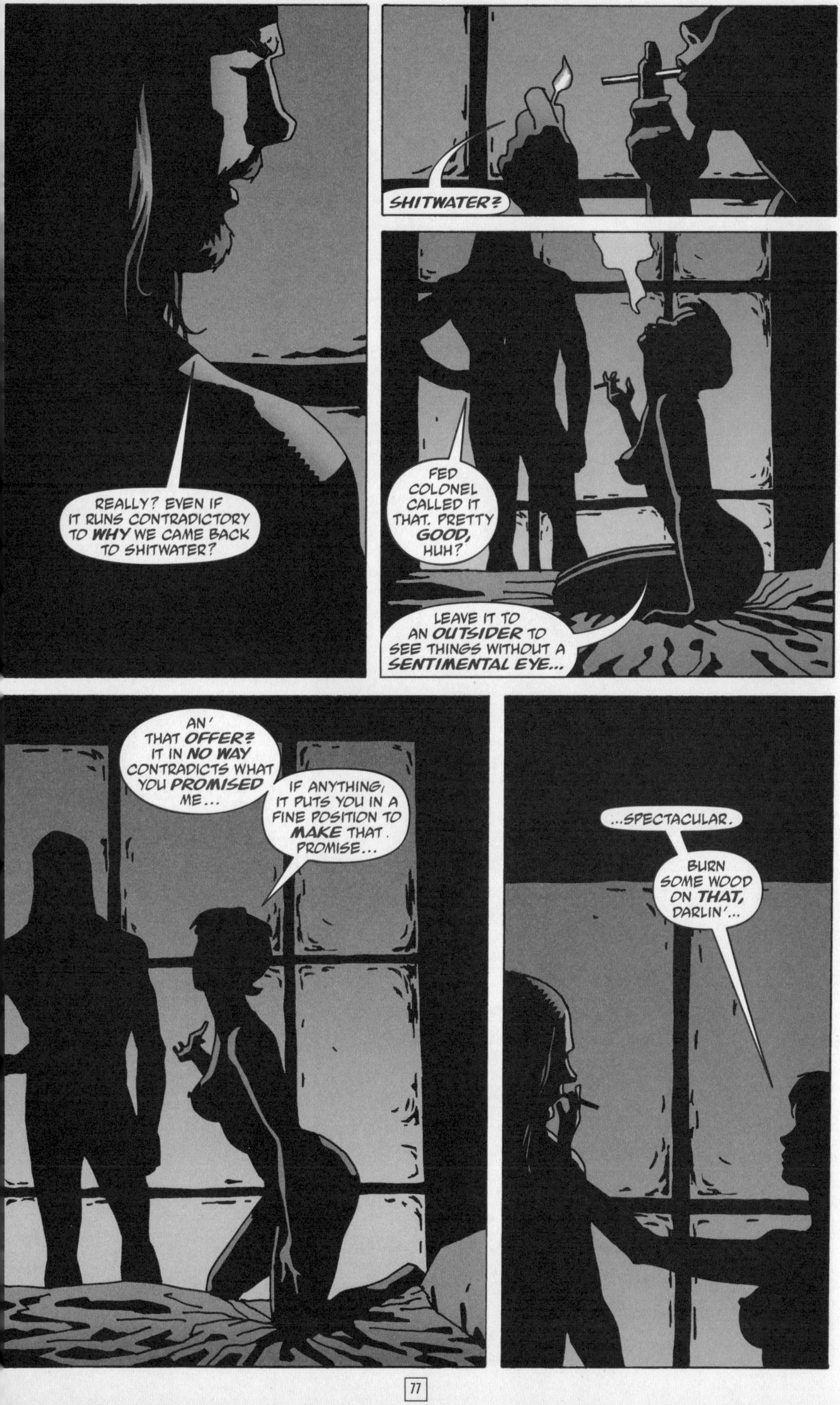
SHITWATER?
REALLY? EVEN IF IT RUNS CONTRADICTORY TO WHY WE CAME BACK TO SHITWATER?
FED COLONEL CALLED IT THAT. PRETTY GOOD, HUH?
LEAVE IT TO AN OUTSIDER TO SEE THINGS WITHOUT A SENTIMENTAL EYE...
AN' THAT OFFER? IT IN NO WAY CONTRADICTS WHAT YOU PROMISED ME...
IF ANYTHING, IT PUTS YOU IN A FINE POSITION TO MAKE THAT PROMISE...
...SPECTACULAR.
BURN SOME WOOD ON THAT, DARLIN'...

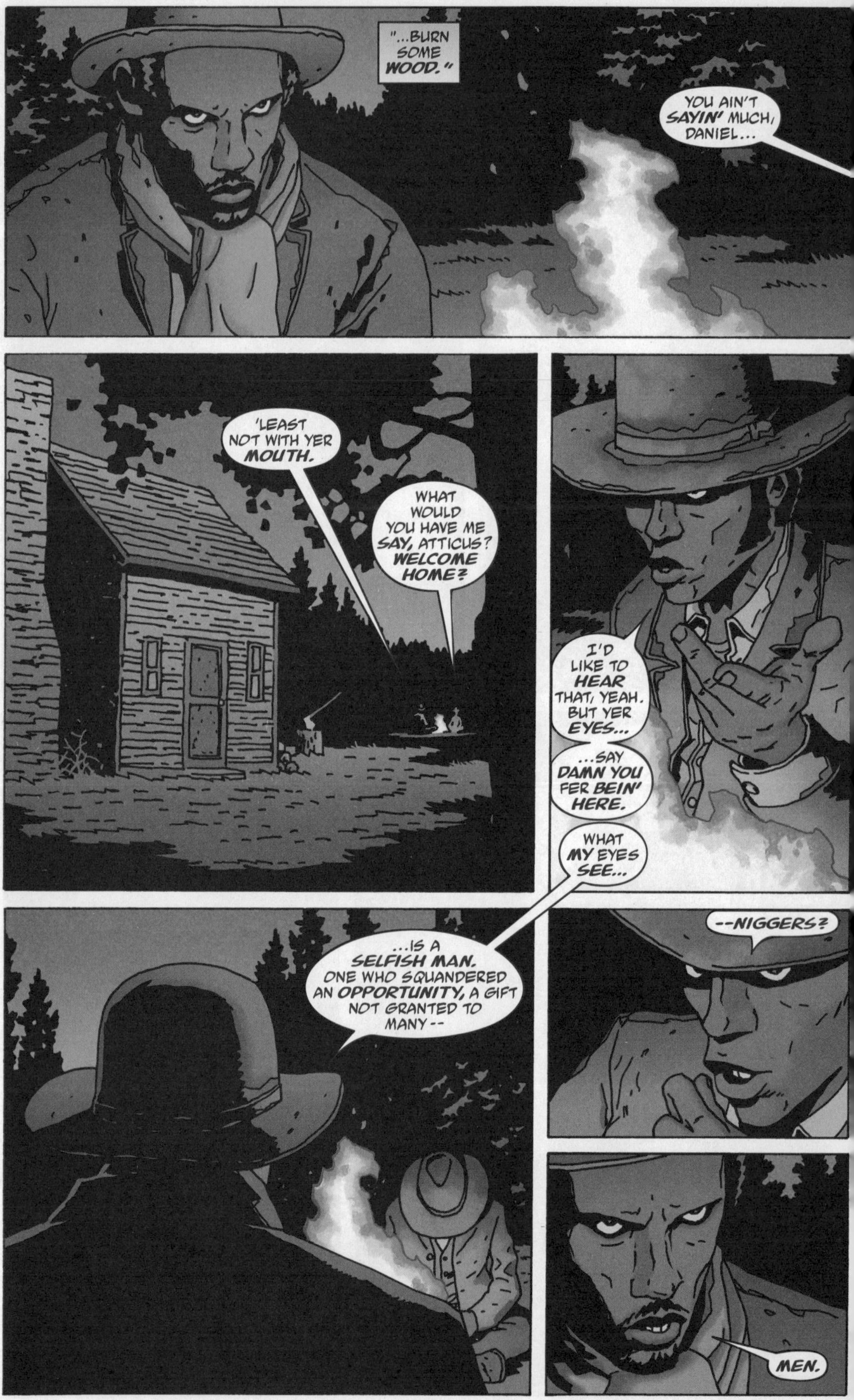
"...BURN SOME WOOD."
YOU AIN'T SAYIN' MUCH, DANIEL...
'LEAST NOT WITH YER MOUTH.
WHAT WOULD YOU HAVE ME SAY, ATTICUS? WELCOME HOME?
I'D LIKE TO HEAR THAT, YEAH. BUT YER EYES...
...SAY DAMN YOU FER BEIN' HERE.
WHAT MY EYES SEE...
...IS A SELFISH MAN. ONE WHO SQUANDERED AN OPPORTUNITY, A GIFT NOT GRANTED TO MANY --
--NIGGERS?
MEN.

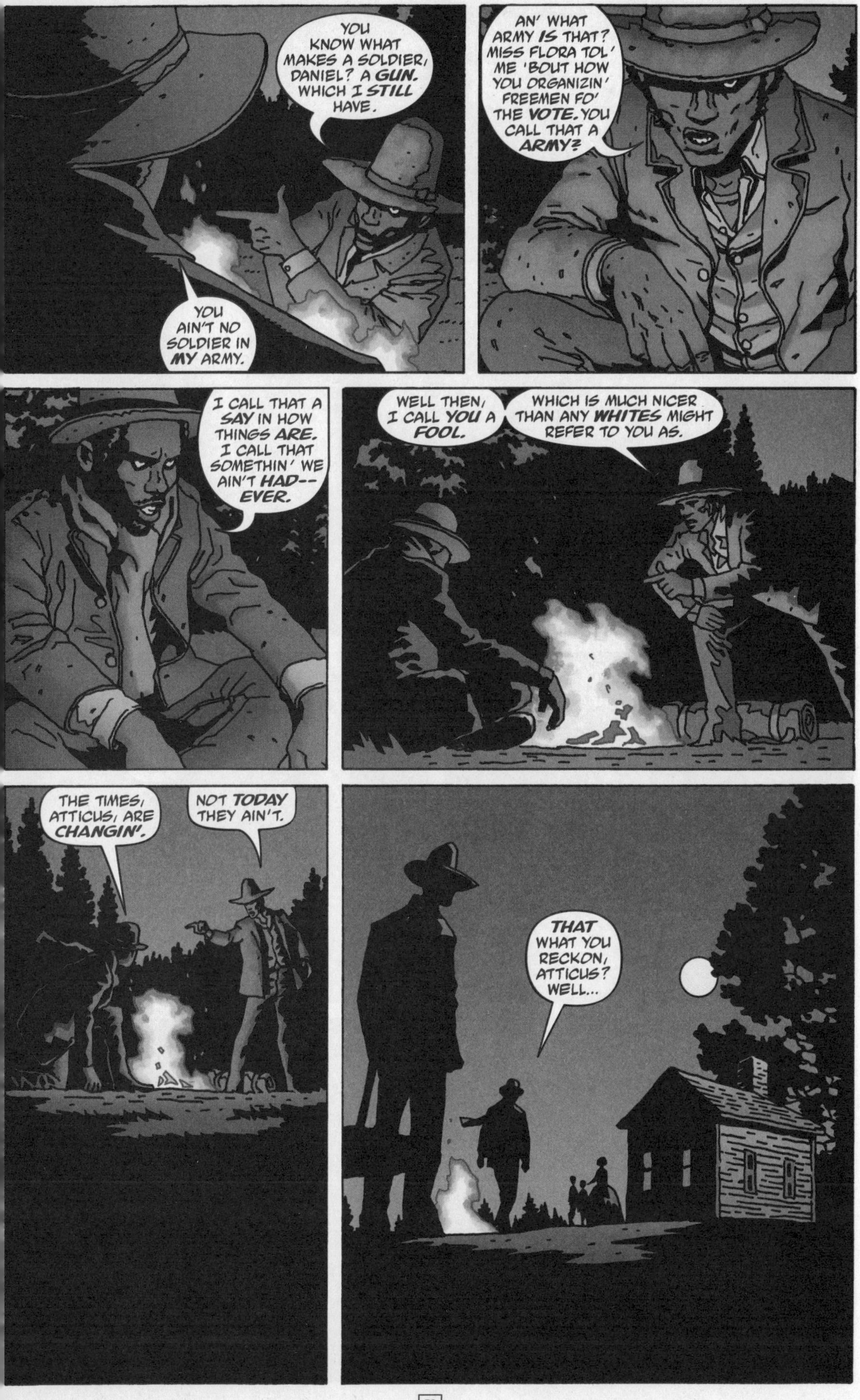
YOU KNOW WHAT MAKES A SOLDIER, DANIEL? A GUN. WHICH I STILL HAVE.
YOU AIN'T NO SOLDIER IN MY ARMY.
AN' WHAT ARMY IS THAT? MISS FLORA TOL' ME 'BOUT HOW YOU ORGANIZIN' FREEMEN FO' THE VOTE. YOU CALL THAT A ARMY?
I CALL THAT A SAY IN HOW THINGS ARE. I CALL THAT SOMETHIN' WE AIN'T HAD-- EVER.
WELL THEN, I CALL YOU A FOOL.
WHICH IS MUCH NICER THAN ANY WHITES MIGHT REFER TO YOU AS.
THE TIMES, ATTICUS, ARE CHANGIN'.
NOT TODAY THEY AIN'T.
THAT WHAT YOU RECKON, ATTICUS? WELL...

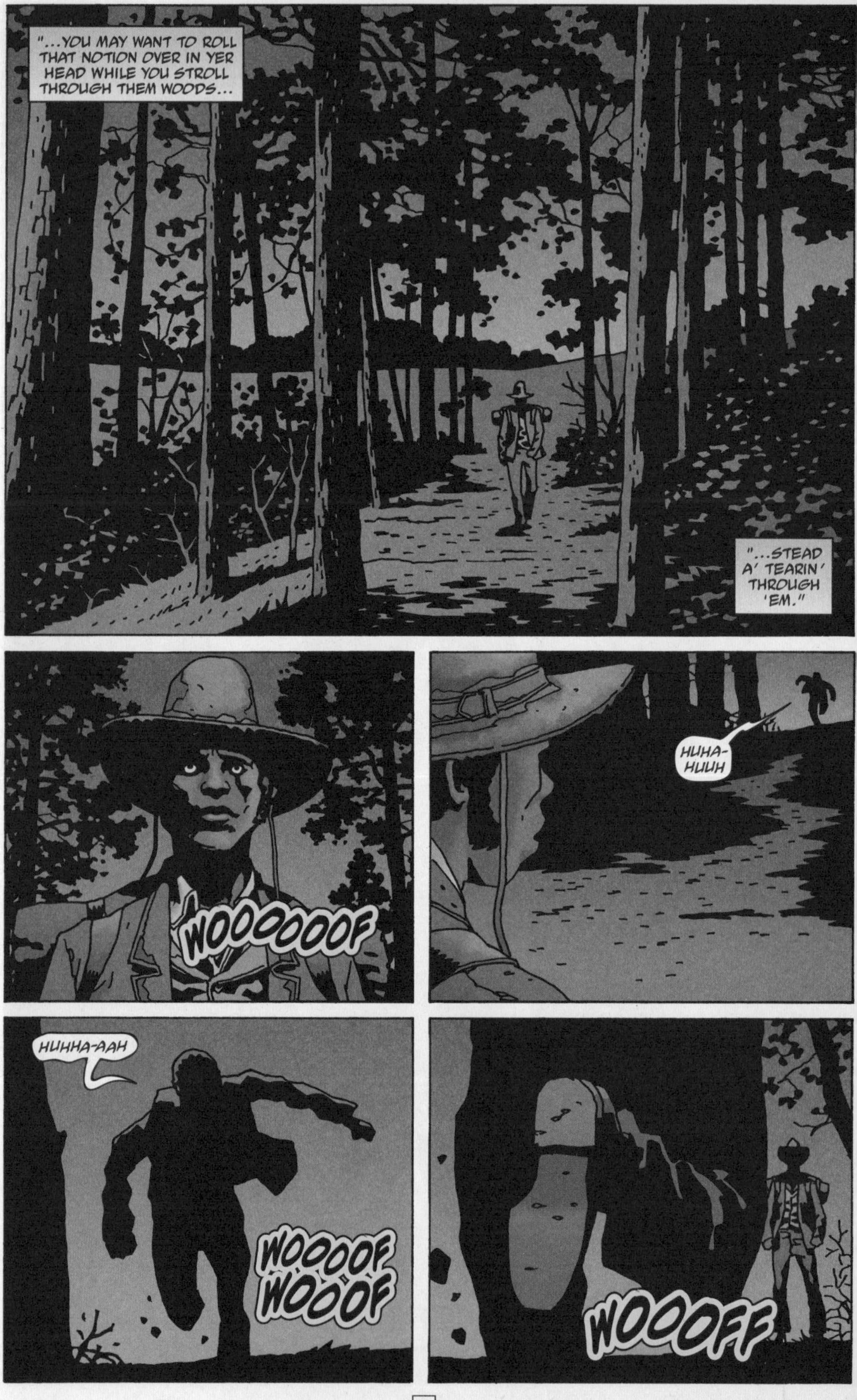
"...YOU MAY WANT TO ROLL THAT NOTION OVER IN YER HEAD WHILE YOU STROLL THROUGH THEM WOODS...
"...STEAD A' TEARIN' THROUGH 'EM."
WOOOOOOF
HUHA-HUUH
HUHHA-AAH
WOOOOF WOOOF
WOOOFF

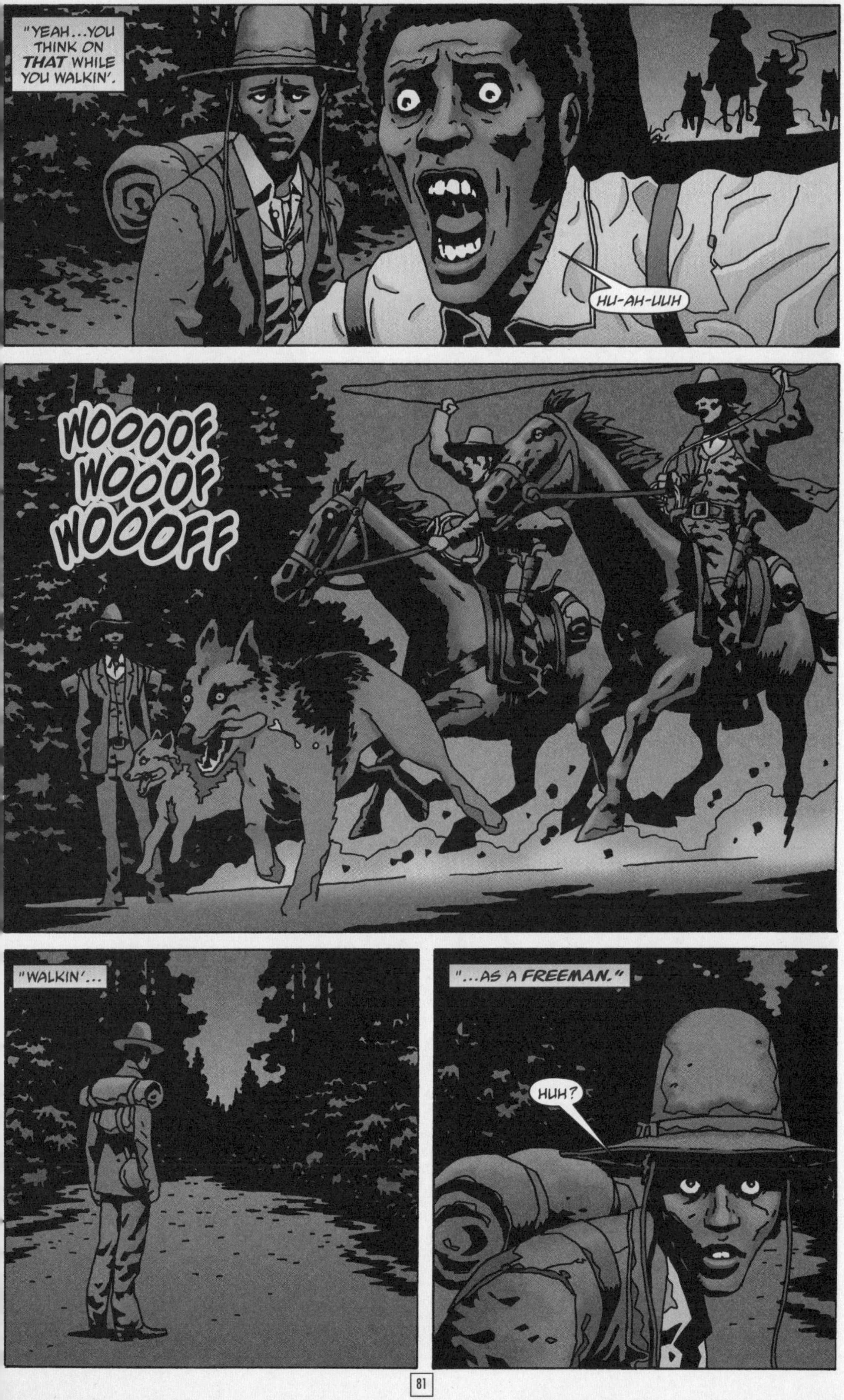
"YEAH...YOU THINK ON THAT WHILE YOU WALKIN'.
HU-AH-UUH
WOOOOF WOOOF WOOOFF
"WALKIN'...
"...AS A FREEMAN."
HUH?

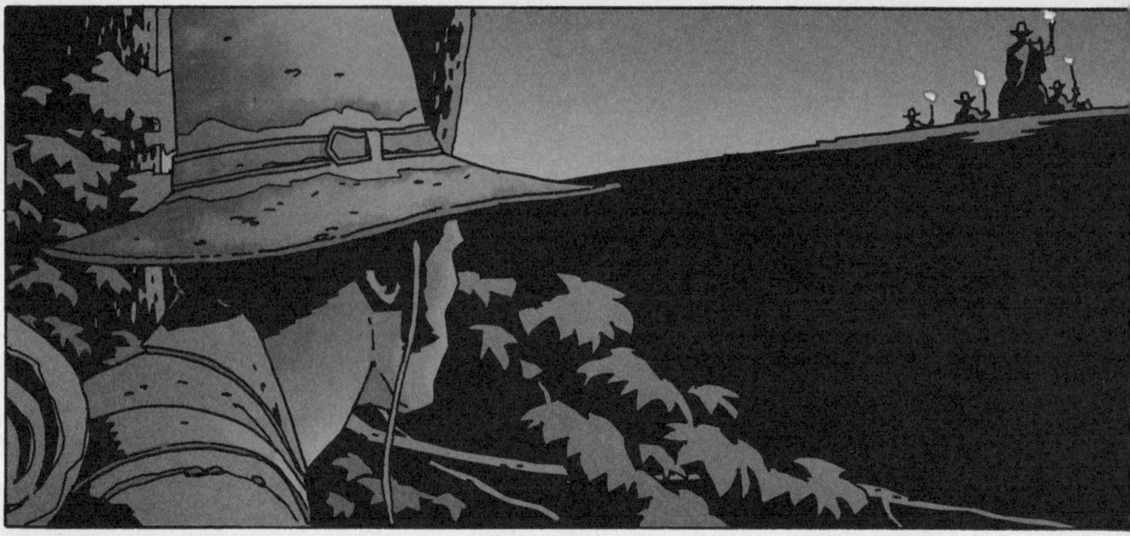

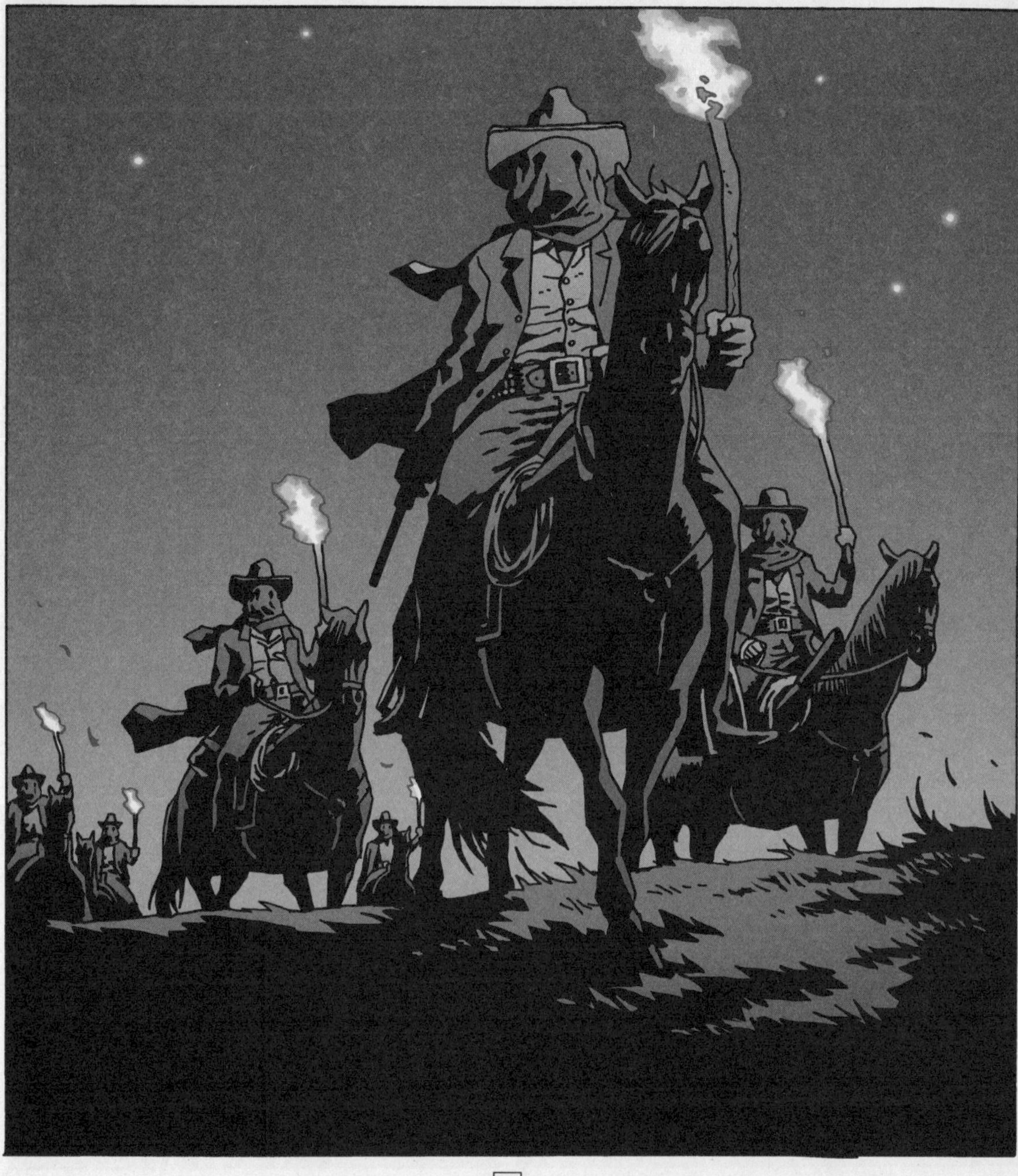

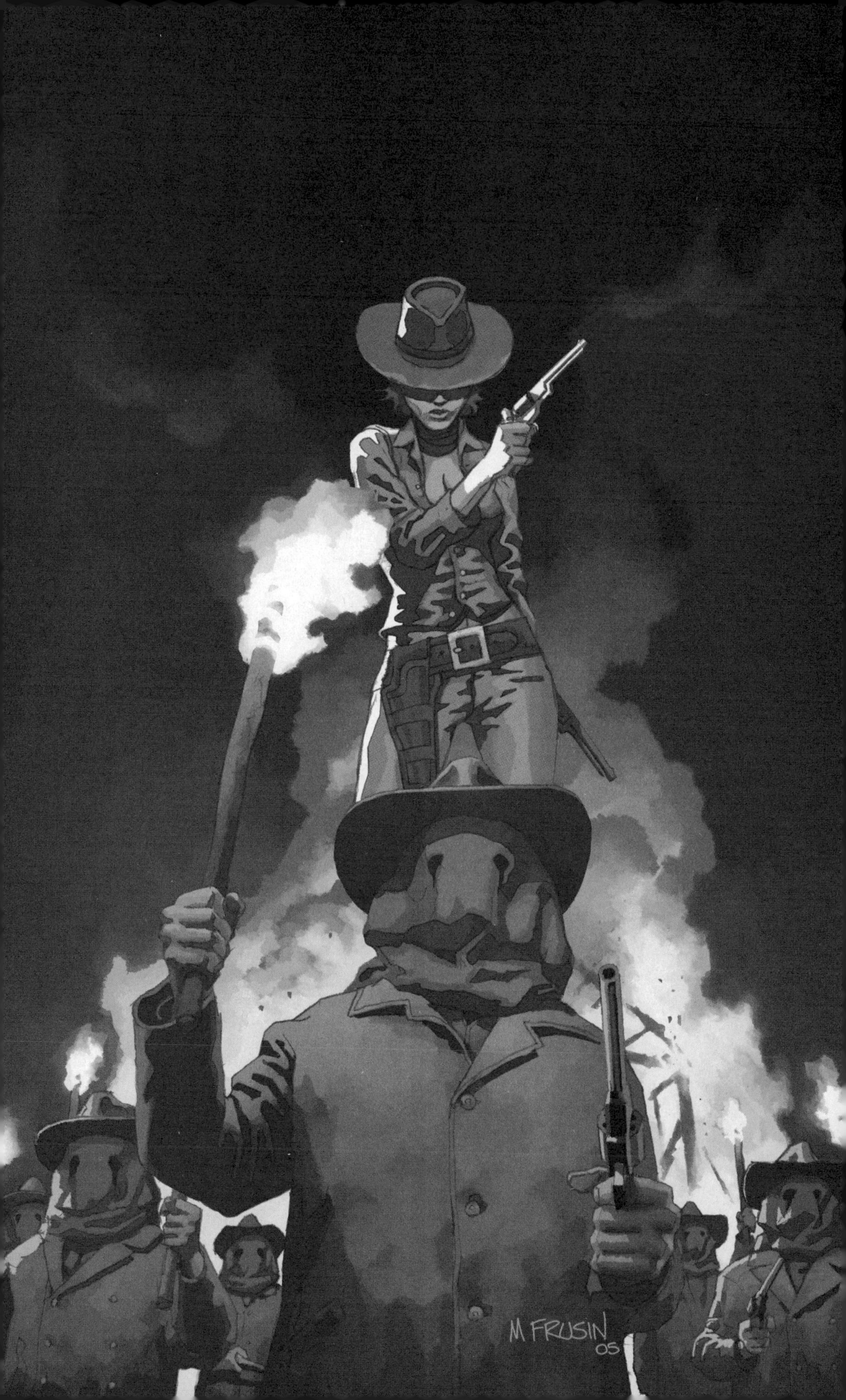
M FRUSIN
05

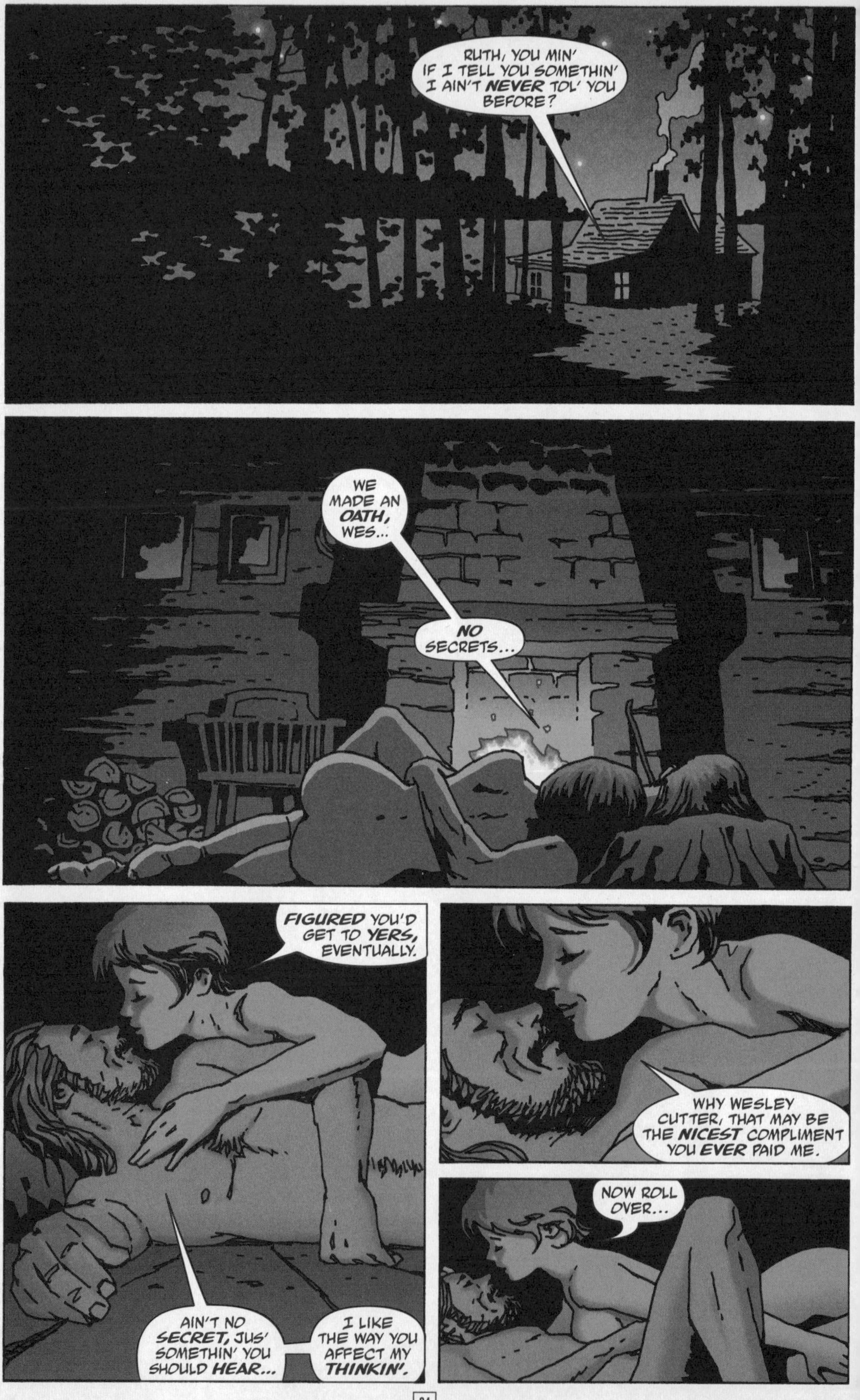
RUTH, YOU MIN' IF I TELL YOU SOMETHIN' I AIN'T NEVER TOL' YOU BEFORE?
WE MADE AN OATH, WES...
NO SECRETS...
FIGURED YOU'D GET TO YERS, EVENTUALLY.
AIN'T NO SECRET, JUS' SOMETHIN' YOU SHOULD HEAR...
I LIKE THE WAY YOU AFFECT MY THINKIN'.
WHY WESLEY CUTTER, THAT MAY BE THE NICEST COMPLIMENT YOU EVER PAID ME.
NOW ROLL OVER...

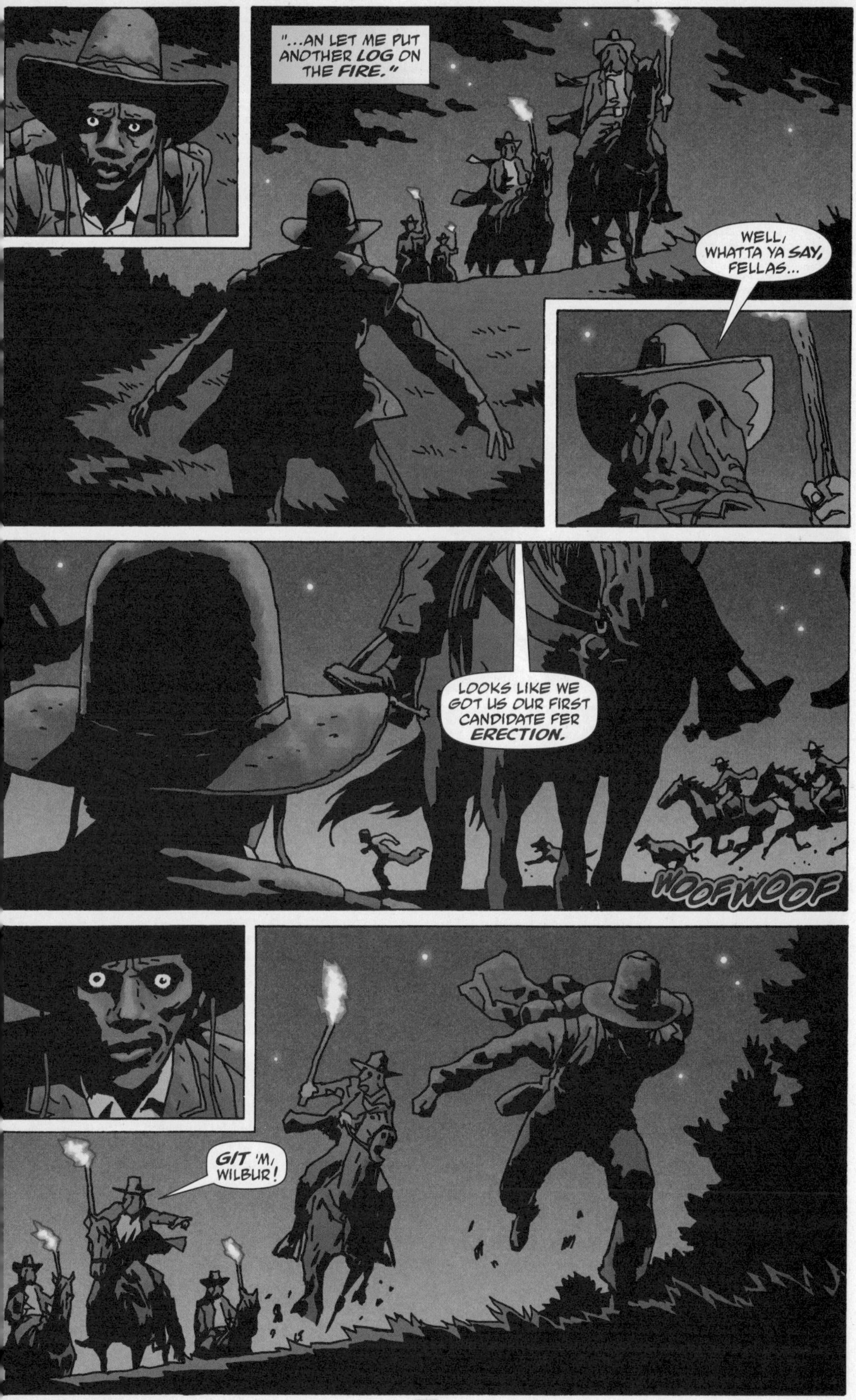
"...AN LET ME PUT ANOTHER LOG ON THE FIRE."
WELL, WHATTA YA SAY, FELLAS...
LOOKS LIKE WE GOT US OUR FIRST CANDIDATE FER ERECTION.
WOOFWOOF
GIT 'M, WILBUR!

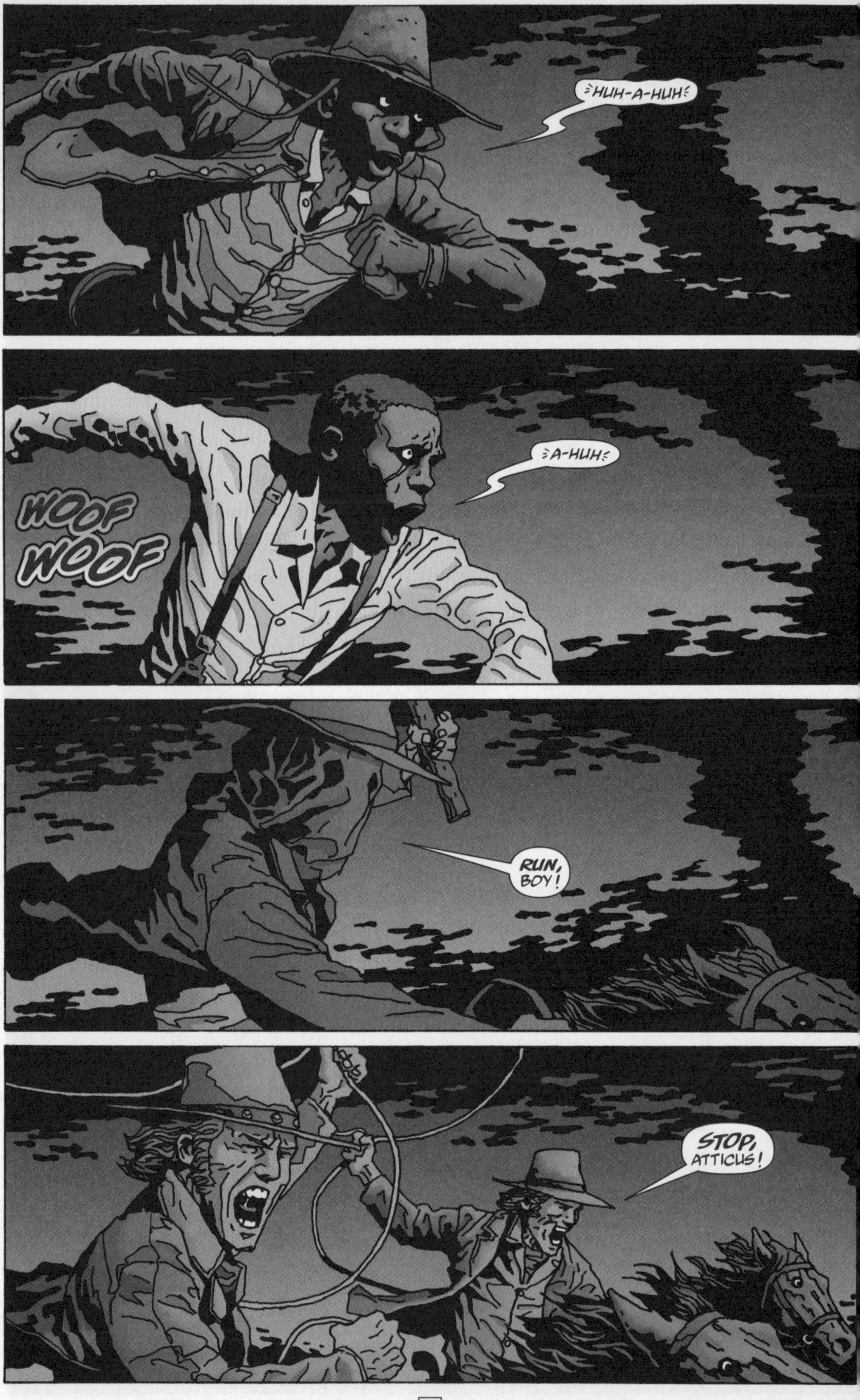
HUH-A-HUH
A-HUH
WOOF WOOF
RUN, BOY!
STOP, ATTICUS!

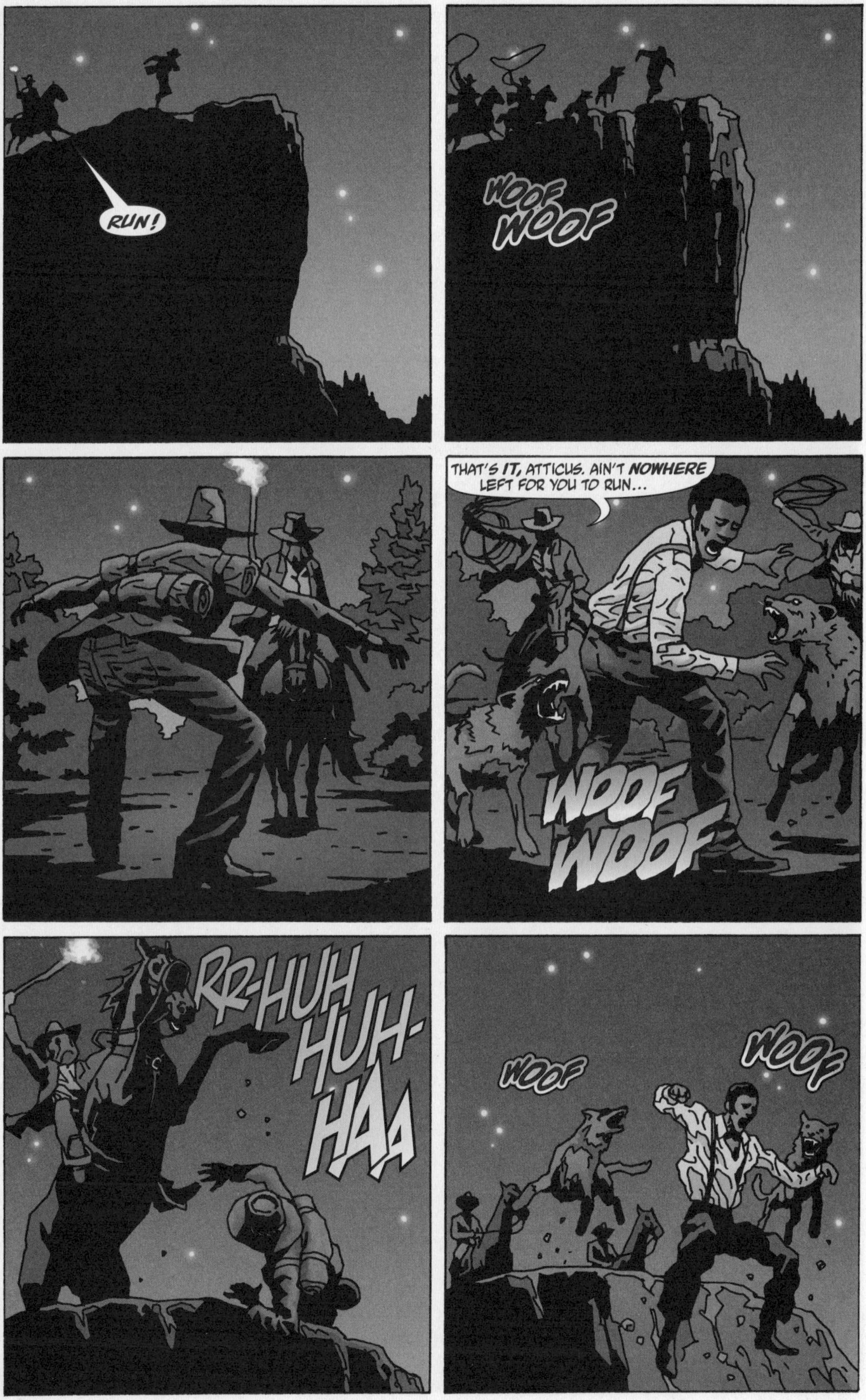
RUN!
WOOF WOOF
THAT'S IT, ATTICUS. AIN'T NOWHERE LEFT FOR YOU TO RUN...
WOOF WOOF
RR-HUH HUH-HAA
WOOF
WOOF

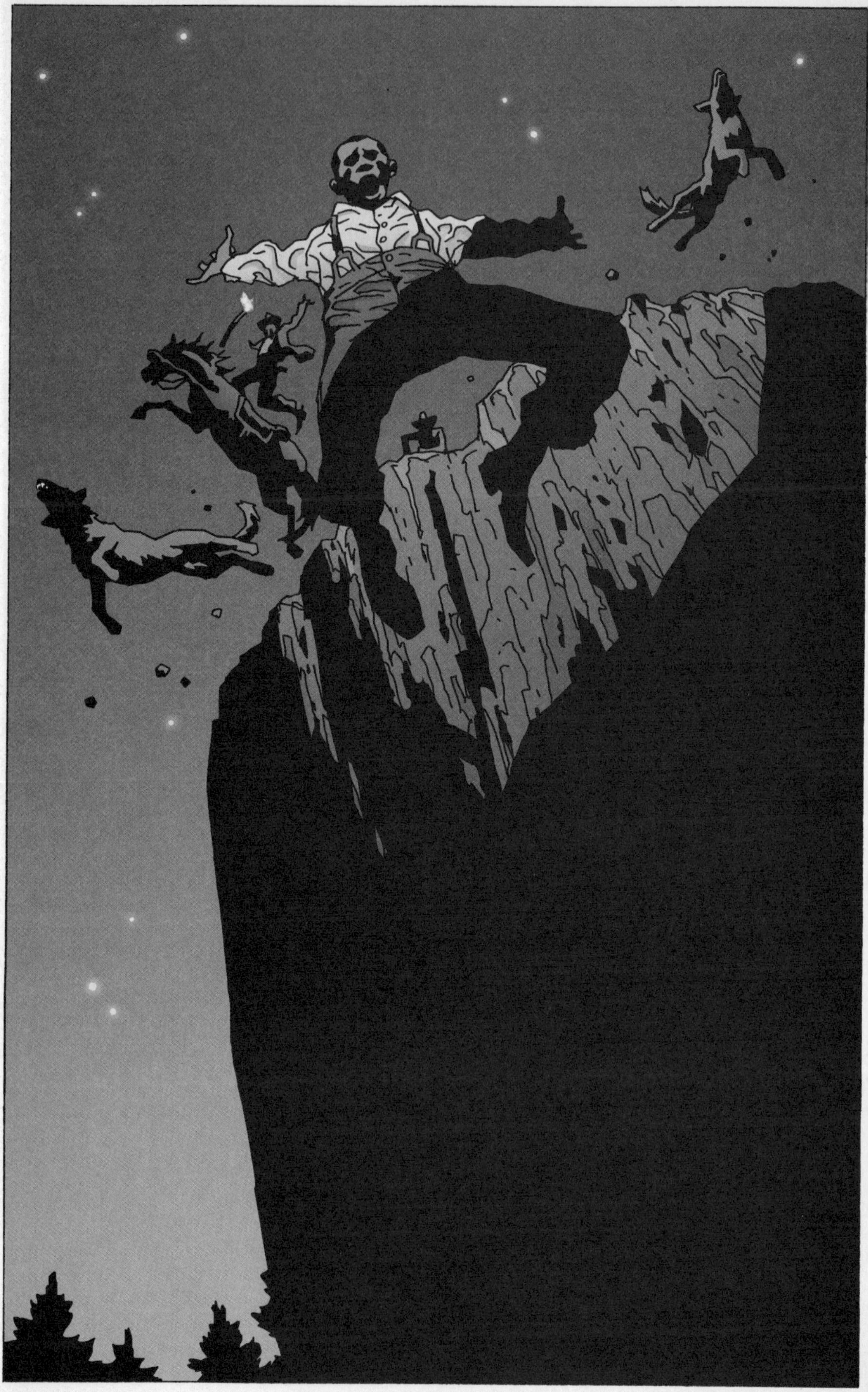

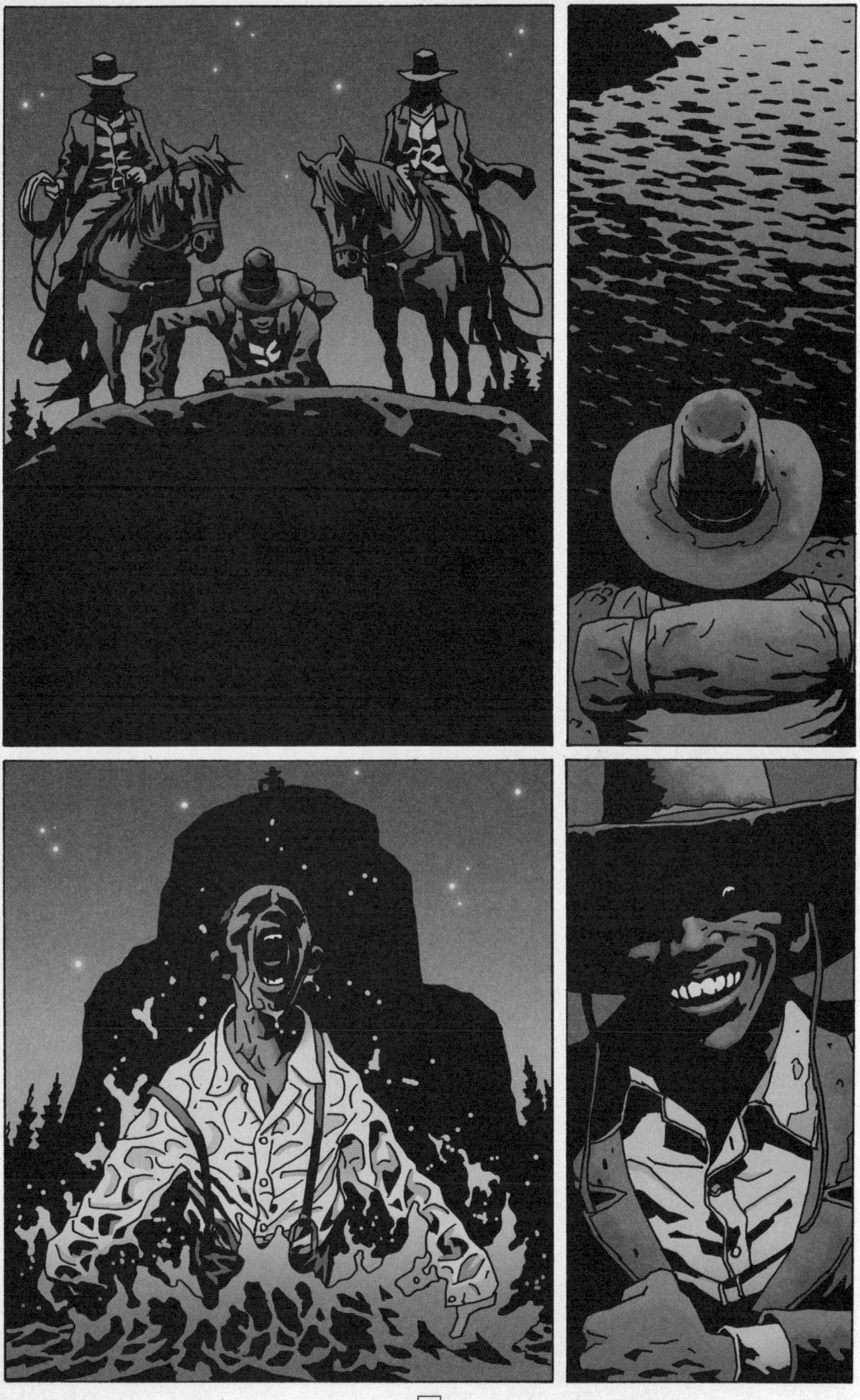

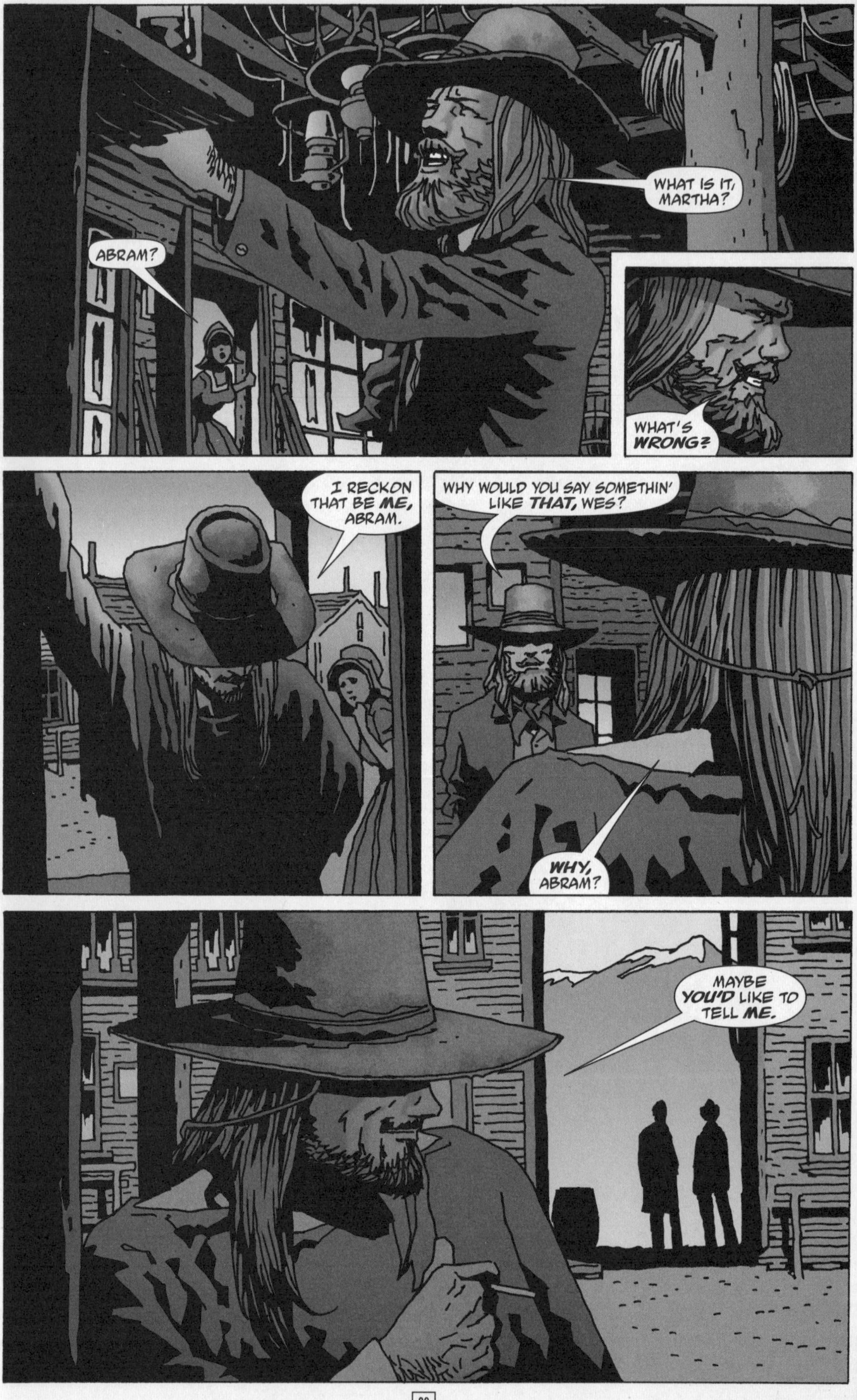
ABRAM?
WHAT IS IT, MARTHA?
WHAT'S WRONG?
I RECKON THAT BE ME, ABRAM.
WHY WOULD YOU SAY SOMETHIN' LIKE THAT, WES?
WHY, ABRAM?
MAYBE YOU'D LIKE TO TELL ME.

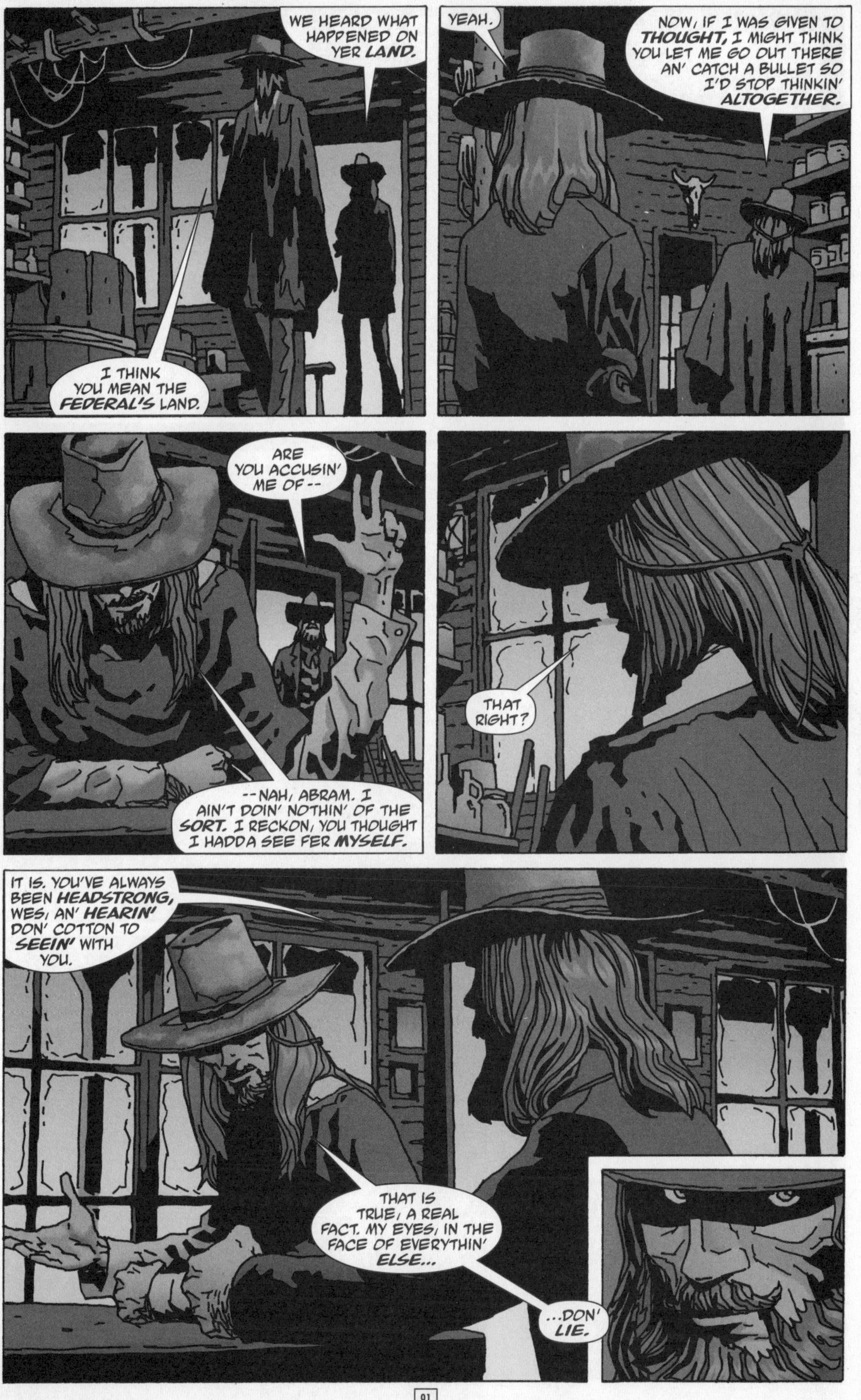
WE HEARD WHAT HAPPENED ON YER LAND.
I THINK YOU MEAN THE FEDERAL'S LAND.
YEAH.
NOW, IF I WAS GIVEN TO THOUGHT, I MIGHT THINK YOU LET ME GO OUT THERE AN' CATCH A BULLET SO I'D STOP THINKIN' ALTOGETHER.
ARE YOU ACCUSIN' ME OF --
--NAH, ABRAM. I AIN'T DOIN' NOTHIN' OF THE SORT. I RECKON, YOU THOUGHT I HADDA SEE FER MYSELF.
THAT RIGHT?
IT IS. YOU'VE ALWAYS BEEN HEADSTRONG, WES, AN' HEARIN' DON' COTTON TO SEEIN' WITH YOU.
THAT IS TRUE, A REAL FACT. MY EYES, IN THE FACE OF EVERYTHIN' ELSE...
...DON' LIE.

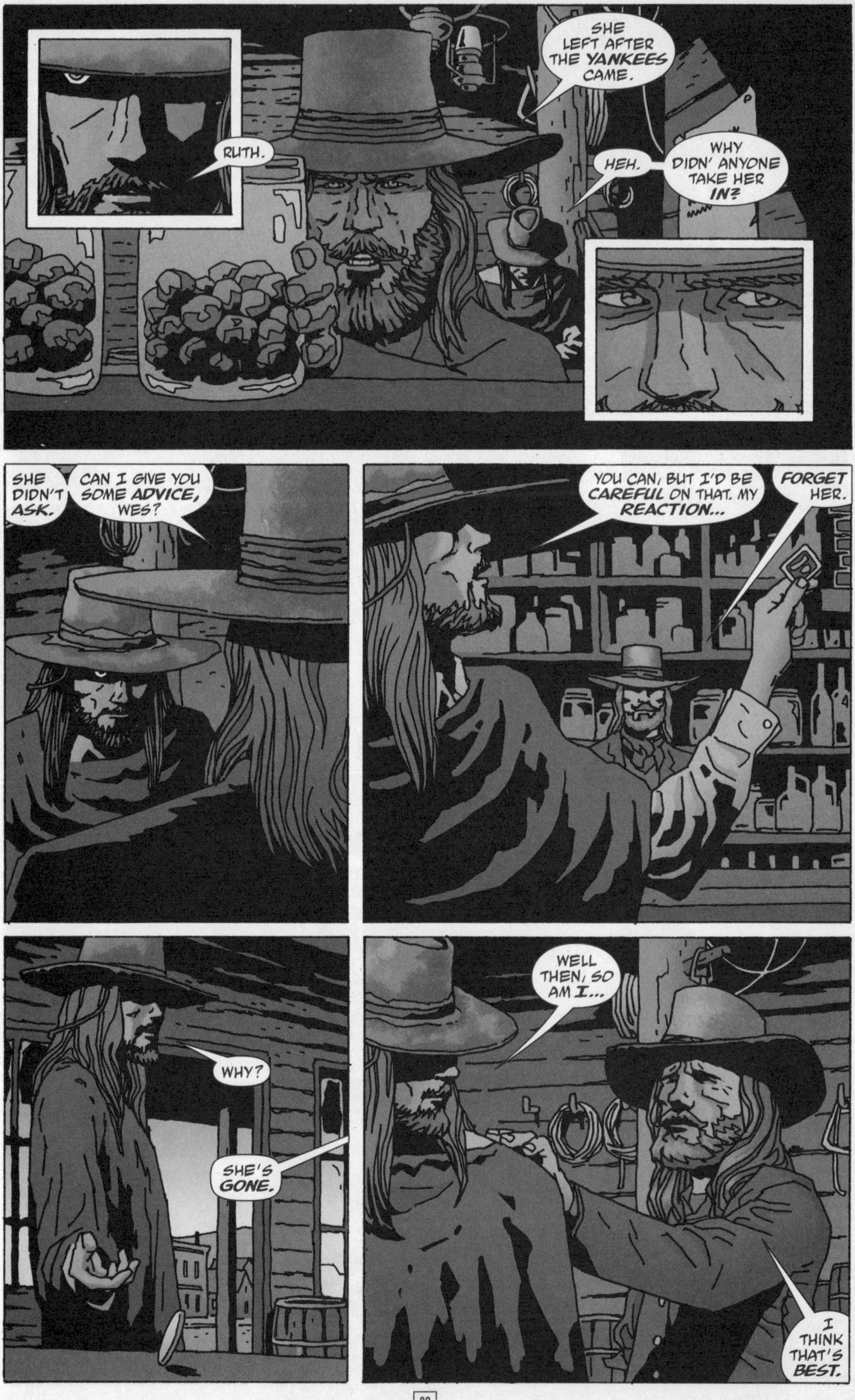
RUTH.
SHE LEFT AFTER THE YANKEES CAME.
HEH.
WHY DIDN' ANYONE TAKE HER IN?
SHE DIDN'T ASK.
CAN I GIVE YOU SOME ADVICE, WES?
YOU CAN, BUT I'D BE CAREFUL ON THAT. MY REACTION...
FORGET HER.
WHY?
SHE'S GONE.
WELL THEN, SO AM I...
I THINK THAT'S BEST.

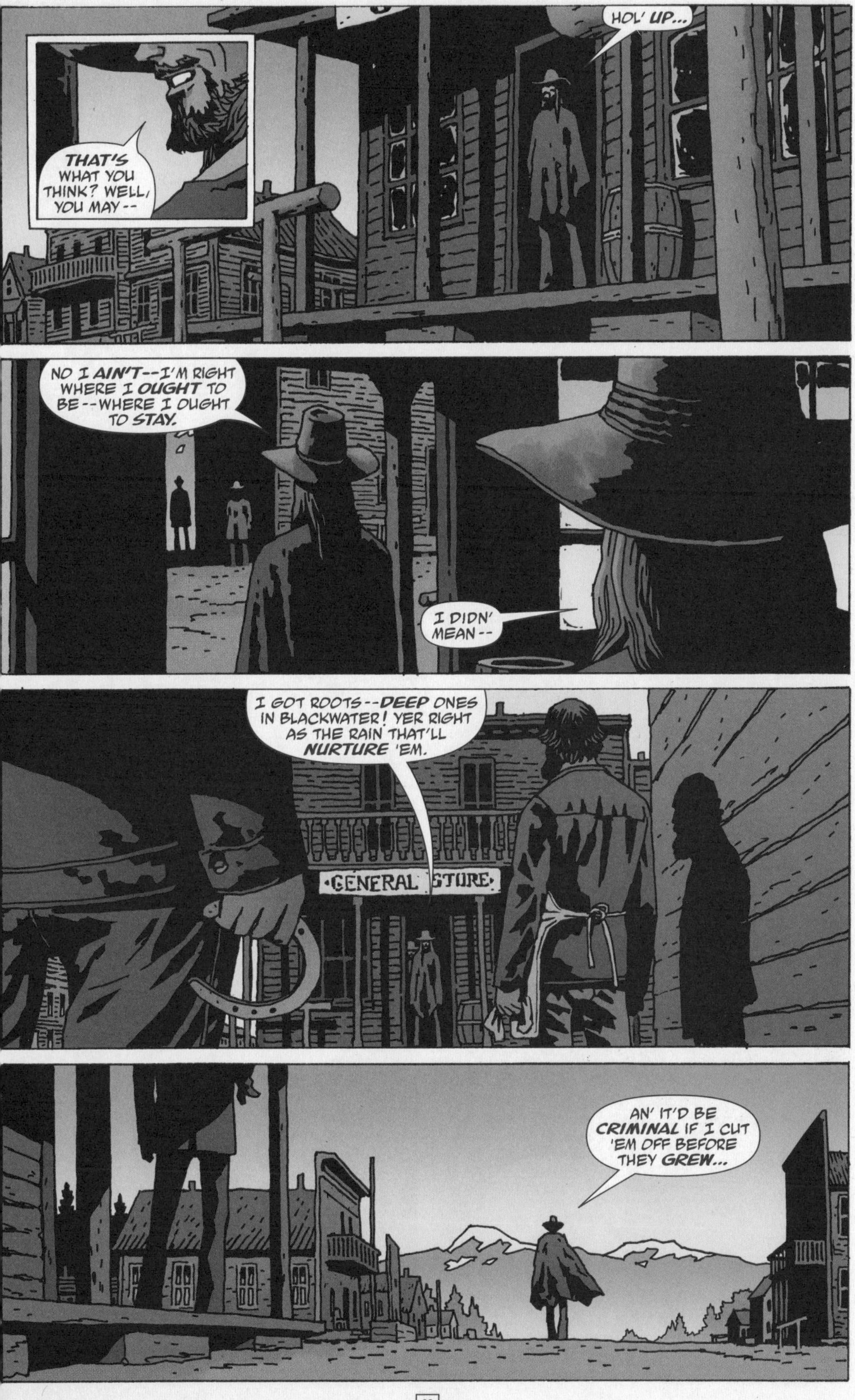
THAT'S WHAT YOU THINK? WELL, YOU MAY --
HOL' UP...
NO I AIN'T -- I'M RIGHT WHERE I OUGHT TO BE -- WHERE I OUGHT TO STAY.
I DIDN' MEAN --
I GOT ROOTS -- DEEP ONES IN BLACKWATER! YER RIGHT AS THE RAIN THAT'LL NURTURE 'EM.
GENERAL STORE
AN' IT'D BE CRIMINAL IF I CUT 'EM OFF BEFORE THEY GREW...

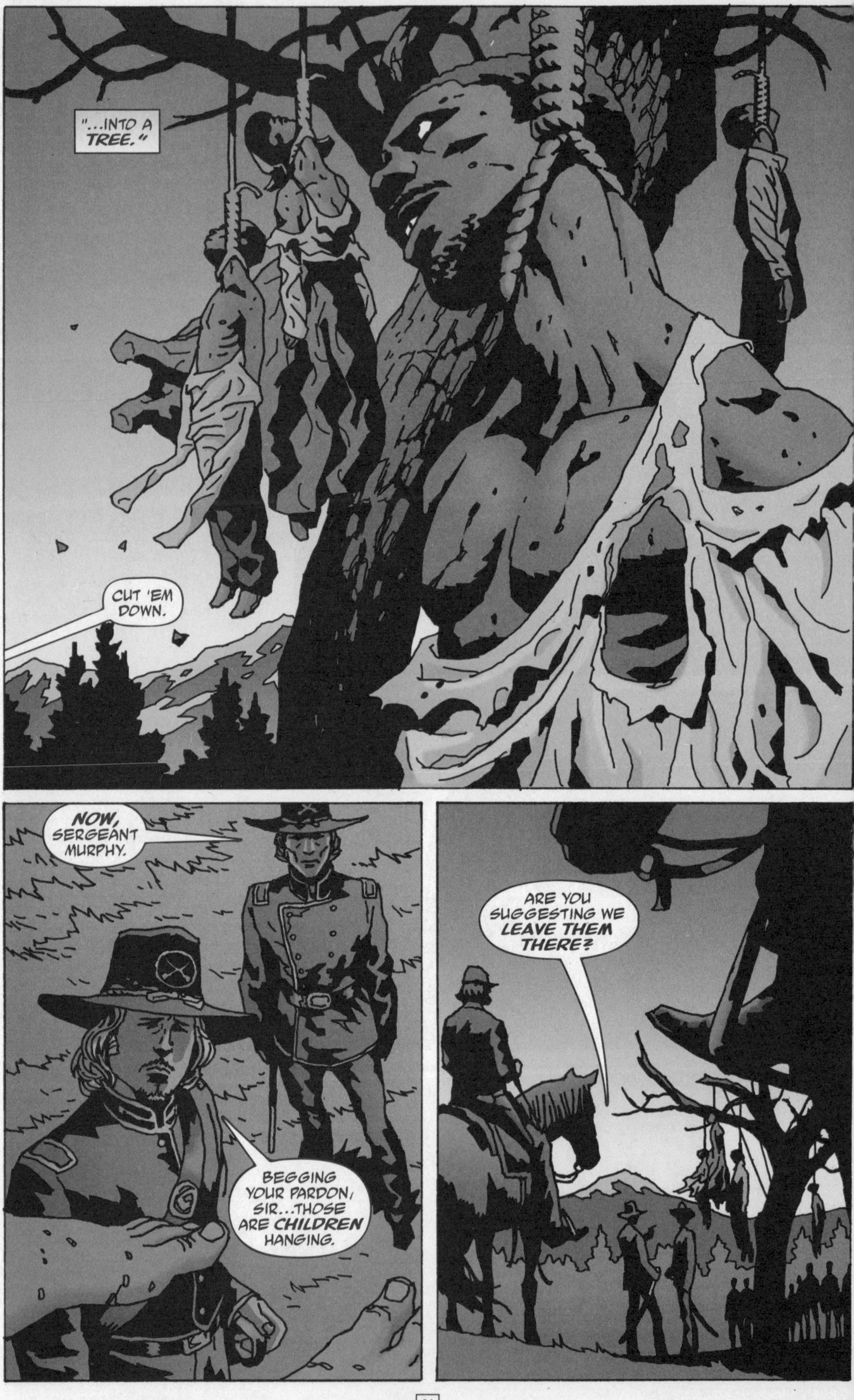
"...INTO A TREE."
CUT 'EM DOWN.
NOW, SERGEANT MURPHY.
BEGGING YOUR PARDON, SIR...THOSE ARE CHILDREN HANGING.
ARE YOU SUGGESTING WE LEAVE THEM THERE?

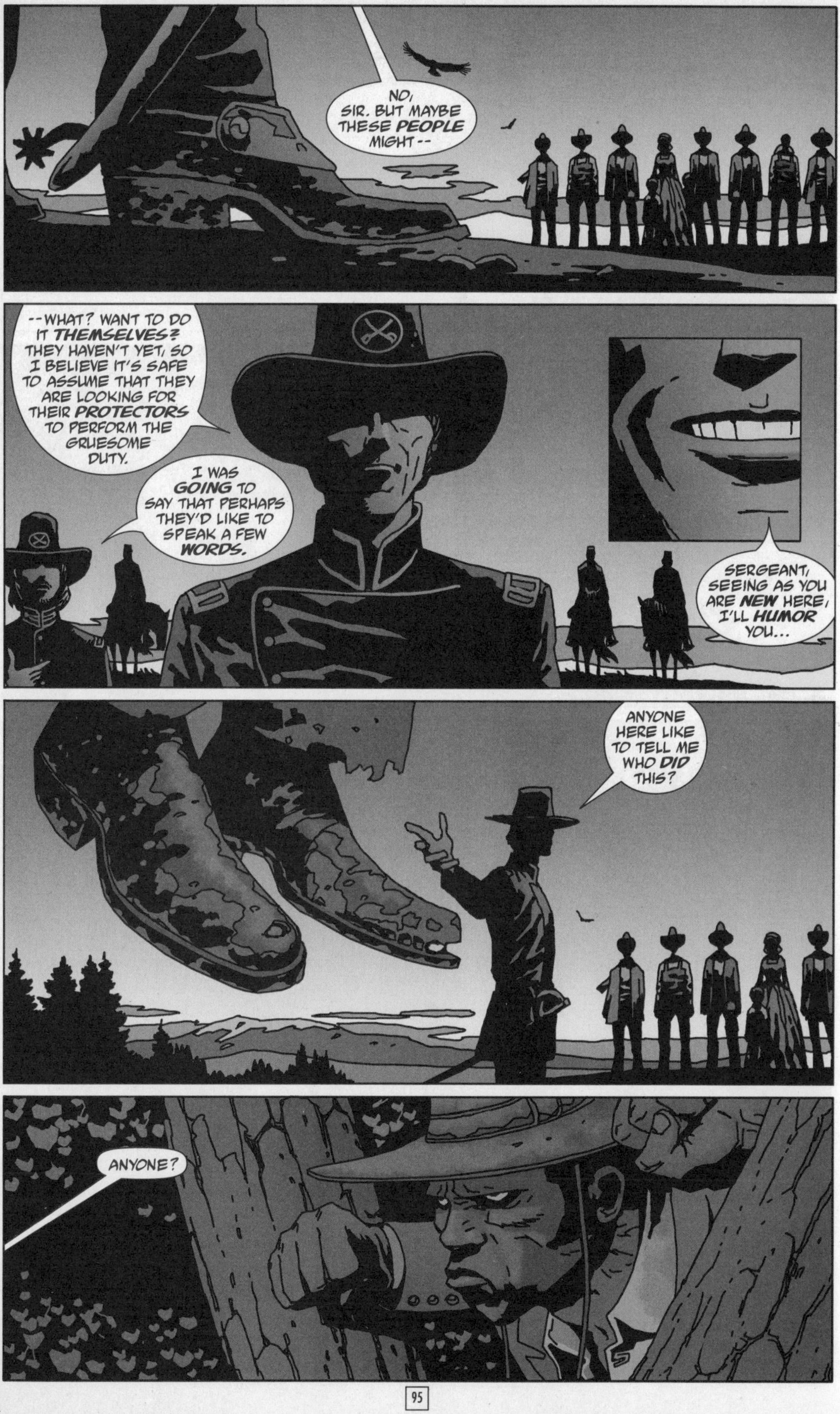
NO, SIR. BUT MAYBE THESE PEOPLE MIGHT--
--WHAT? WANT TO DO IT THEMSELVES? THEY HAVEN'T YET, SO I BELIEVE IT'S SAFE TO ASSUME THAT THEY ARE LOOKING FOR THEIR PROTECTORS TO PERFORM THE GRUESOME DUTY.
I WAS GOING TO SAY THAT PERHAPS THEY'D LIKE TO SPEAK A FEW WORDS.
SERGEANT, SEEING AS YOU ARE NEW HERE, I'LL HUMOR YOU...
ANYONE HERE LIKE TO TELL ME WHO DID THIS?
ANYONE?

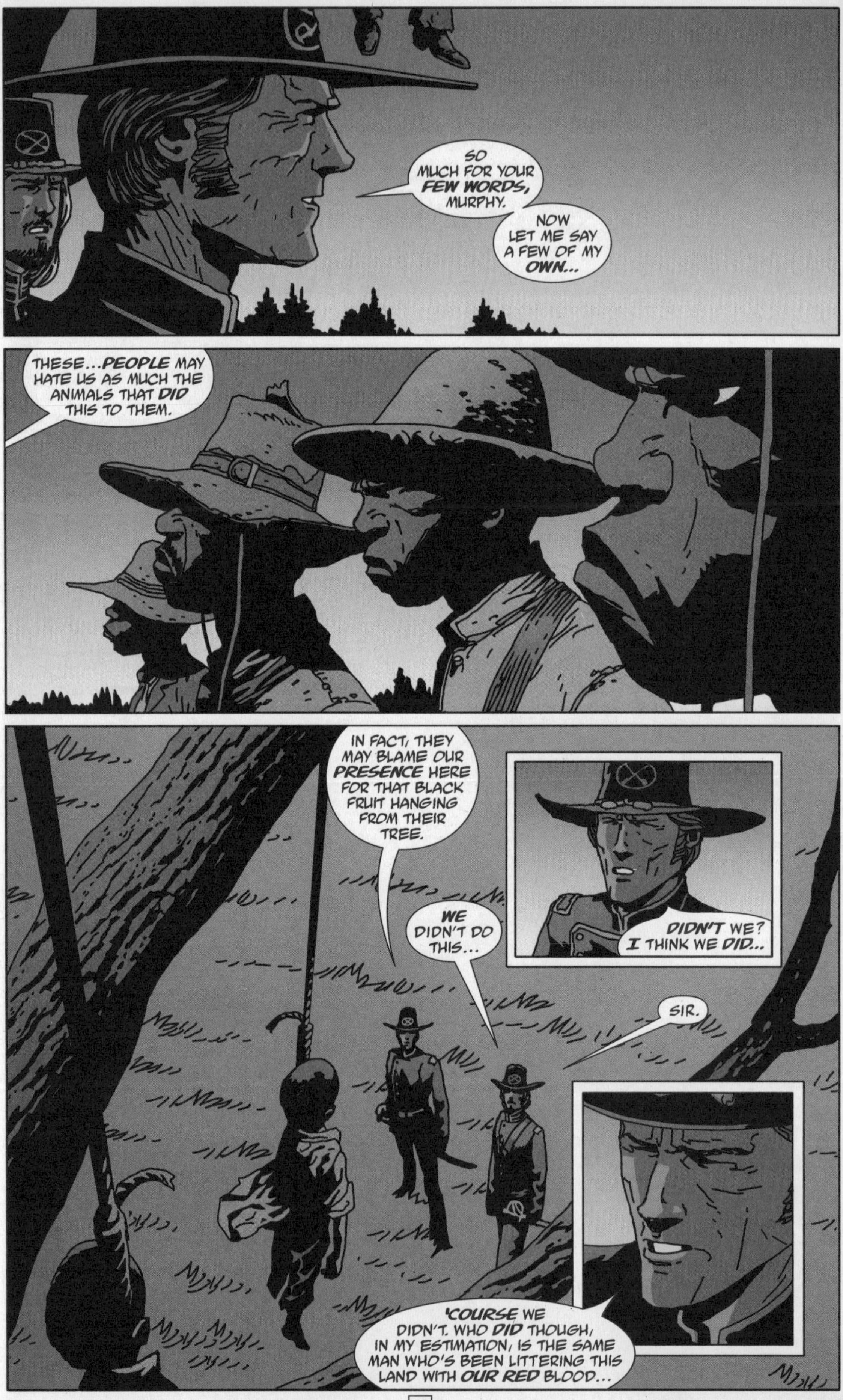

SO MUCH FOR YOUR **FEW WORDS,** MURPHY.
NOW LET ME SAY A FEW OF MY **OWN...**
THESE...**PEOPLE** MAY HATE US AS MUCH THE ANIMALS THAT **DID** THIS TO THEM.
IN FACT, THEY MAY BLAME OUR **PRESENCE** HERE FOR THAT BLACK FRUIT HANGING FROM THEIR TREE.
WE DIDN'T DO THIS...
DIDN'T WE? **I** THINK WE **DID...**
SIR.
'COURSE WE DIDN'T. WHO **DID** THOUGH, IN MY ESTIMATION, IS THE SAME MAN WHO'S BEEN LITTERING THIS LAND WITH **OUR RED** BLOOD...

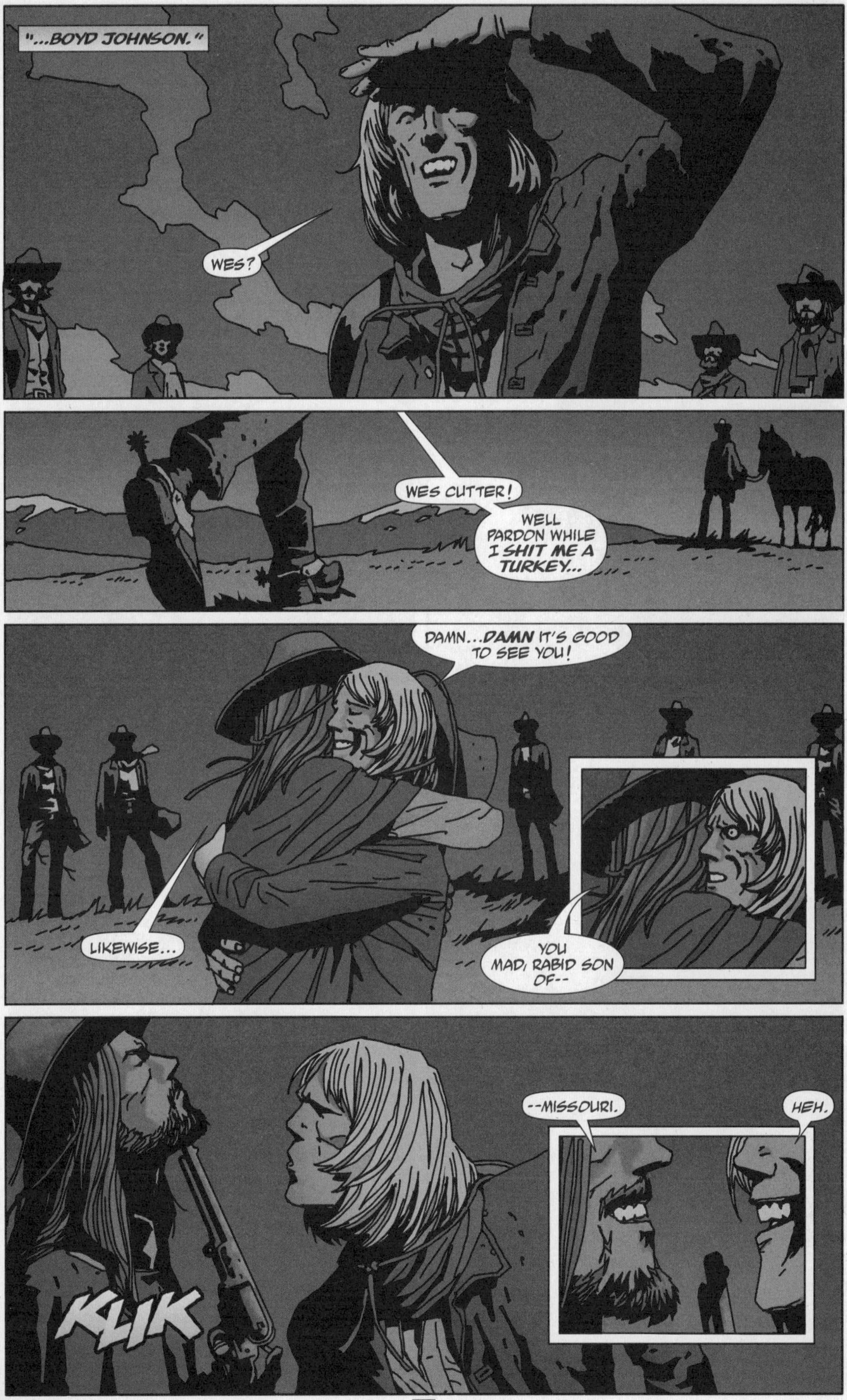
"...BOYD JOHNSON."
WES?
WES CUTTER!
WELL PARDON WHILE I SHIT ME A TURKEY...
DAMN...DAMN IT'S GOOD TO SEE YOU!
LIKEWISE...
YOU MAD, RABID SON OF--
--MISSOURI.
HEH.
KLIK

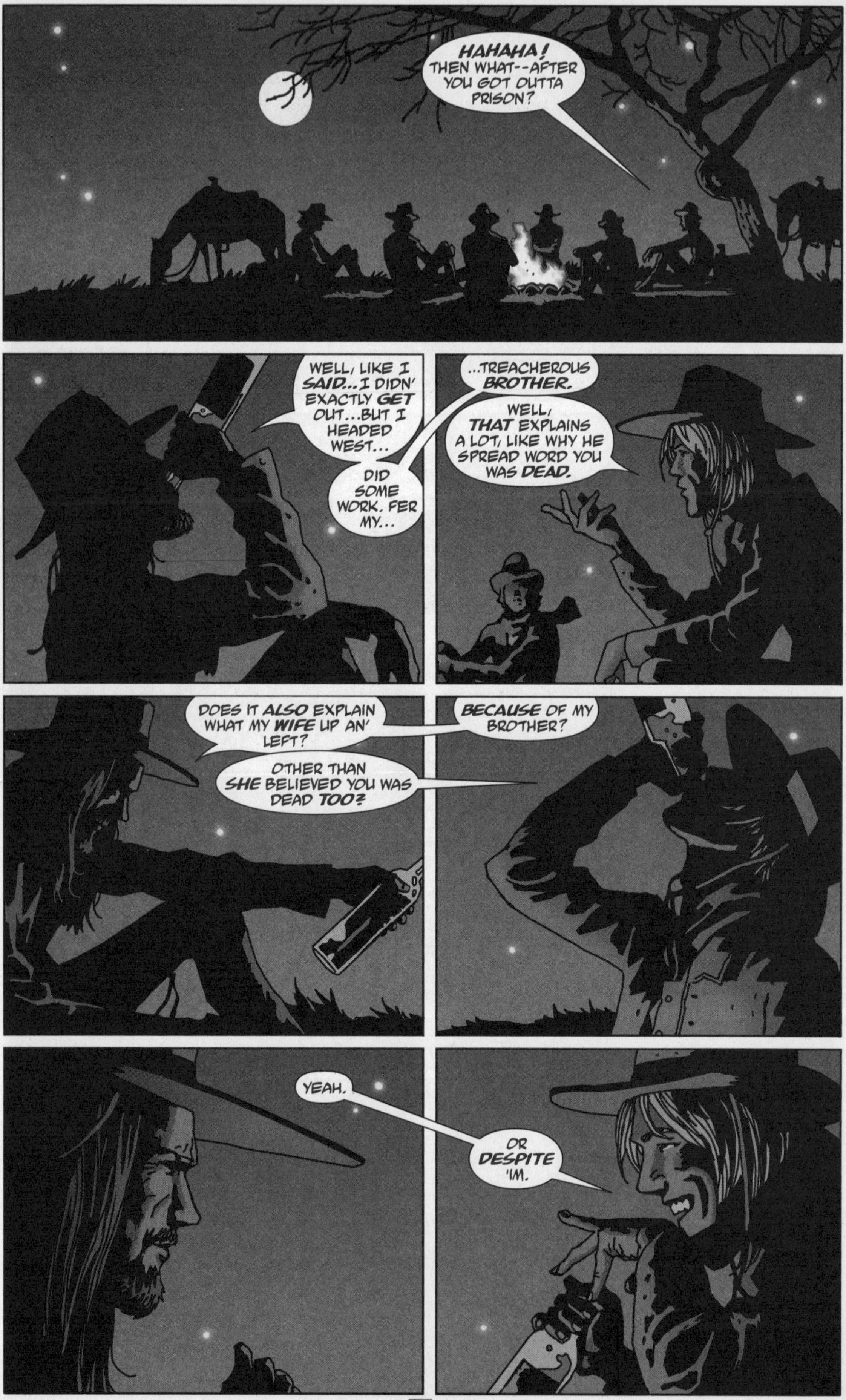
HAHAHA! THEN WHAT--AFTER YOU GOT OUTTA PRISON?
WELL, LIKE I SAID...I DIDN' EXACTLY GET OUT...BUT I HEADED WEST...
DID SOME WORK. FER MY...
...TREACHEROUS BROTHER.
WELL, THAT EXPLAINS A LOT, LIKE WHY HE SPREAD WORD YOU WAS DEAD.
DOES IT ALSO EXPLAIN WHAT MY WIFE UP AN' LEFT?
OTHER THAN SHE BELIEVED YOU WAS DEAD TOO?
BECAUSE OF MY BROTHER?
YEAH.
OR DESPITE 'IM.

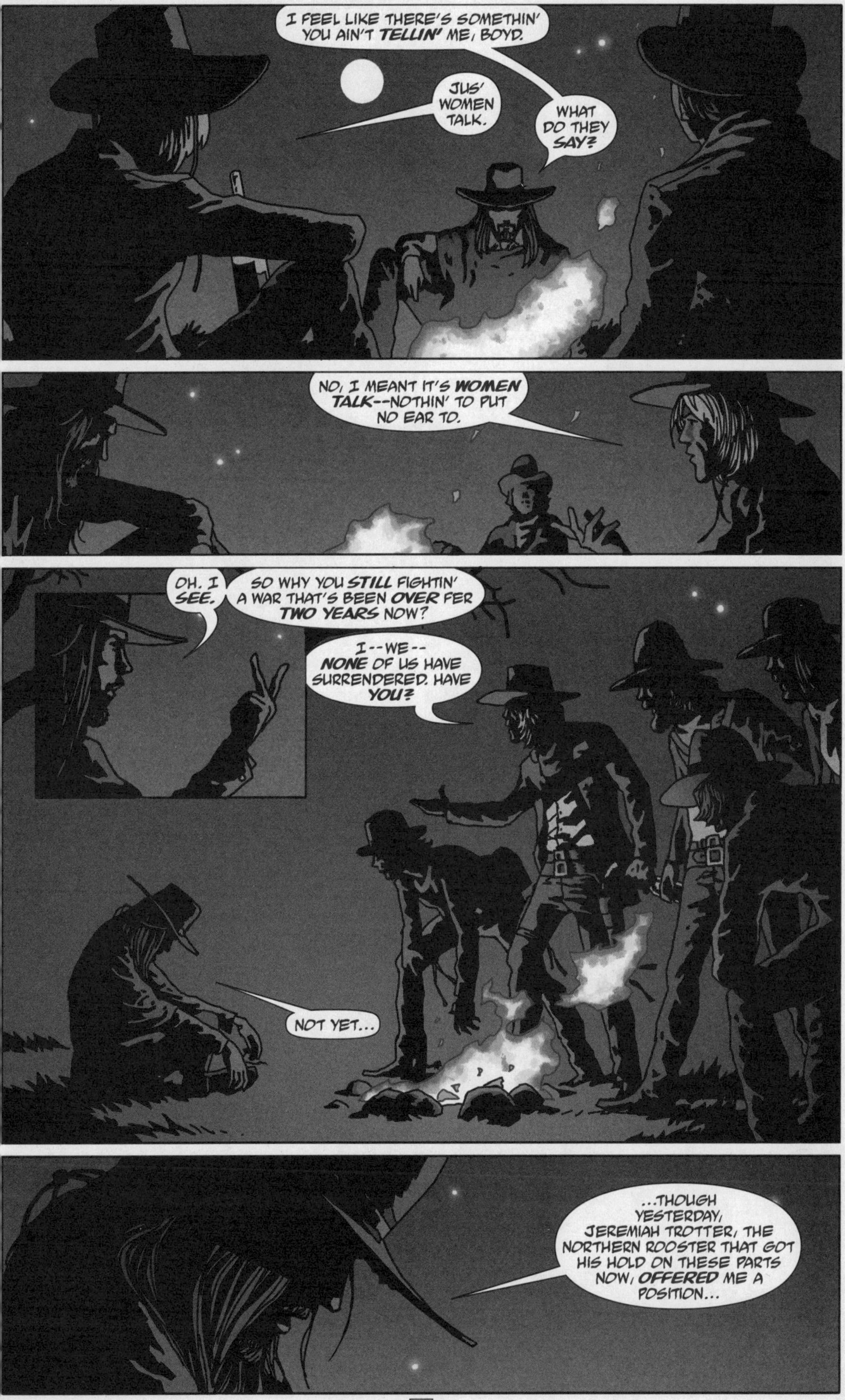
I FEEL LIKE THERE'S SOMETHIN' YOU AIN'T TELLIN' ME, BOYD.
JUS' WOMEN TALK.
WHAT DO THEY SAY?
NO, I MEANT IT'S WOMEN TALK--NOTHIN' TO PUT NO EAR TO.
OH. I SEE.
SO WHY YOU STILL FIGHTIN' A WAR THAT'S BEEN OVER FER TWO YEARS NOW?
I--WE-- NONE OF US HAVE SURRENDERED. HAVE YOU?
NOT YET...
...THOUGH YESTERDAY, JEREMIAH TROTTER, THE NORTHERN ROOSTER THAT GOT HIS HOLD ON THESE PARTS NOW, OFFERED ME A POSITION...

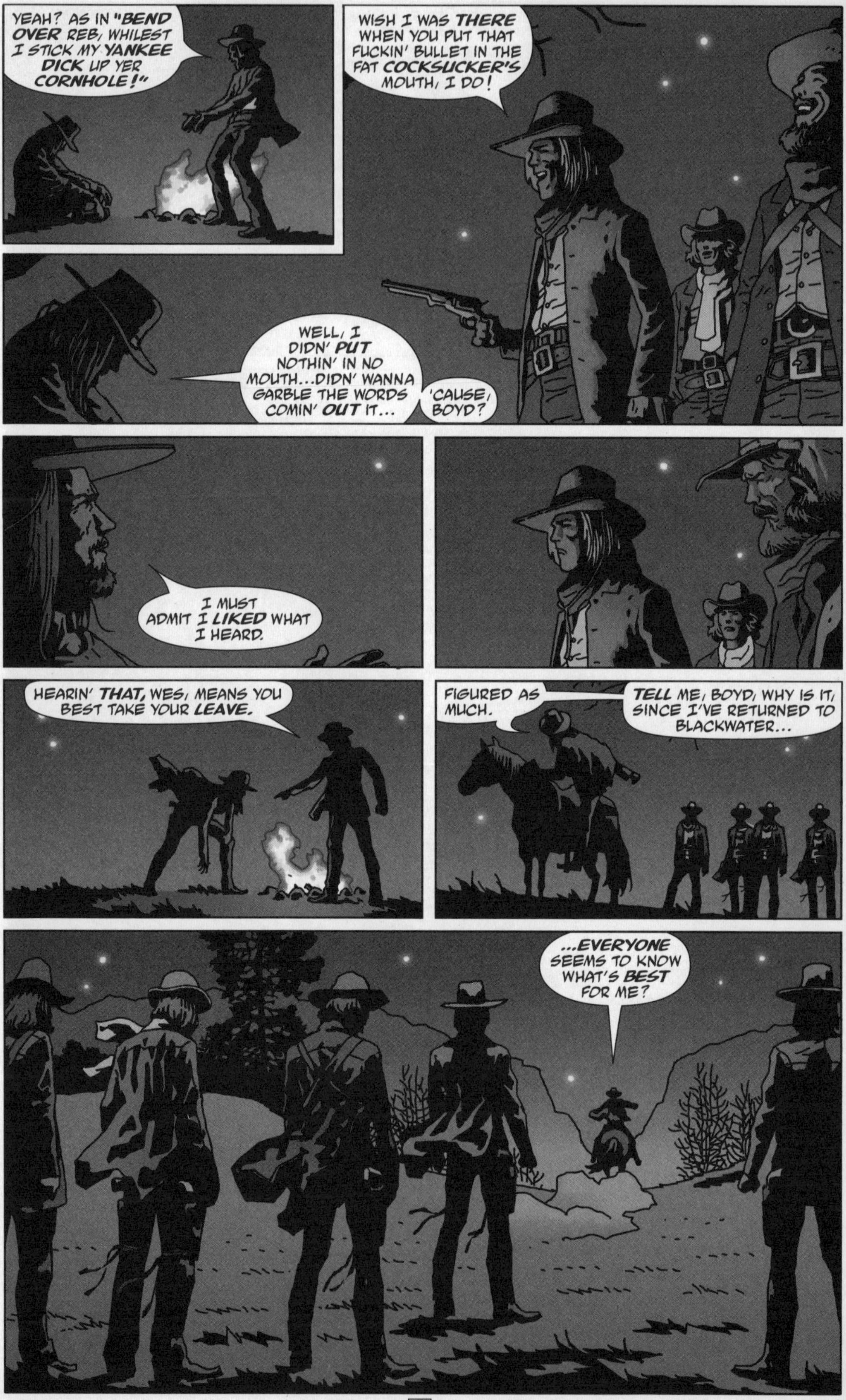
YEAH? AS IN "BEND OVER REB, WHILEST I STICK MY YANKEE DICK UP YER CORNHOLE!"
WISH I WAS THERE WHEN YOU PUT THAT FUCKIN' BULLET IN THE FAT COCKSUCKER'S MOUTH, I DO!
WELL, I DIDN' PUT NOTHIN' IN NO MOUTH...DIDN' WANNA GARBLE THE WORDS COMIN' OUT IT...
'CAUSE, BOYD?
I MUST ADMIT I LIKED WHAT I HEARD.
HEARIN' THAT, WES, MEANS YOU BEST TAKE YOUR LEAVE.
FIGURED AS MUCH.
TELL ME, BOYD, WHY IS IT, SINCE I'VE RETURNED TO BLACKWATER...
...EVERYONE SEEMS TO KNOW WHAT'S BEST FOR ME?

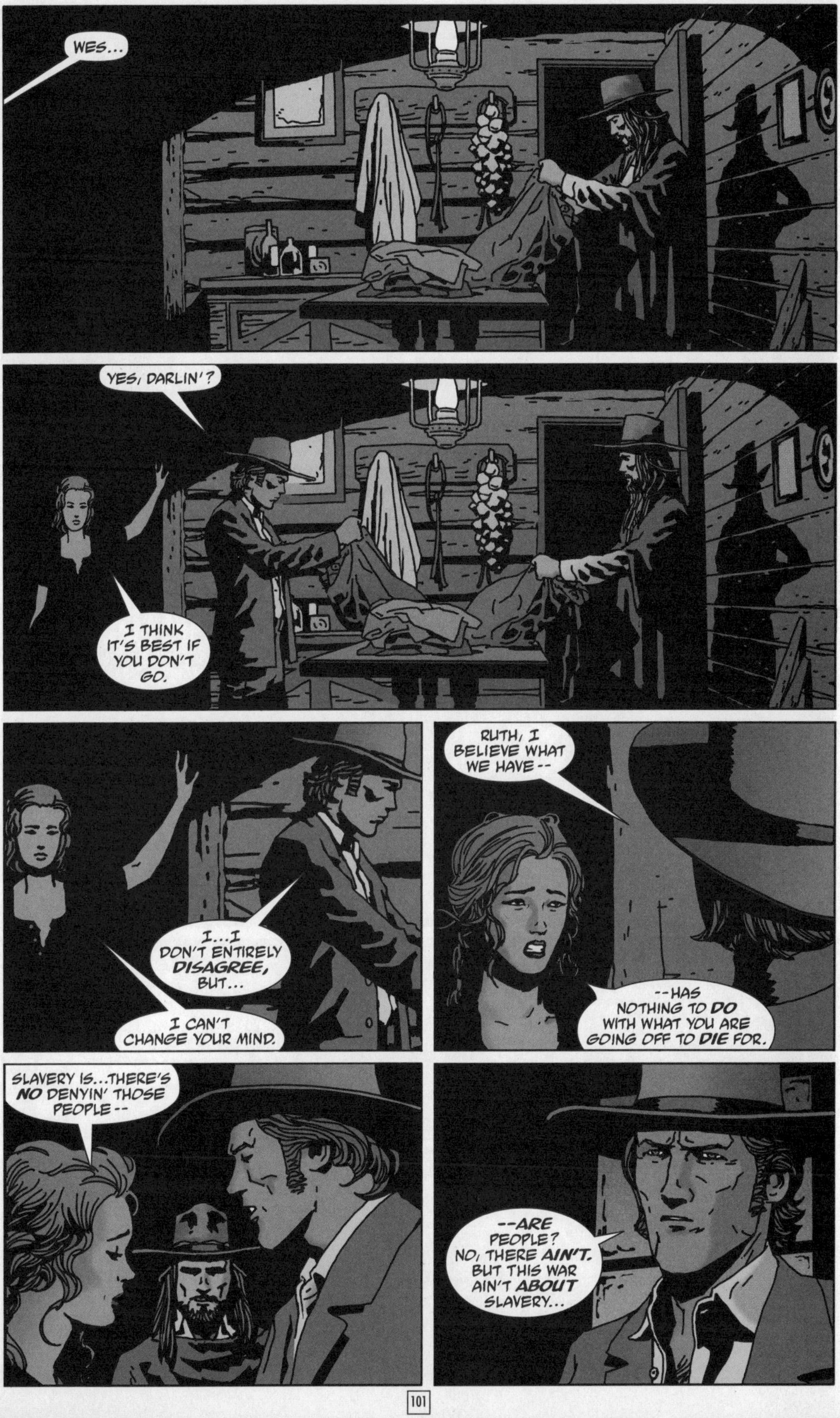
WES...
YES, DARLIN'?
I THINK IT'S BEST IF YOU DON'T GO.
I...I DON'T ENTIRELY DISAGREE, BUT...
I CAN'T CHANGE YOUR MIND.
RUTH, I BELIEVE WHAT WE HAVE --
--HAS NOTHING TO DO WITH WHAT YOU ARE GOING OFF TO DIE FOR.
SLAVERY IS...THERE'S NO DENYIN' THOSE PEOPLE --
--ARE PEOPLE? NO, THERE AIN'T. BUT THIS WAR AIN'T ABOUT SLAVERY...

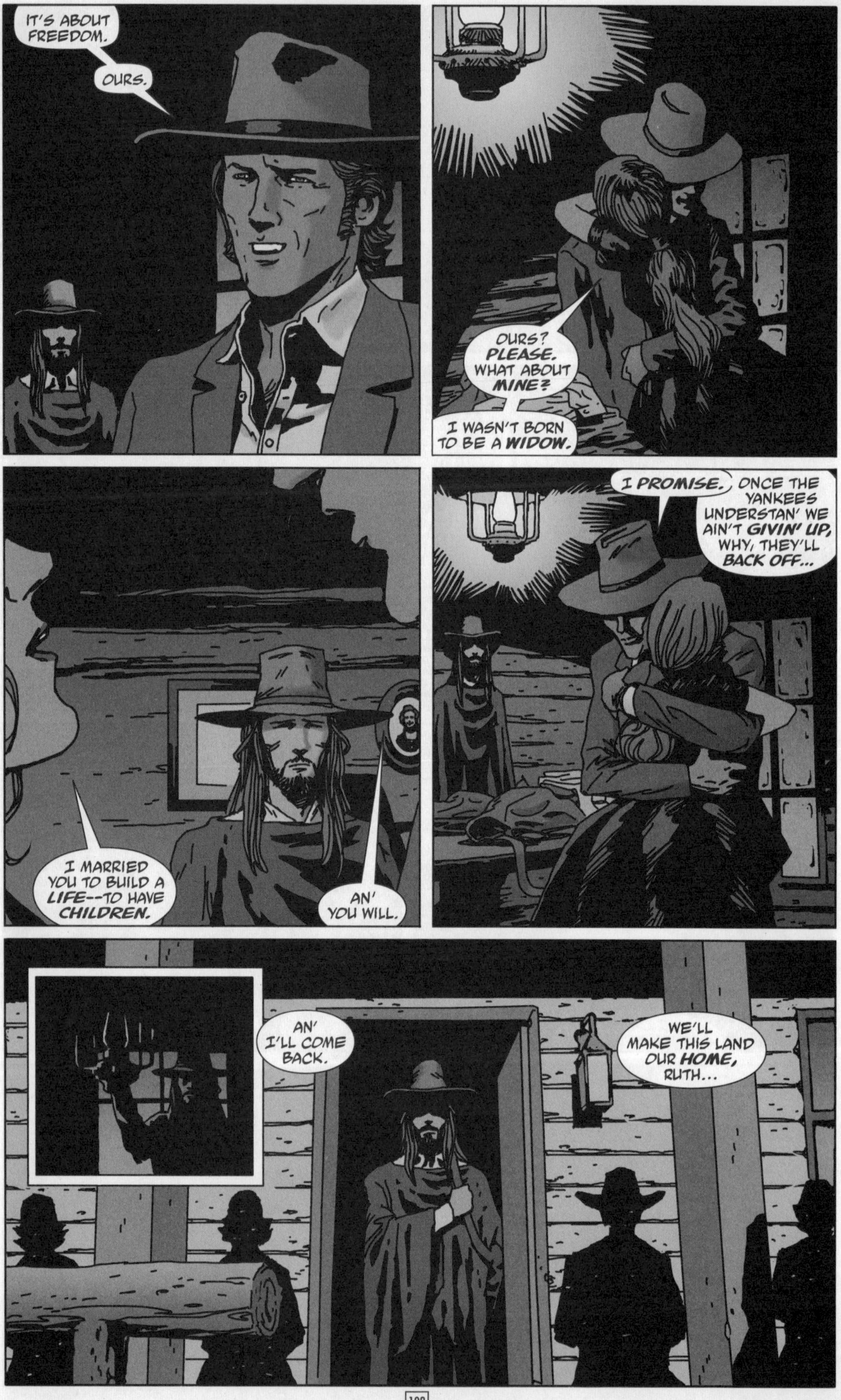
IT'S ABOUT FREEDOM.
OURS.
OURS? PLEASE. WHAT ABOUT MINE?
I WASN'T BORN TO BE A WIDOW.
I MARRIED YOU TO BUILD A LIFE--TO HAVE CHILDREN.
AN' YOU WILL.
I PROMISE.
ONCE THE YANKEES UNDERSTAN' WE AIN'T GIVIN' UP, WHY, THEY'LL BACK OFF...
AN' I'LL COME BACK.
WE'LL MAKE THIS LAND OUR HOME, RUTH...

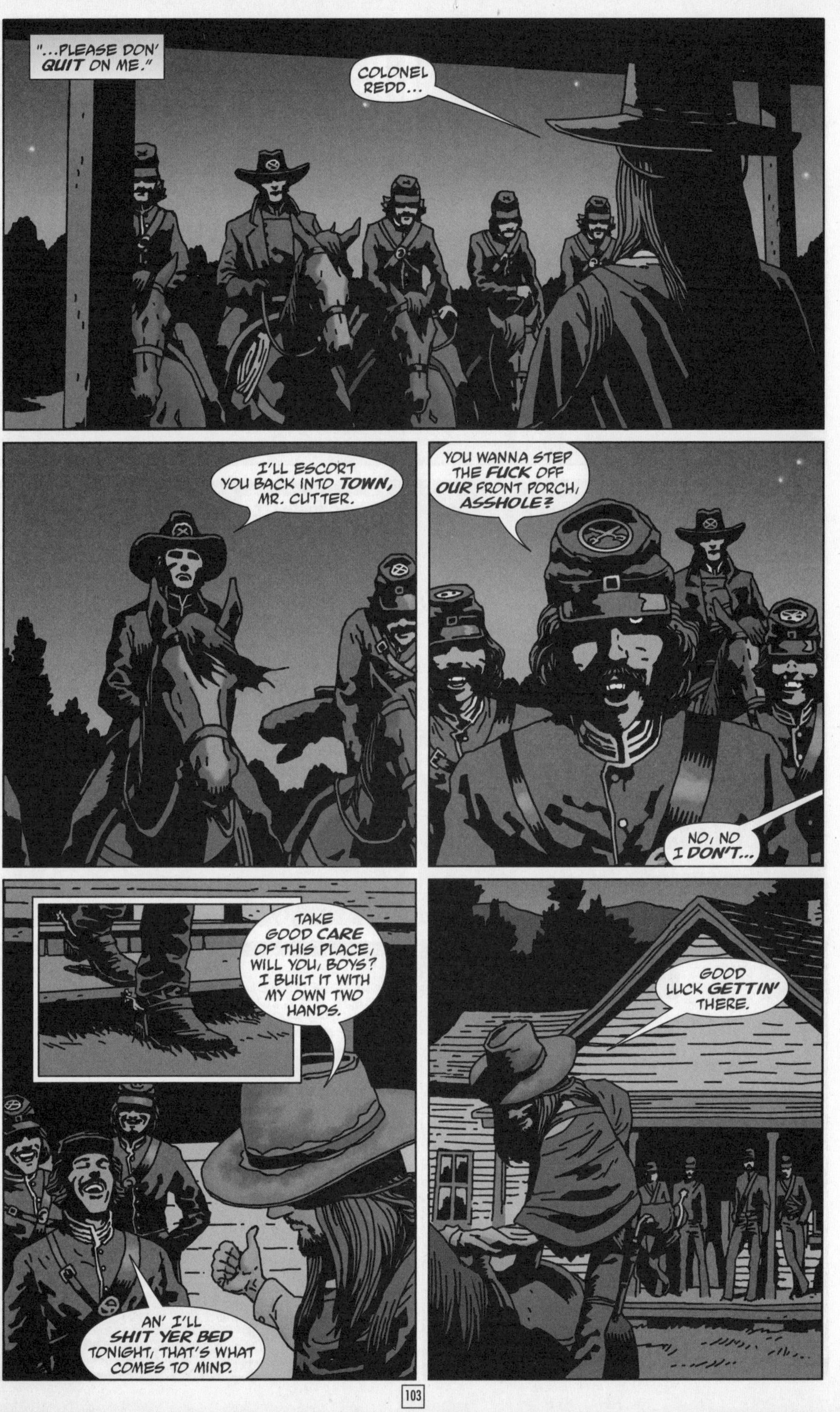
"...PLEASE DON' QUIT ON ME."
COLONEL REDD...
I'LL ESCORT YOU BACK INTO TOWN, MR. CUTTER.
YOU WANNA STEP THE FUCK OFF OUR FRONT PORCH, ASSHOLE?
NO, NO I DON'T...
TAKE GOOD CARE OF THIS PLACE, WILL YOU, BOYS? I BUILT IT WITH MY OWN TWO HANDS.
AN' I'LL SHIT YER BED TONIGHT, THAT'S WHAT COMES TO MIND.
GOOD LUCK GETTIN' THERE.

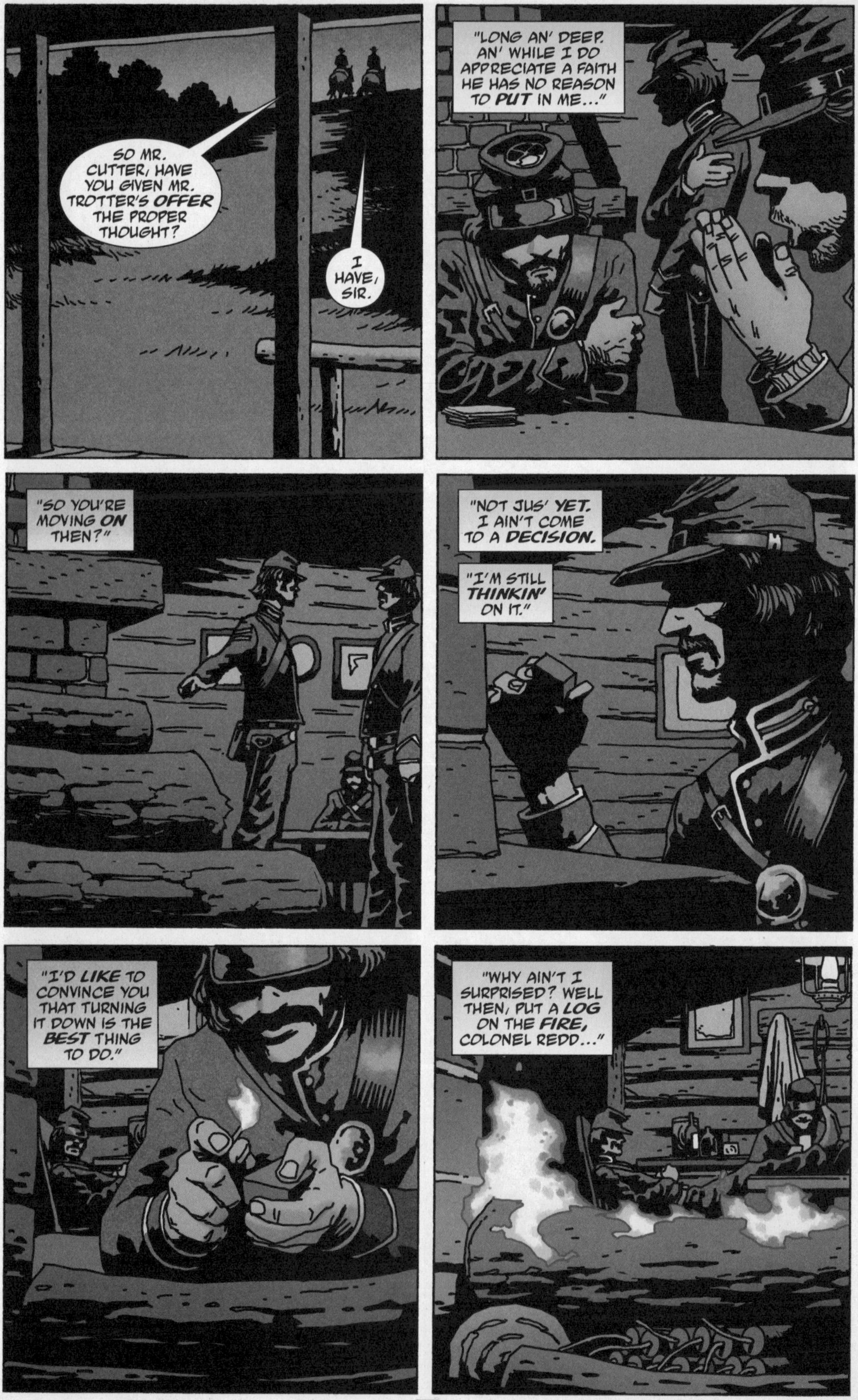

SO MR. CUTTER, HAVE YOU GIVEN MR. TROTTER'S OFFER THE PROPER THOUGHT?
I HAVE, SIR.
"LONG AN' DEEP. AN' WHILE I DO APPRECIATE A FAITH HE HAS NO REASON TO PUT IN ME..."
"SO YOU'RE MOVING ON THEN?"
"NOT JUS' YET. I AIN'T COME TO A DECISION.
"I'M STILL THINKIN' ON IT."
"I'D LIKE TO CONVINCE YOU THAT TURNING IT DOWN IS THE BEST THING TO DO."
"WHY AIN'T I SURPRISED? WELL THEN, PUT A LOG ON THE FIRE, COLONEL REDD..."

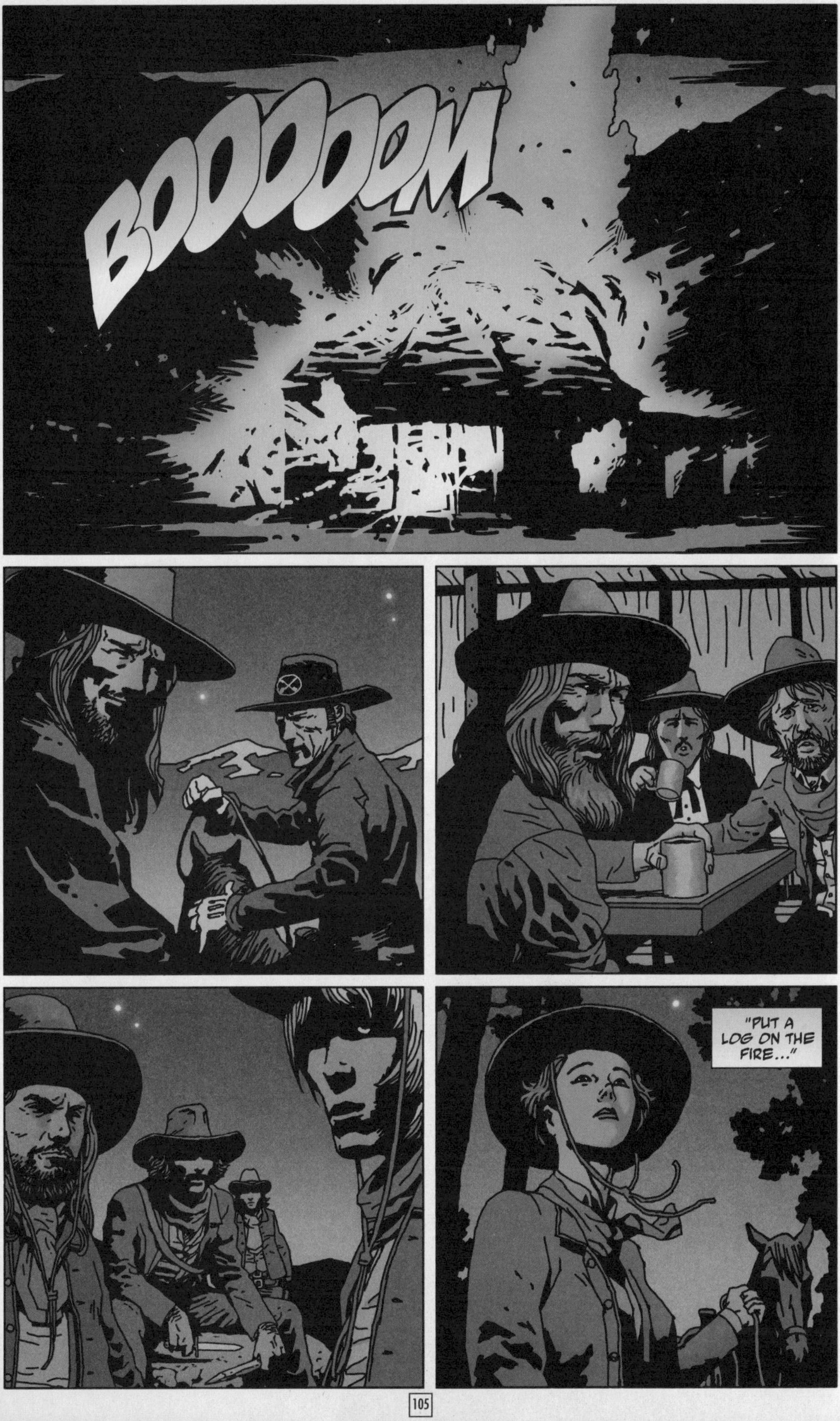
BOOOOOM
"PUT A LOG ON THE FIRE..."

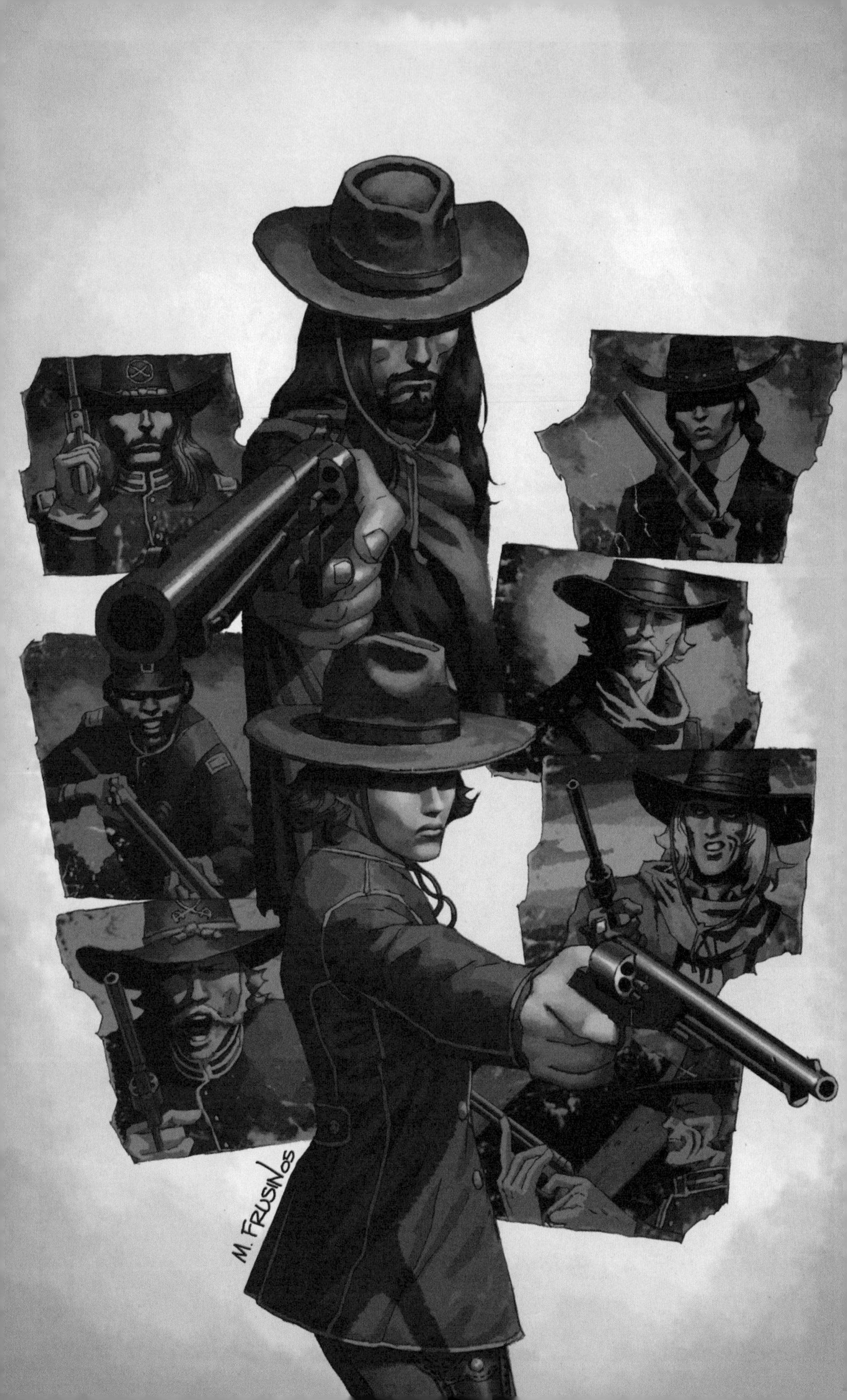
M. FRUSINO05

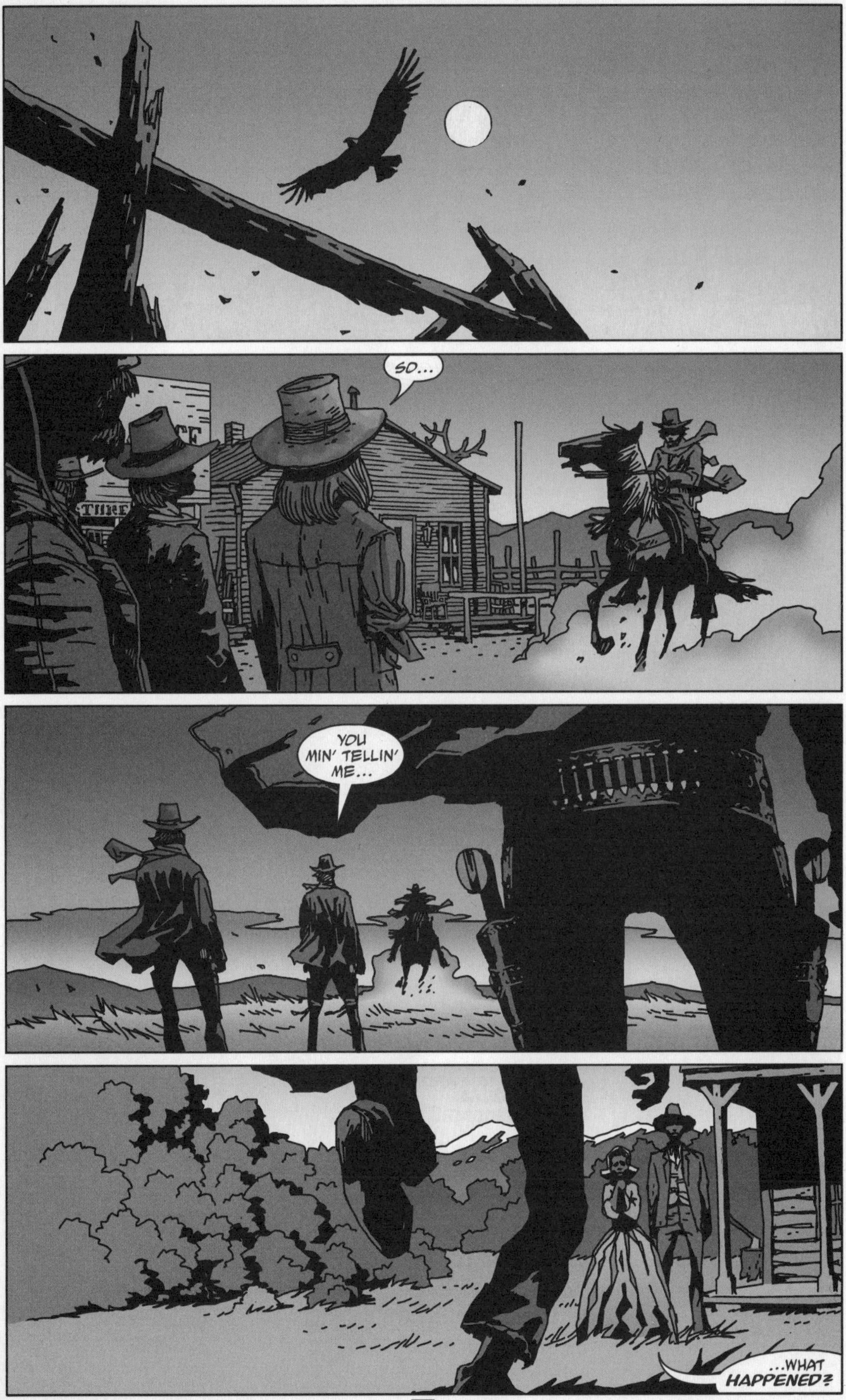
SO...
YOU MIN' TELLIN' ME...
...WHAT HAPPENED?

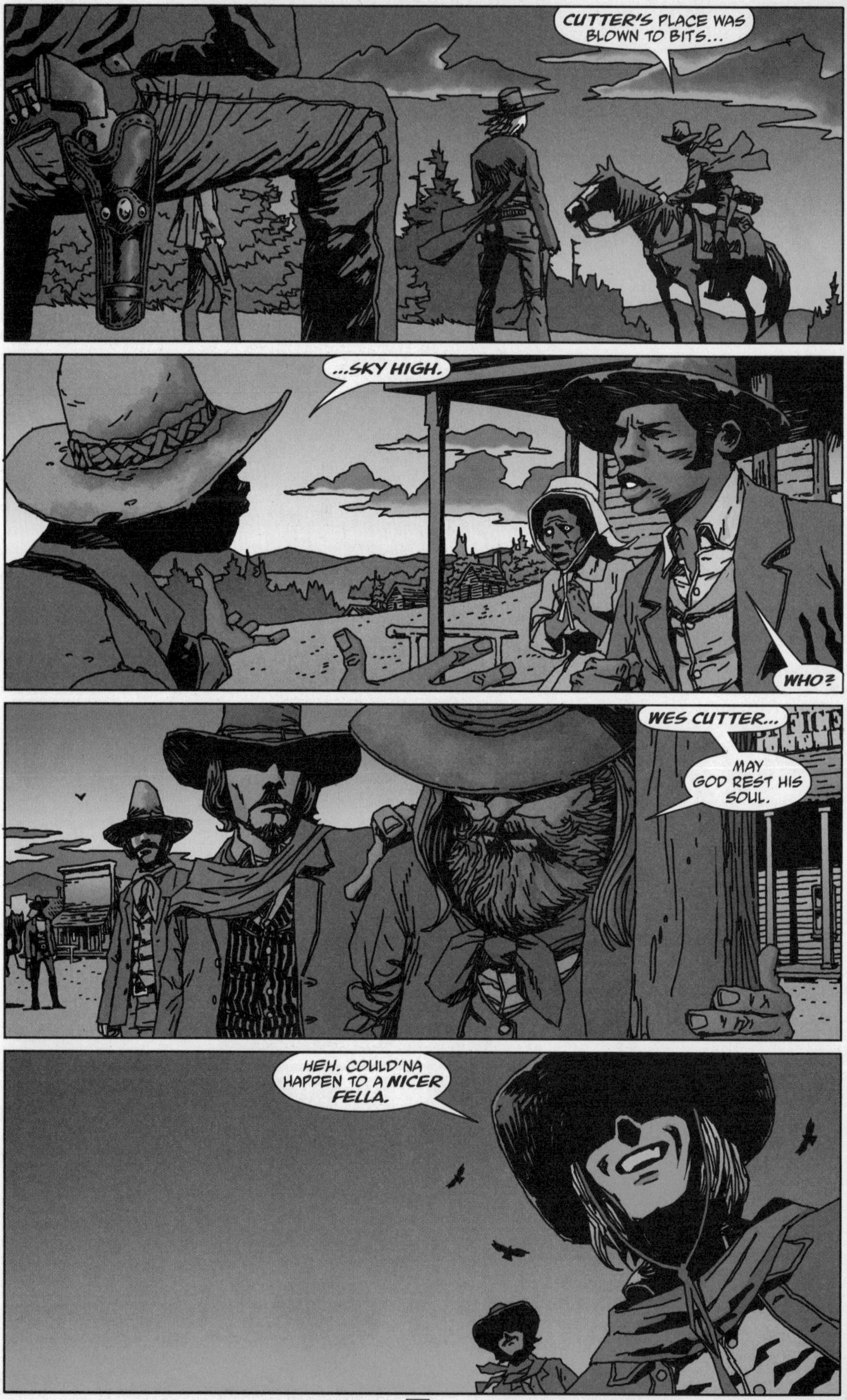
CUTTER'S PLACE WAS BLOWN TO BITS...
...SKY HIGH.
WHO?
WES CUTTER...
MAY GOD REST HIS SOUL.
HEH. COULD'NA HAPPEN TO A NICER FELLA.

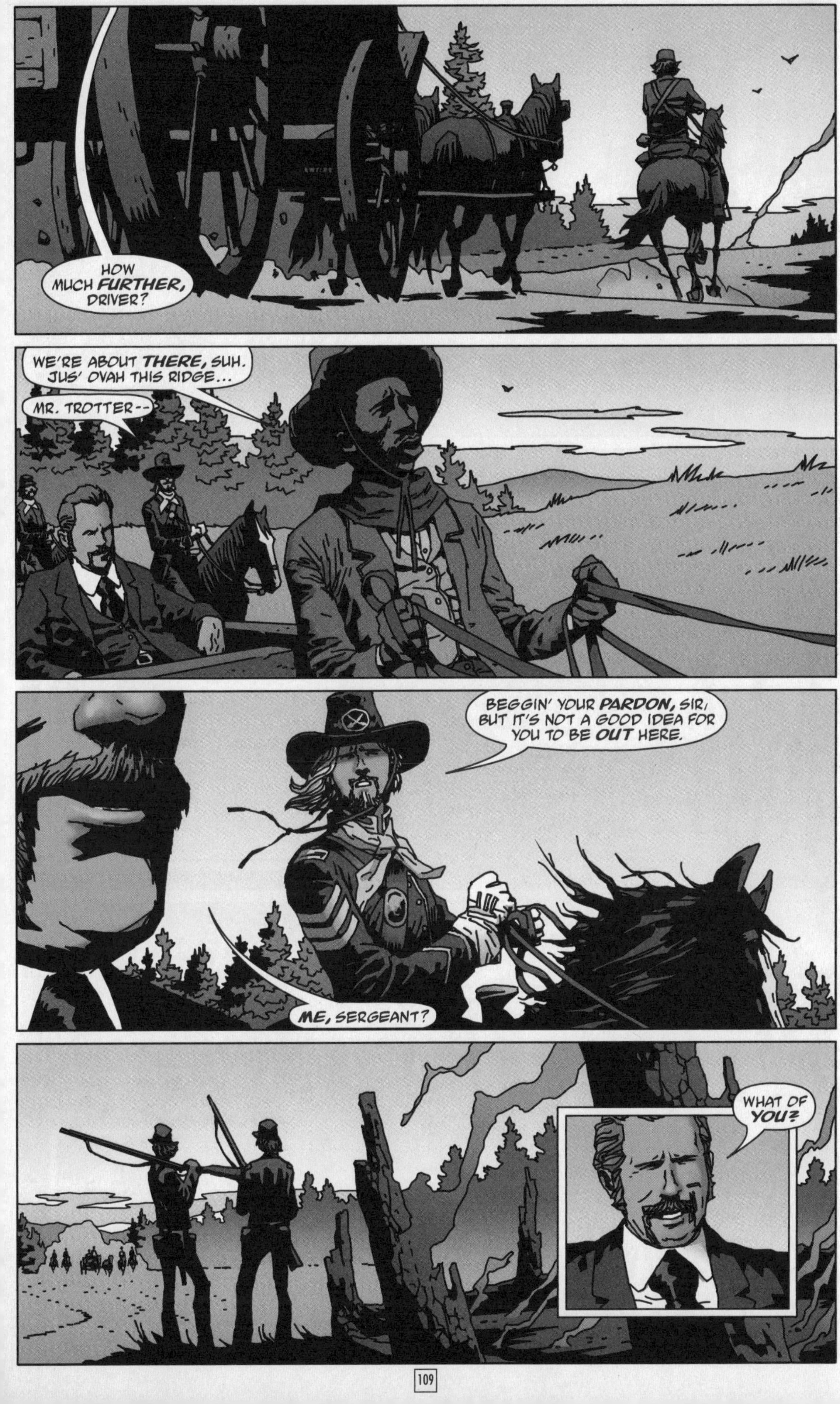
HOW MUCH FURTHER, DRIVER?
WE'RE ABOUT THERE, SUH. JUS' OVAH THIS RIDGE...
MR. TROTTER--
BEGGIN' YOUR PARDON, SIR, BUT IT'S NOT A GOOD IDEA FOR YOU TO BE OUT HERE.
ME, SERGEANT?
WHAT OF YOU?

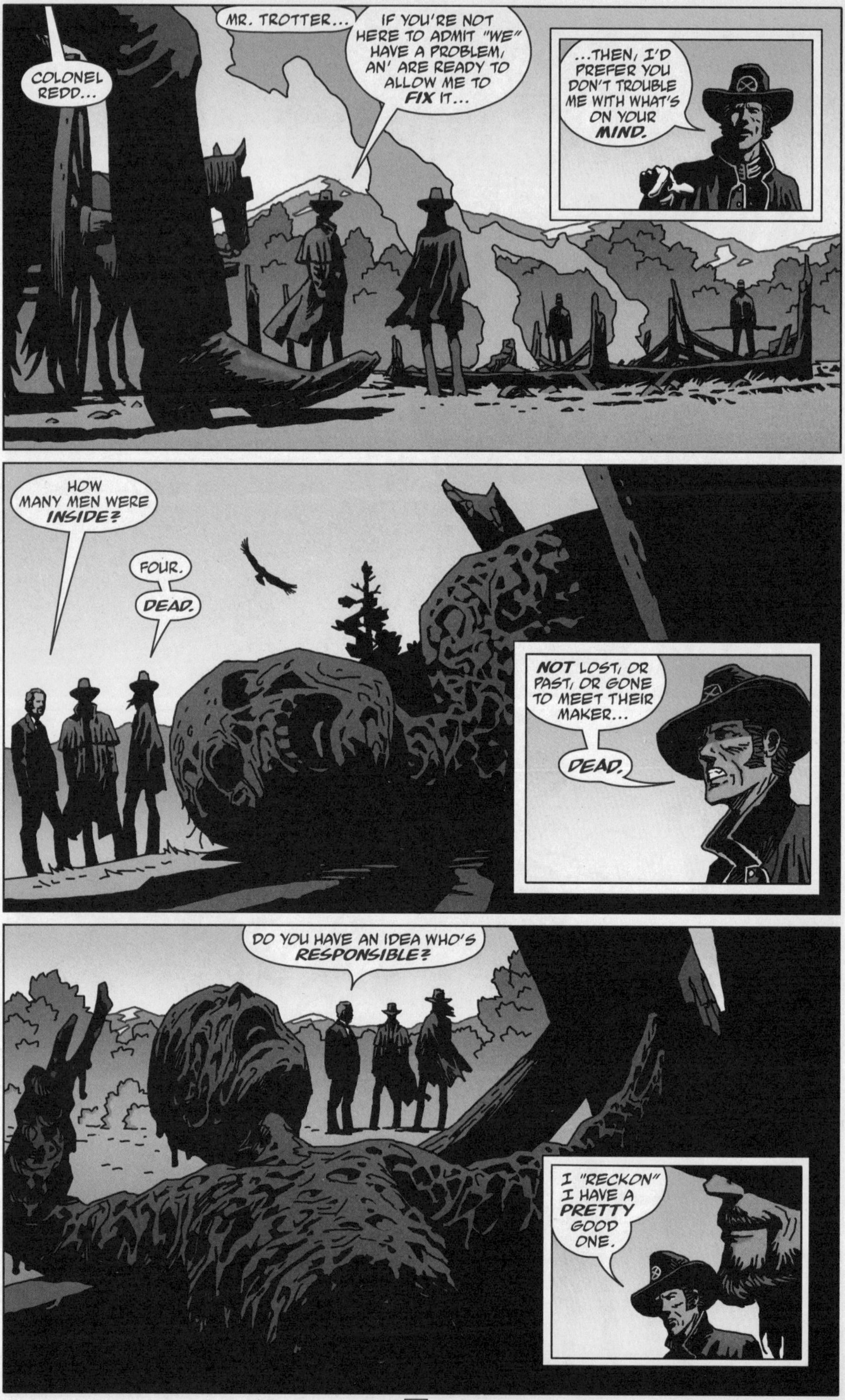
COLONEL REDD...
MR. TROTTER...
IF YOU'RE NOT HERE TO ADMIT "WE" HAVE A PROBLEM, AN' ARE READY TO ALLOW ME TO FIX IT...
...THEN, I'D PREFER YOU DON'T TROUBLE ME WITH WHAT'S ON YOUR MIND.
HOW MANY MEN WERE INSIDE?
FOUR.
DEAD.
NOT LOST, OR PAST, OR GONE TO MEET THEIR MAKER...
DEAD.
DO YOU HAVE AN IDEA WHO'S RESPONSIBLE?
I "RECKON" I HAVE A PRETTY GOOD ONE.

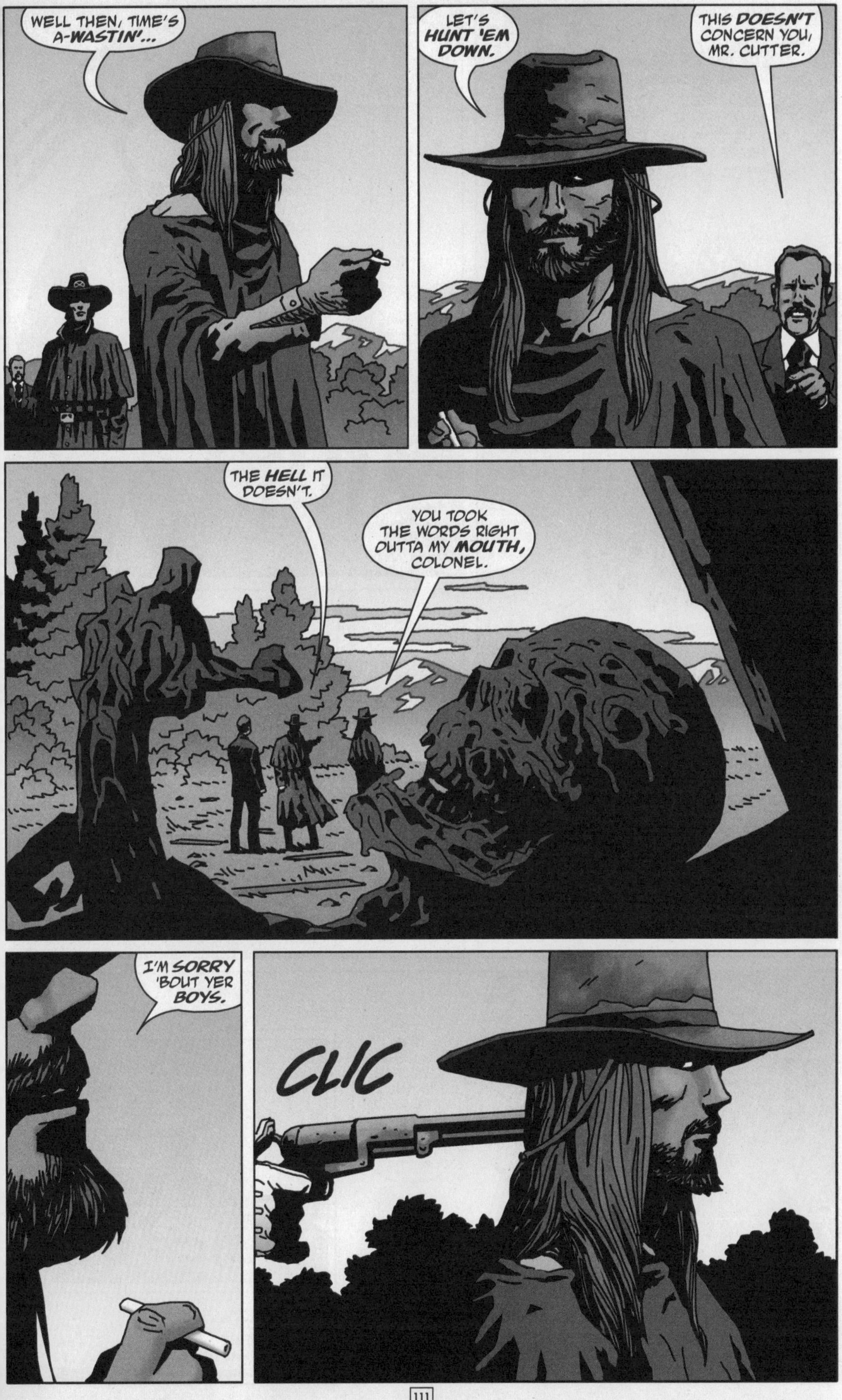
WELL THEN, TIME'S A-WASTIN'...
LET'S HUNT 'EM DOWN.
THIS DOESN'T CONCERN YOU, MR. CUTTER.
THE HELL IT DOESN'T.
YOU TOOK THE WORDS RIGHT OUTTA MY MOUTH, COLONEL.
I'M SORRY 'BOUT YER BOYS.
CLIC

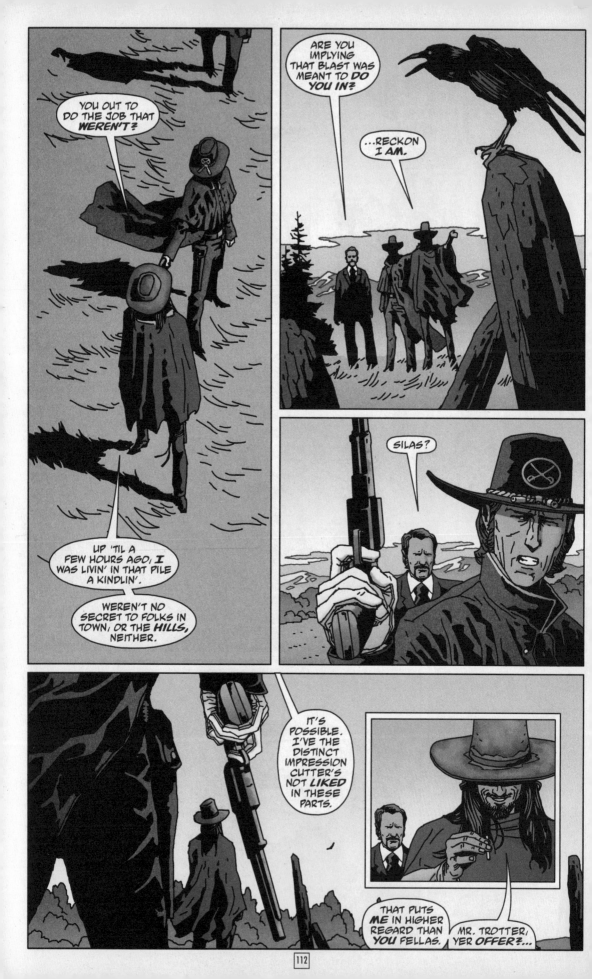

YOU OUT TO DO THE JOB THAT *WEREN'T?*

ARE YOU IMPLYING THAT BLAST WAS MEANT TO *DO YOU IN?*

...RECKON I *AM.*

SILAS?

UP 'TIL A FEW HOURS AGO, I WAS LIVIN' IN THAT PILE A KINDLIN'.

WEREN'T NO SECRET TO FOLKS IN TOWN, OR THE *HILLS,* NEITHER.

IT'S POSSIBLE. I'VE THE DISTINCT IMPRESSION CUTTER'S NOT *LIKED* IN THESE PARTS.

THAT PUTS *ME* IN HIGHER REGARD THAN *YOU* FELLAS.

MR. TROTTER, YER *OFFER?*...

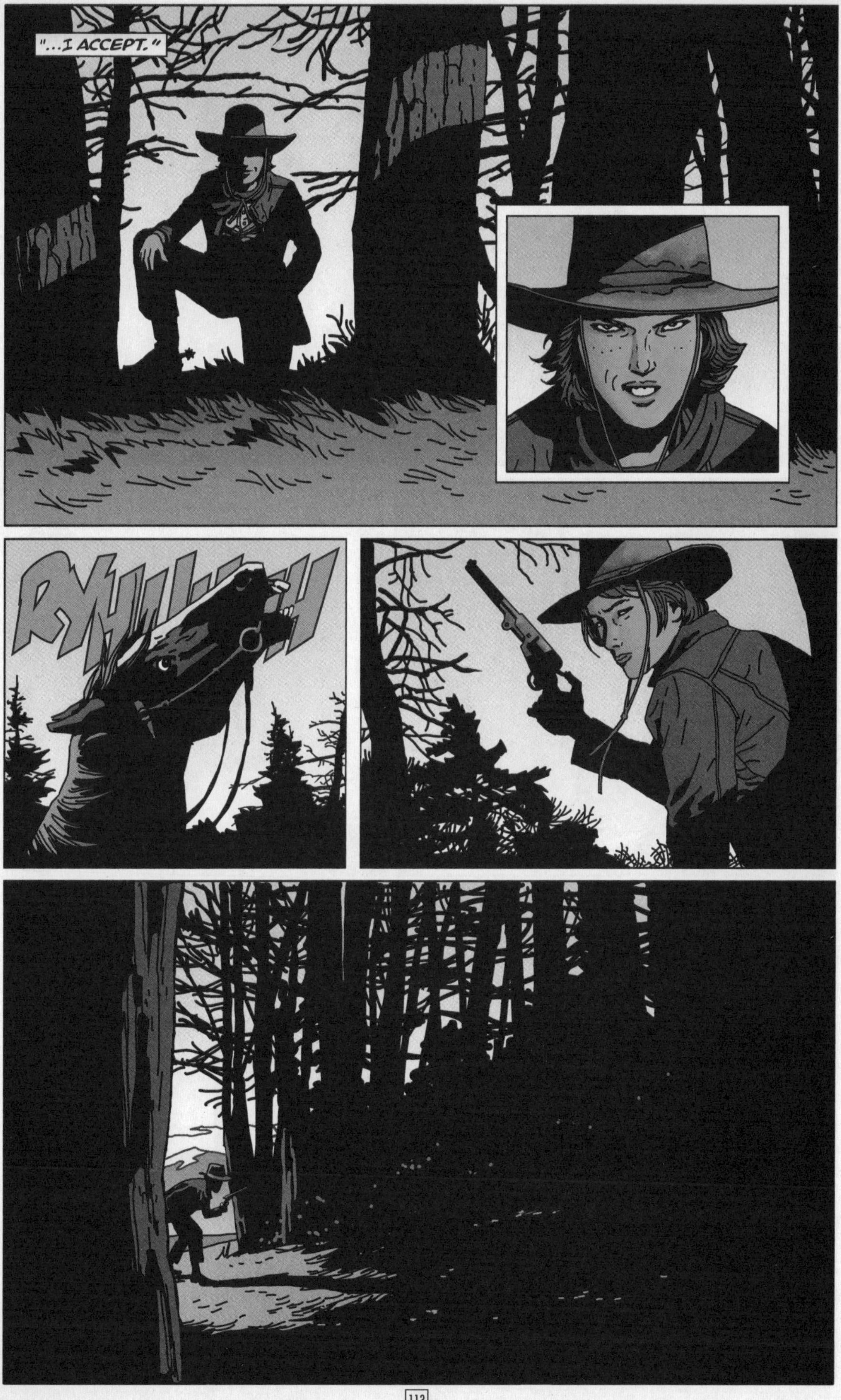
"...I ACCEPT."

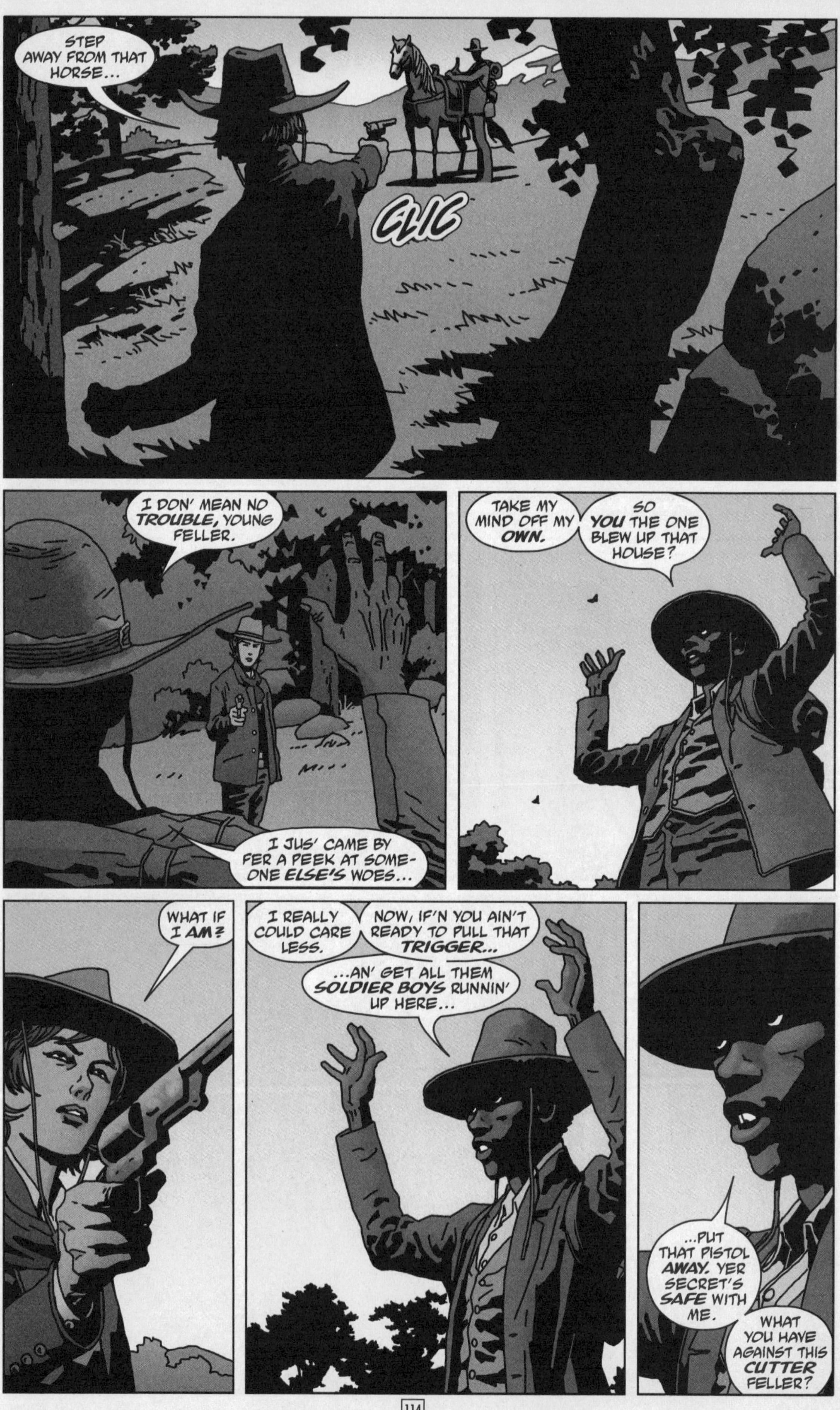

STEP AWAY FROM THAT HORSE...
CLIC
I DON' MEAN NO TROUBLE, YOUNG FELLER.
I JUS' CAME BY FER A PEEK AT SOME-ONE ELSE'S WOES...
TAKE MY MIND OFF MY OWN.
SO YOU THE ONE BLEW UP THAT HOUSE?
WHAT IF I AM?
I REALLY COULD CARE LESS.
NOW, IF'N YOU AIN'T READY TO PULL THAT TRIGGER...
...AN' GET ALL THEM SOLDIER BOYS RUNNIN' UP HERE...
...PUT THAT PISTOL AWAY. YER SECRET'S SAFE WITH ME.
WHAT YOU HAVE AGAINST THIS CUTTER FELLER?

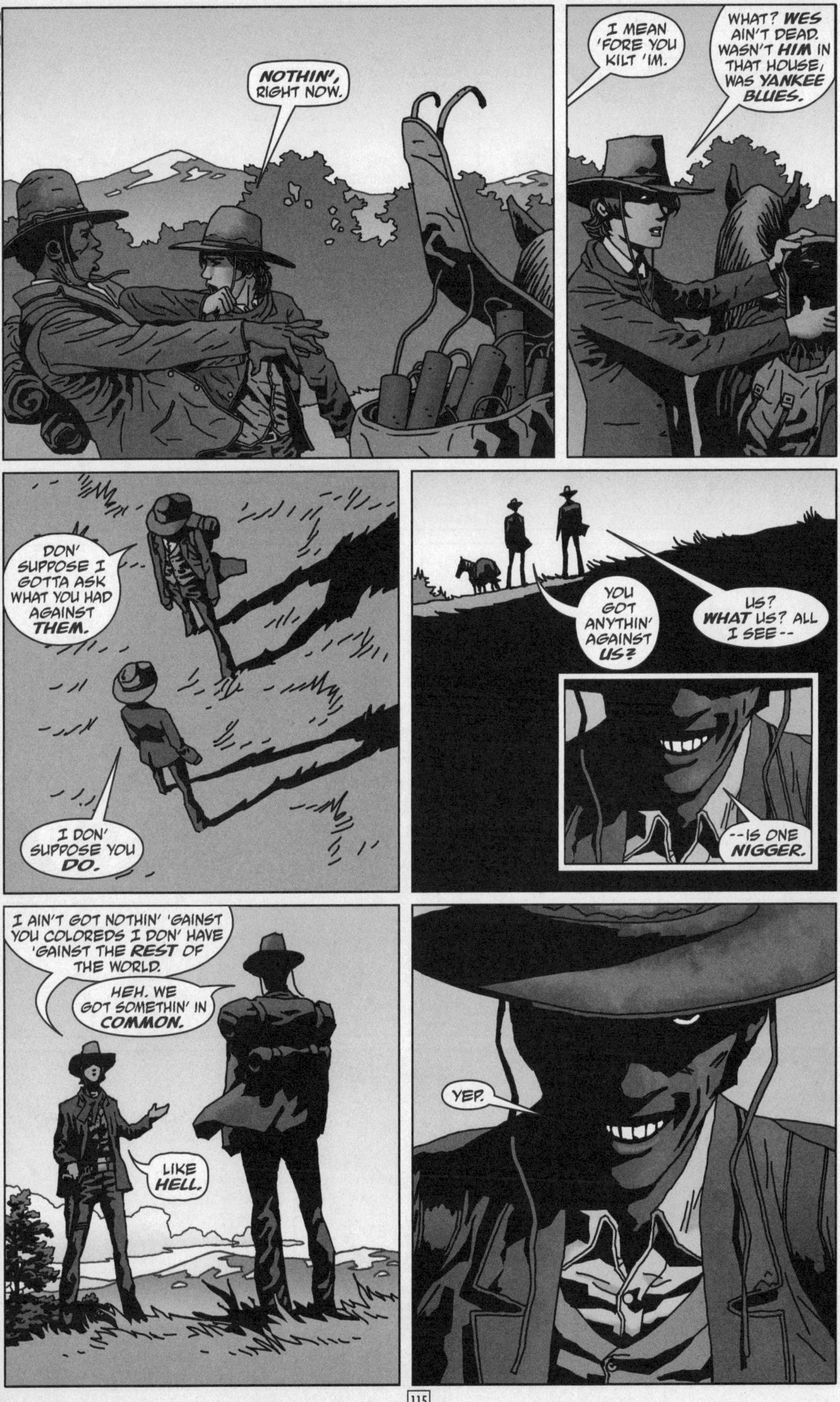
NOTHIN', RIGHT NOW.
I MEAN 'FORE YOU KILT 'IM.
WHAT? WES AIN'T DEAD. WASN'T HIM IN THAT HOUSE, WAS YANKEE BLUES.
DON' SUPPOSE I GOTTA ASK WHAT YOU HAD AGAINST THEM.
I DON' SUPPOSE YOU DO.
YOU GOT ANYTHIN' AGAINST US?
US? WHAT US? ALL I SEE--
--IS ONE NIGGER.
I AIN'T GOT NOTHIN' 'GAINST YOU COLOREDS I DON' HAVE 'GAINST THE REST OF THE WORLD.
HEH. WE GOT SOMETHIN' IN COMMON.
LIKE HELL.
YEP.

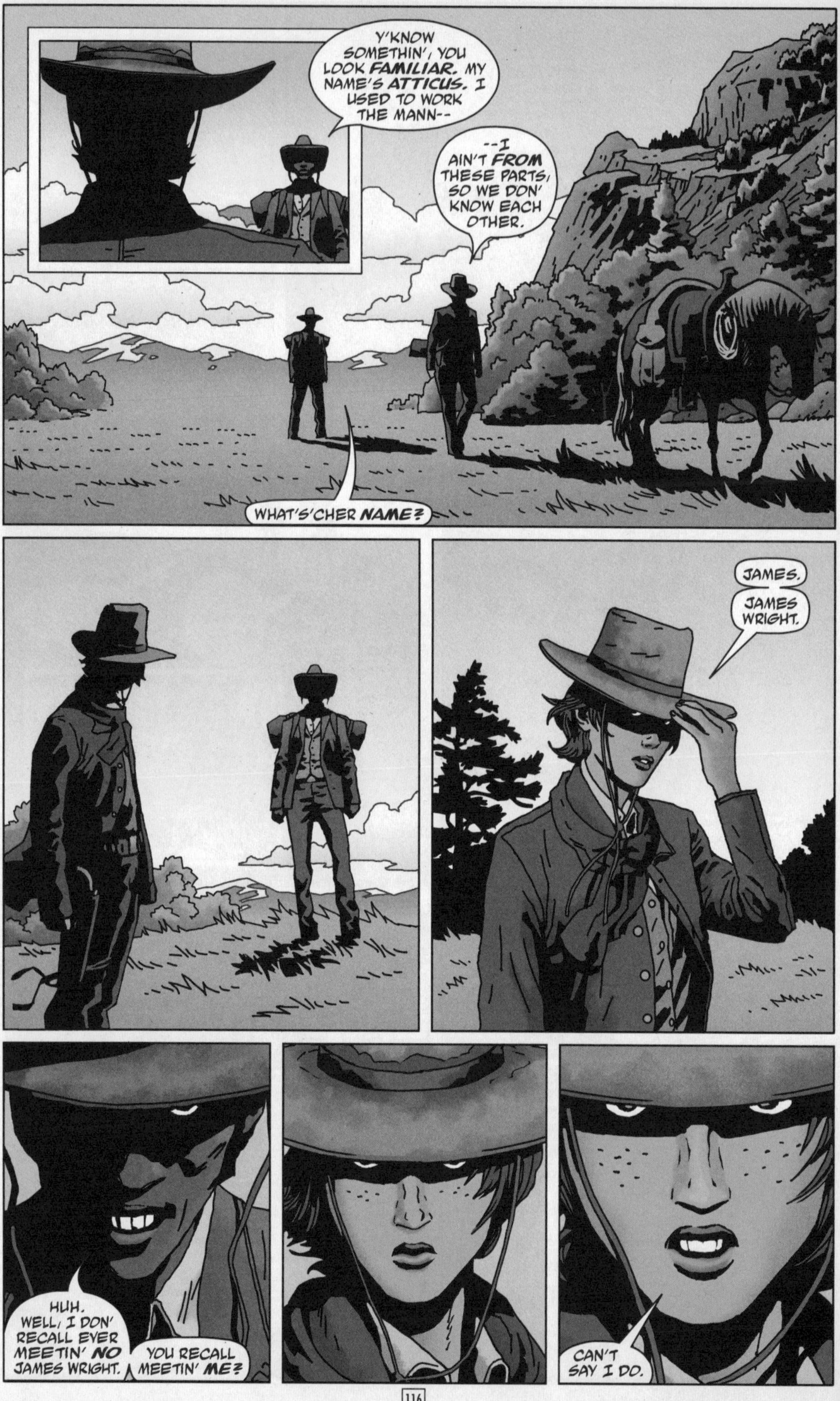
Y'KNOW SOMETHIN', YOU LOOK FAMILIAR. MY NAME'S ATTICUS. I USED TO WORK THE MANN--
--I AIN'T FROM THESE PARTS, SO WE DON' KNOW EACH OTHER.
WHAT'S'CHER NAME?
JAMES.
JAMES WRIGHT.
HUH. WELL, I DON' RECALL EVER MEETIN' NO JAMES WRIGHT.
YOU RECALL MEETIN' ME?
CAN'T SAY I DO.

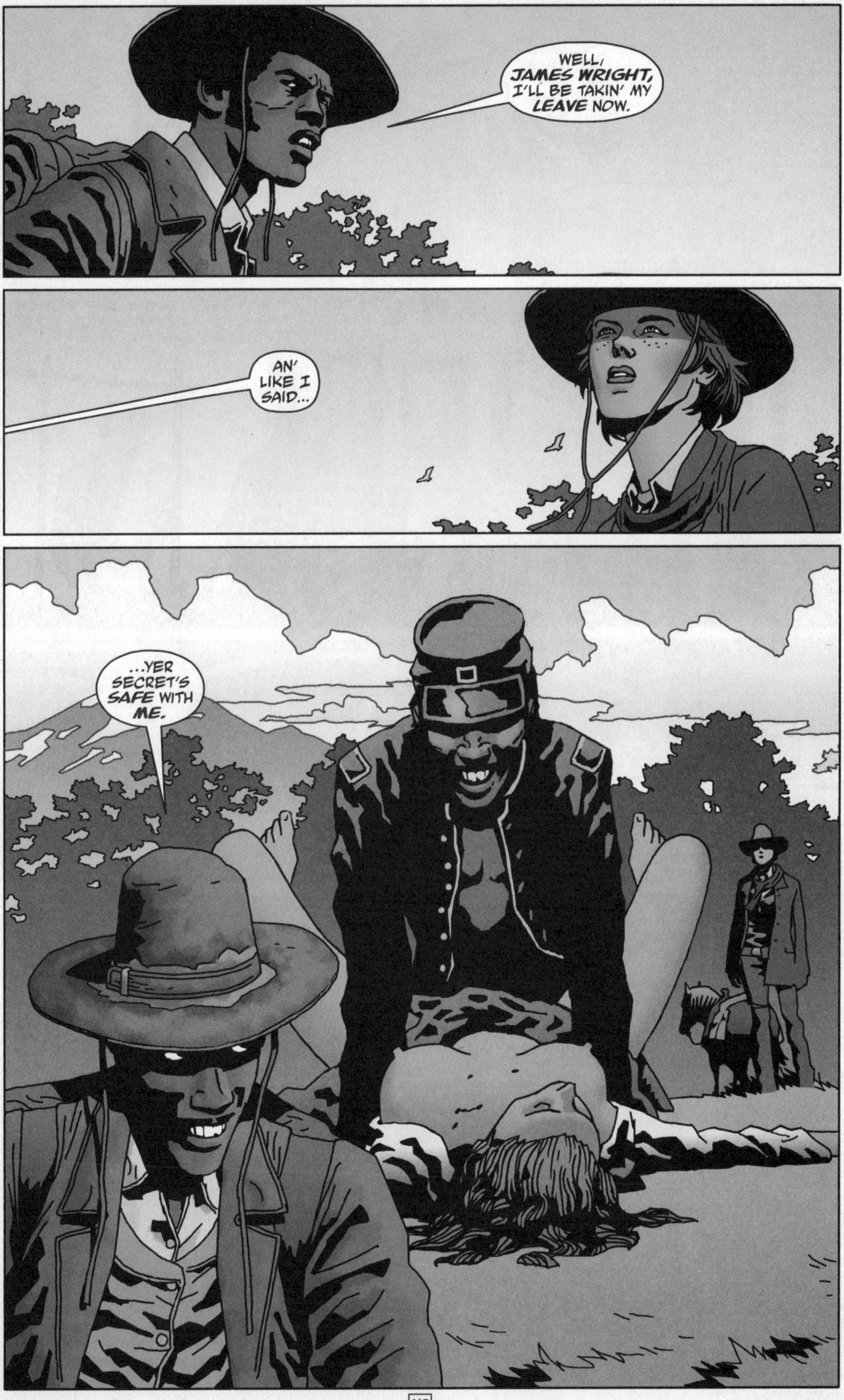
WELL, JAMES WRIGHT, I'LL BE TAKIN' MY LEAVE NOW.
AN' LIKE I SAID...
...YER SECRET'S SAFE WITH ME.

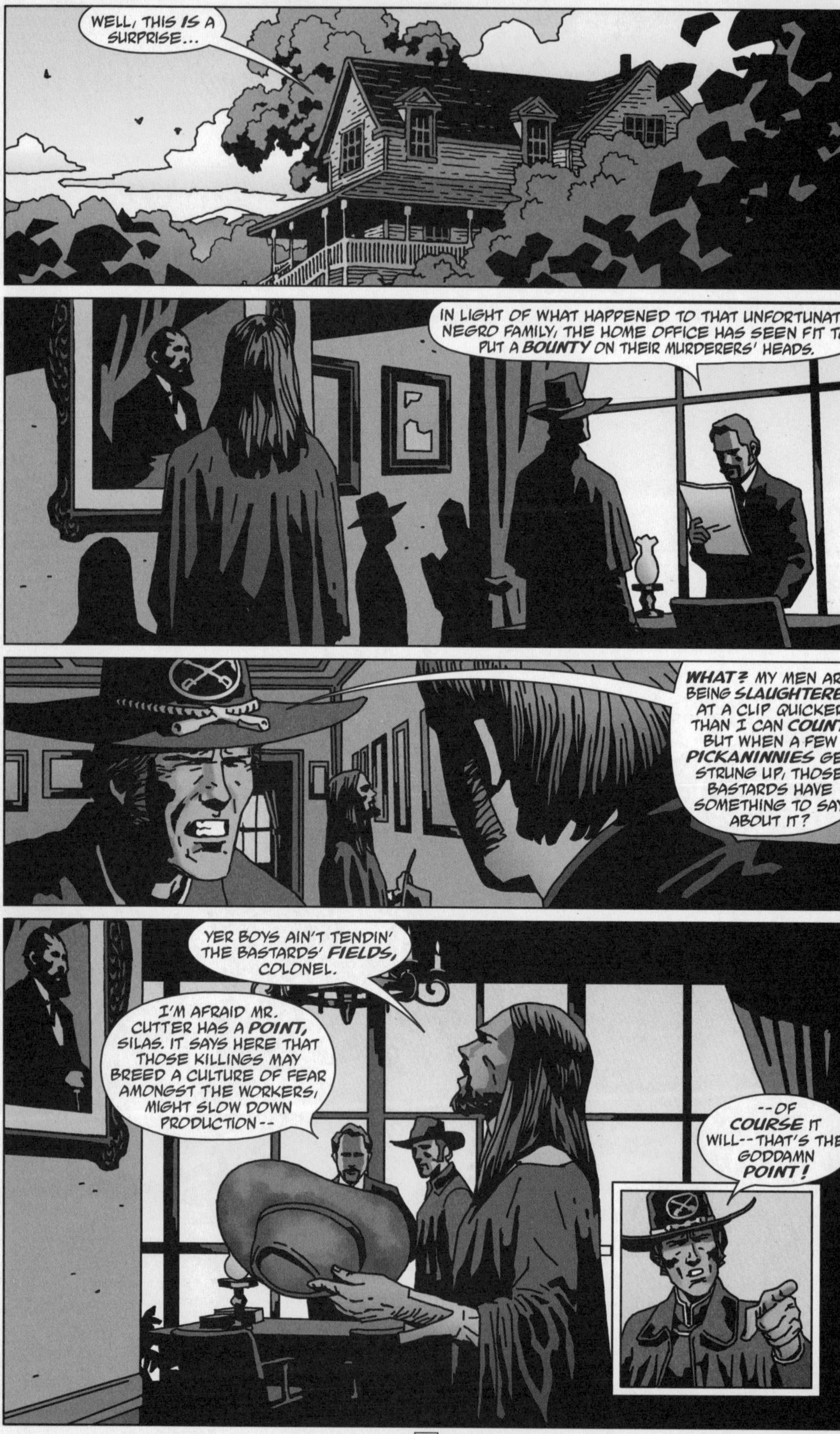
WELL, THIS IS A SURPRISE...
IN LIGHT OF WHAT HAPPENED TO THAT UNFORTUNATE NEGRO FAMILY, THE HOME OFFICE HAS SEEN FIT TO PUT A BOUNTY ON THEIR MURDERERS' HEADS.
WHAT? MY MEN ARE BEING SLAUGHTERED AT A CLIP QUICKER THAN I CAN COUNT, BUT WHEN A FEW PICKANINNIES GET STRUNG UP, THOSE BASTARDS HAVE SOMETHING TO SAY ABOUT IT?
YER BOYS AIN'T TENDIN' THE BASTARDS' FIELDS, COLONEL.
I'M AFRAID MR. CUTTER HAS A POINT, SILAS. IT SAYS HERE THAT THOSE KILLINGS MAY BREED A CULTURE OF FEAR AMONGST THE WORKERS, MIGHT SLOW DOWN PRODUCTION--
--OF COURSE IT WILL--THAT'S THE GODDAMN POINT!

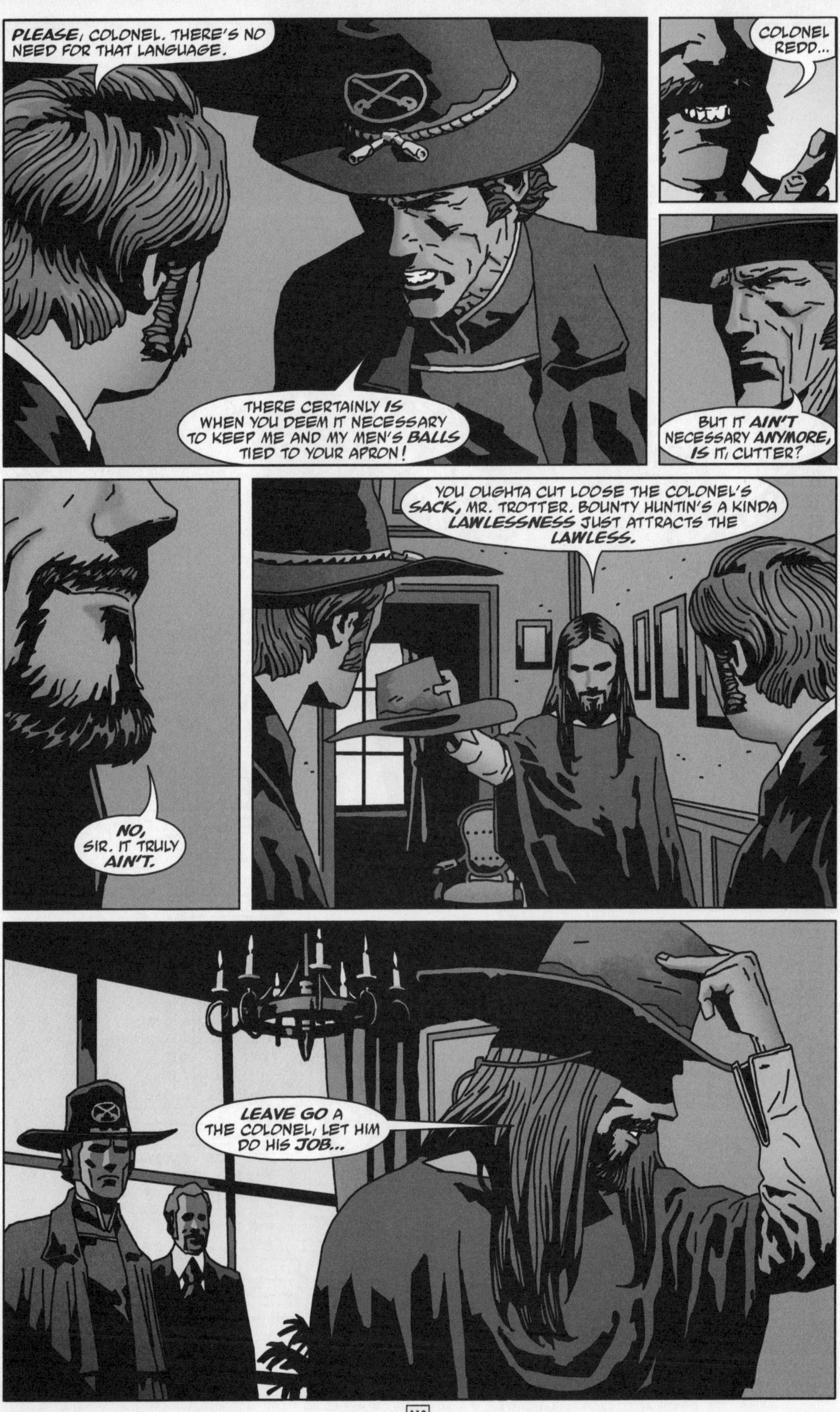
PLEASE, COLONEL. THERE'S NO NEED FOR THAT LANGUAGE.
COLONEL REDD...
THERE CERTAINLY IS WHEN YOU DEEM IT NECESSARY TO KEEP ME AND MY MEN'S BALLS TIED TO YOUR APRON!
BUT IT AIN'T NECESSARY ANYMORE, IS IT, CUTTER?
NO, SIR. IT TRULY AIN'T.
YOU OUGHTA CUT LOOSE THE COLONEL'S SACK, MR. TROTTER. BOUNTY HUNTIN'S A KINDA LAWLESSNESS JUST ATTRACTS THE LAWLESS.
LEAVE GO A THE COLONEL, LET HIM DO HIS JOB...

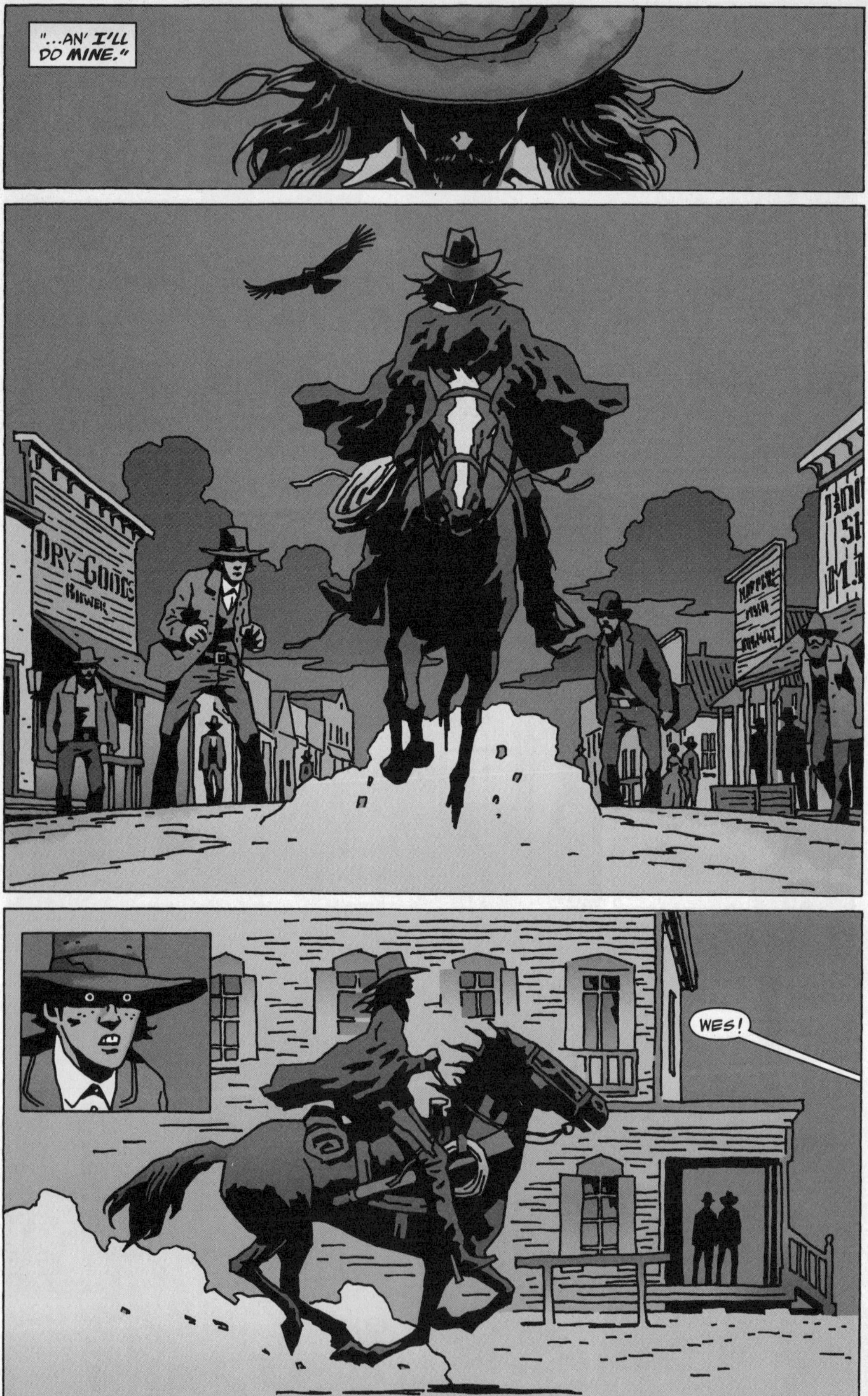
"...AN' I'LL DO MINE."
DRY GOODS
WES!

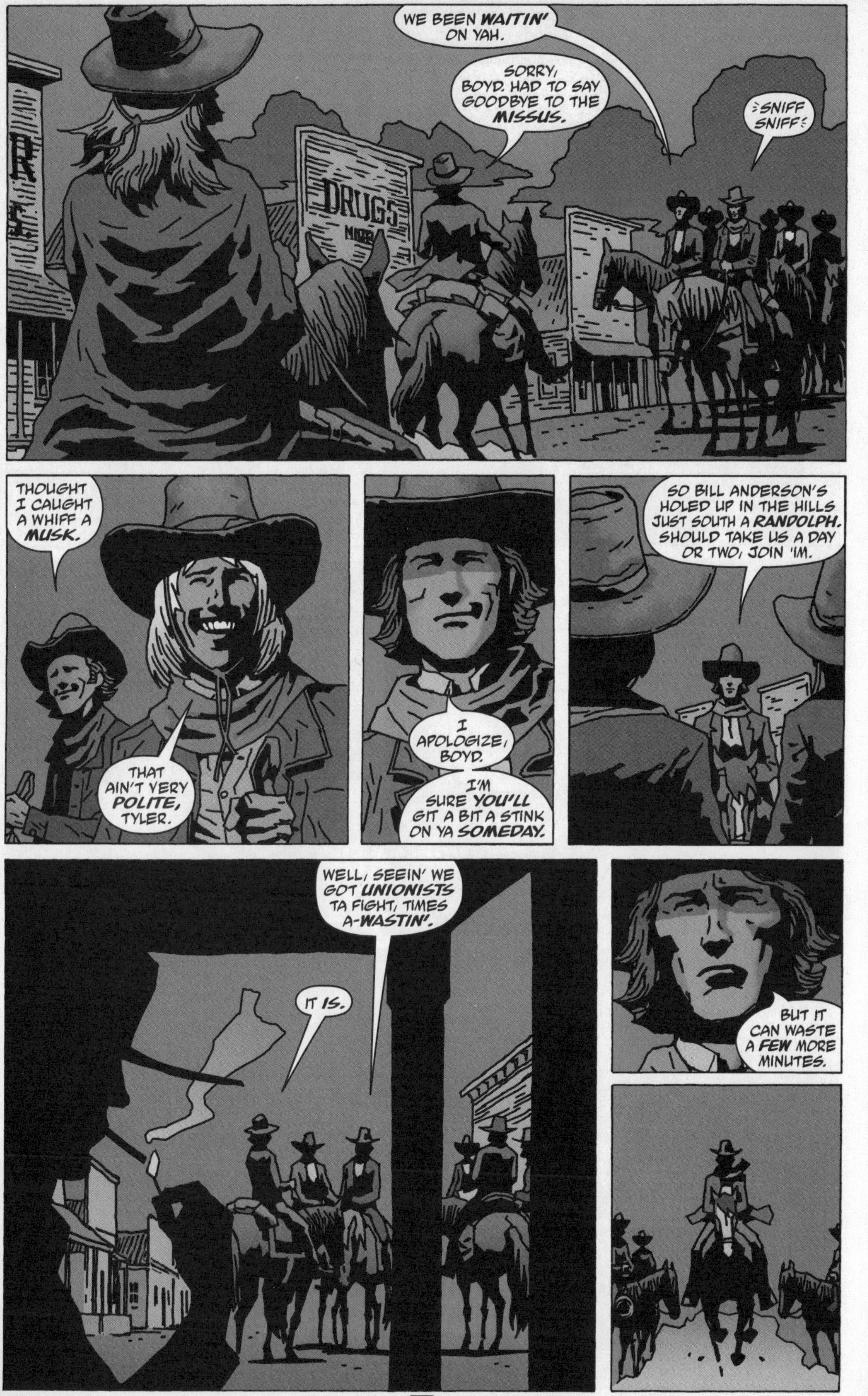
WE BEEN WAITIN' ON YAH.
SORRY, BOYD. HAD TO SAY GOODBYE TO THE MISSUS.
SNIFF SNIFF
DRUGS
THOUGHT I CAUGHT A WHIFF A MUSK.
THAT AIN'T VERY POLITE, TYLER.
I APOLOGIZE, BOYD.
I'M SURE YOU'LL GIT A BIT A STINK ON YA SOMEDAY.
SO BILL ANDERSON'S HOLED UP IN THE HILLS JUST SOUTH A RANDOLPH. SHOULD TAKE US A DAY OR TWO, JOIN 'IM.
WELL, SEEIN' WE GOT UNIONISTS TA FIGHT, TIMES A-WASTIN'.
IT IS.
BUT IT CAN WASTE A FEW MORE MINUTES.

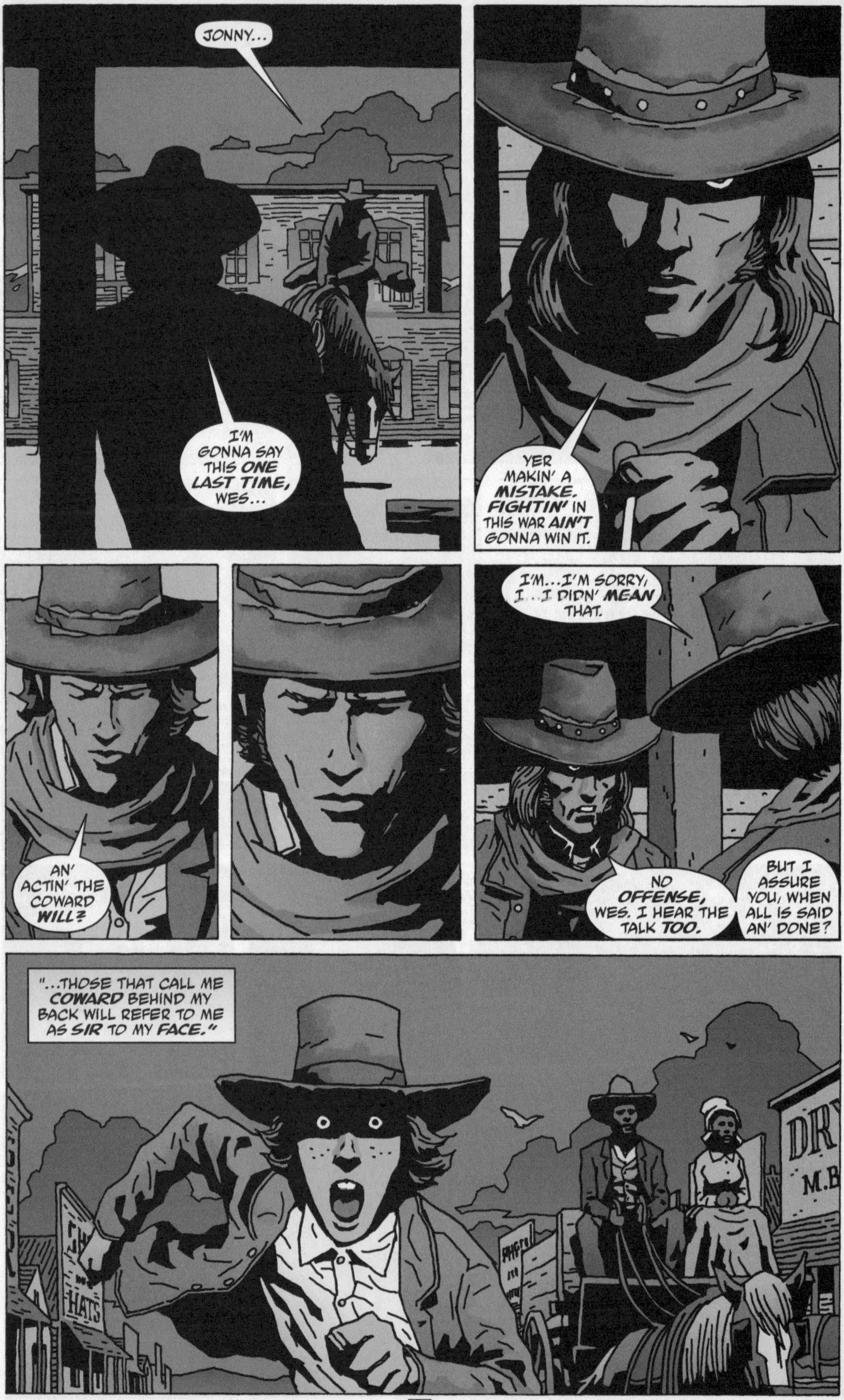
JONNY...
I'M GONNA SAY THIS ONE LAST TIME, WES...
YER MAKIN' A MISTAKE. FIGHTIN' IN THIS WAR AIN'T GONNA WIN IT.
AN' ACTIN' THE COWARD WILL?
I'M... I'M SORRY, I... I DIDN' MEAN THAT.
NO OFFENSE, WES. I HEAR THE TALK TOO.
BUT I ASSURE YOU, WHEN ALL IS SAID AN' DONE?
"...THOSE THAT CALL ME COWARD BEHIND MY BACK WILL REFER TO ME AS SIR TO MY FACE."
HATS

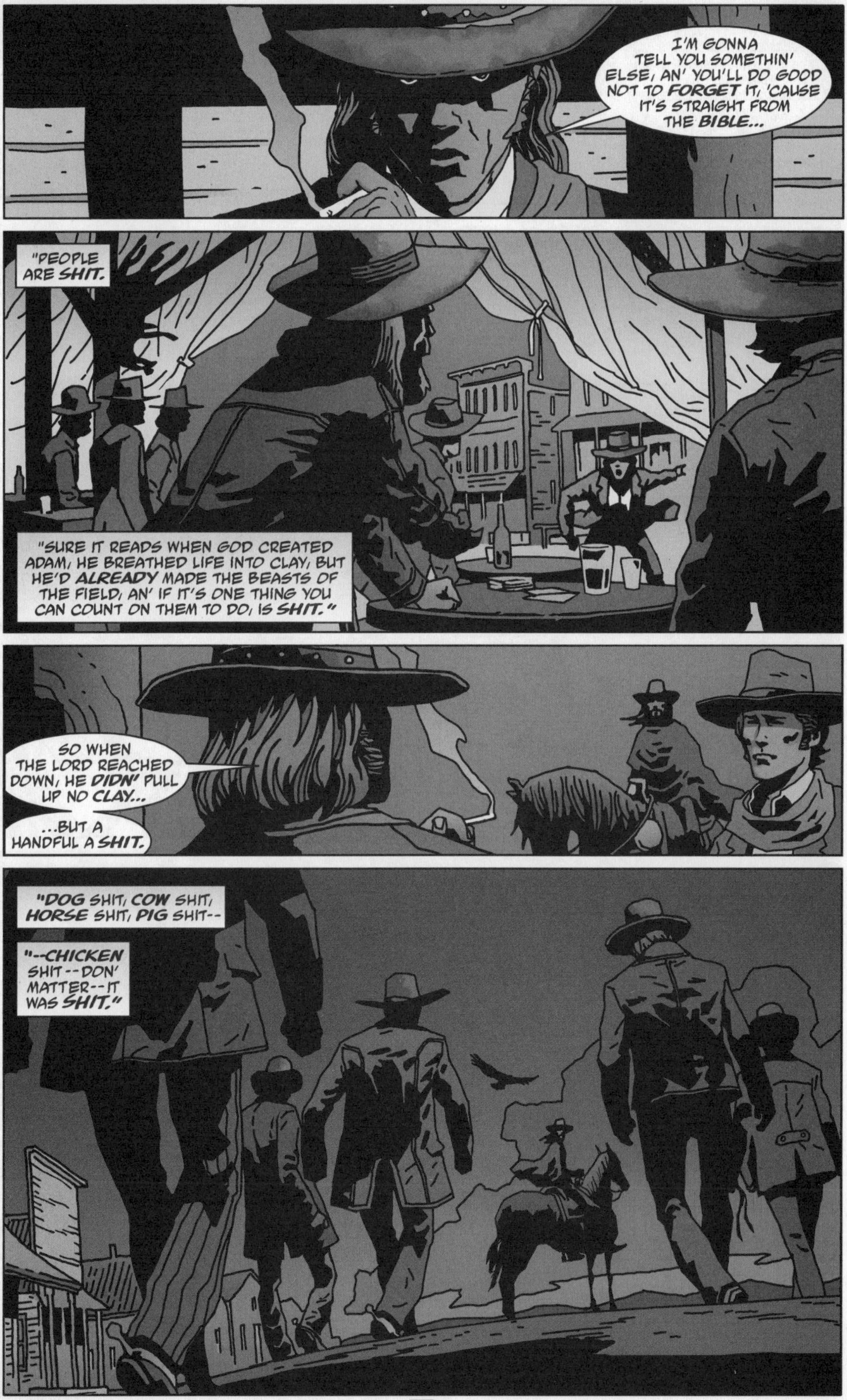
I'M GONNA TELL YOU SOMETHIN' ELSE, AN' YOU'LL DO GOOD NOT TO FORGET IT, 'CAUSE IT'S STRAIGHT FROM THE BIBLE...
"PEOPLE ARE SHIT.
"SURE IT READS WHEN GOD CREATED ADAM, HE BREATHED LIFE INTO CLAY, BUT HE'D ALREADY MADE THE BEASTS OF THE FIELD, AN' IF IT'S ONE THING YOU CAN COUNT ON THEM TO DO, IS SHIT."
SO WHEN THE LORD REACHED DOWN, HE DIDN' PULL UP NO CLAY...
...BUT A HANDFUL A SHIT.
"DOG SHIT, COW SHIT, HORSE SHIT, PIG SHIT--
"--CHICKEN SHIT--DON' MATTER--IT WAS SHIT."

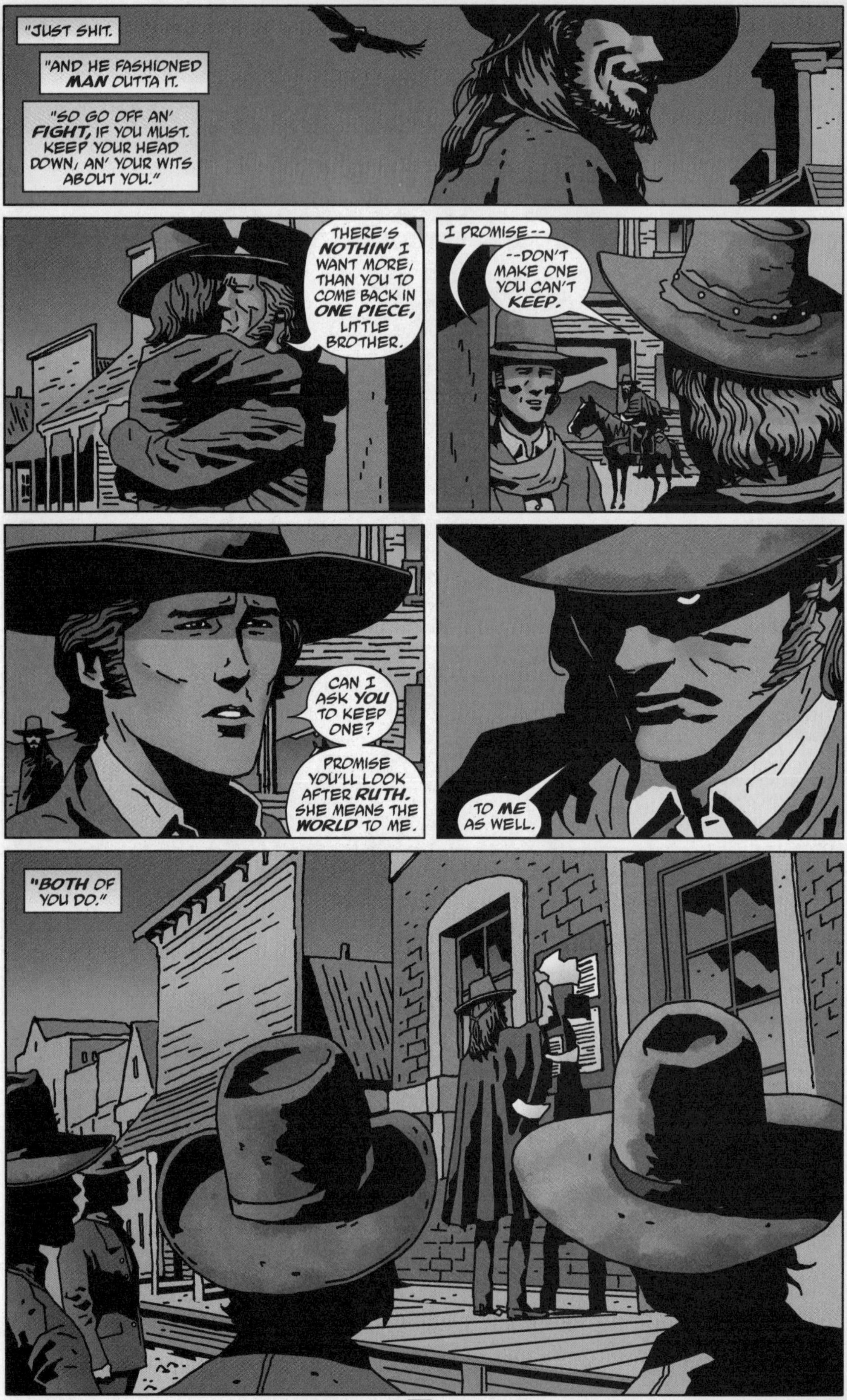
"JUST SHIT.
"AND HE FASHIONED **MAN** OUTTA IT.
"SO GO OFF AN' **FIGHT,** IF YOU MUST. KEEP YOUR HEAD DOWN, AN' YOUR WITS ABOUT YOU."
THERE'S **NOTHIN'** I WANT MORE, THAN YOU TO COME BACK IN **ONE PIECE,** LITTLE BROTHER.
I PROMISE--
--DON'T MAKE ONE YOU CAN'T **KEEP.**
CAN I ASK **YOU** TO KEEP ONE?
PROMISE YOU'LL LOOK AFTER **RUTH.** SHE MEANS THE **WORLD** TO ME.
TO **ME** AS WELL.
"**BOTH** OF YOU DO."

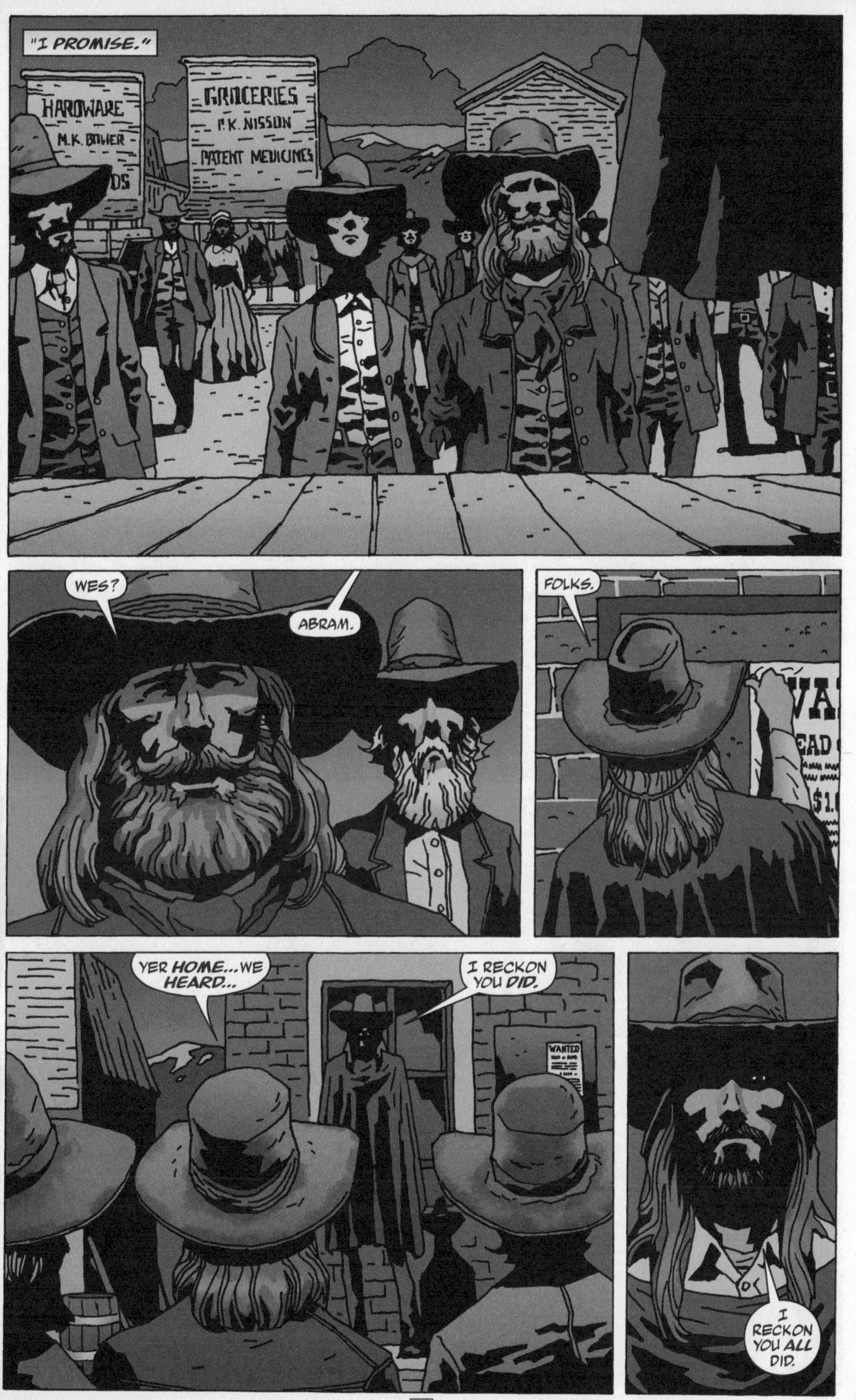
"I PROMISE."
HARDWARE
M.K. BOWER
GROCERIES
C.K. NISSON
PATENT MEDICINES
WES?
ABRAM.
FOLKS.
YER HOME... WE HEARD...
I RECKON YOU DID.
WANTED
I RECKON YOU ALL DID.

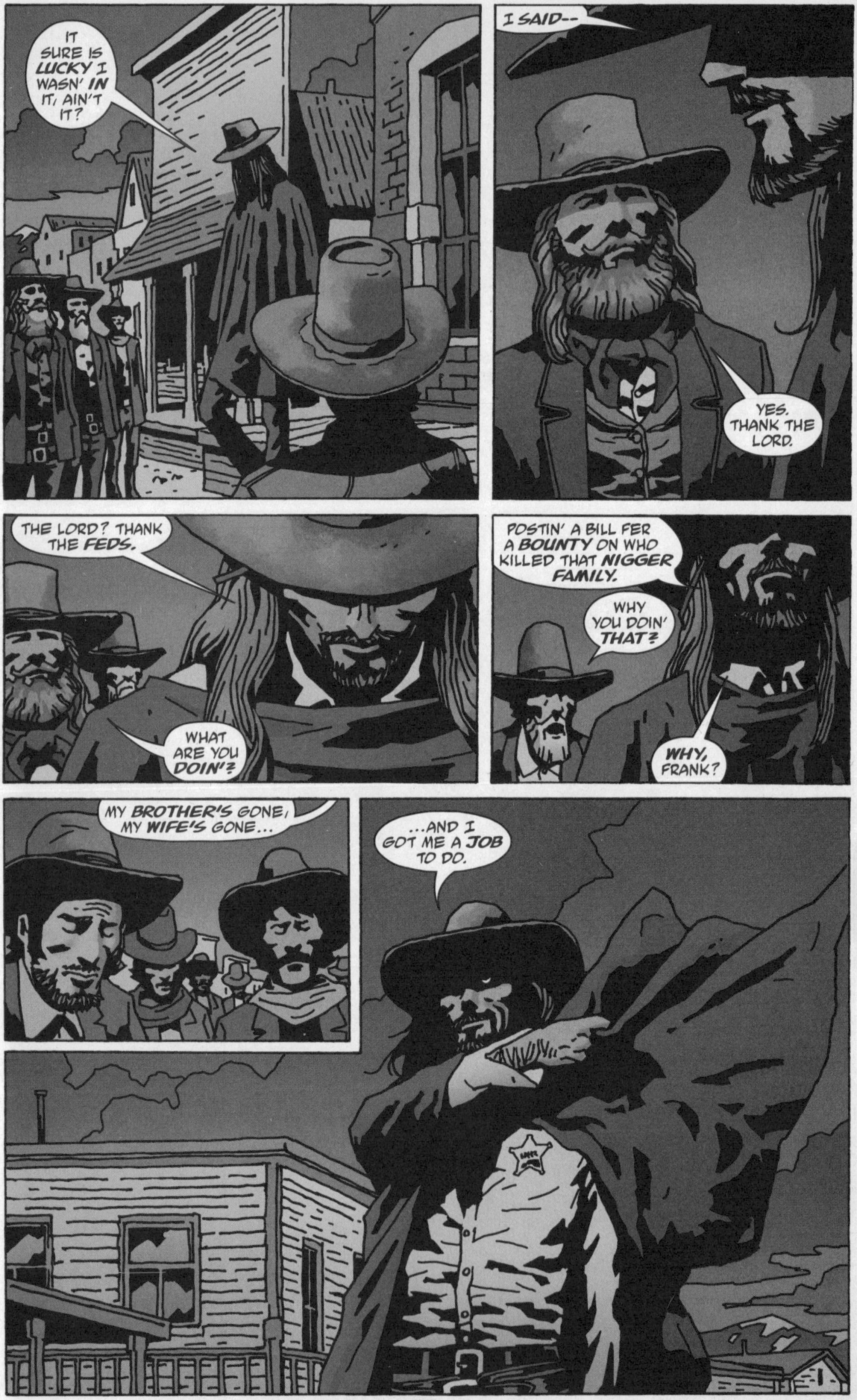
IT SURE IS LUCKY I WASN' IN IT, AIN'T IT?
I SAID--
YES. THANK THE LORD.
THE LORD? THANK THE FEDS.
WHAT ARE YOU DOIN'?
POSTIN' A BILL FER A BOUNTY ON WHO KILLED THAT NIGGER FAMILY.
WHY YOU DOIN' THAT?
WHY, FRANK?
MY BROTHER'S GONE, MY WIFE'S GONE...
...AND I GOT ME A JOB TO DO.

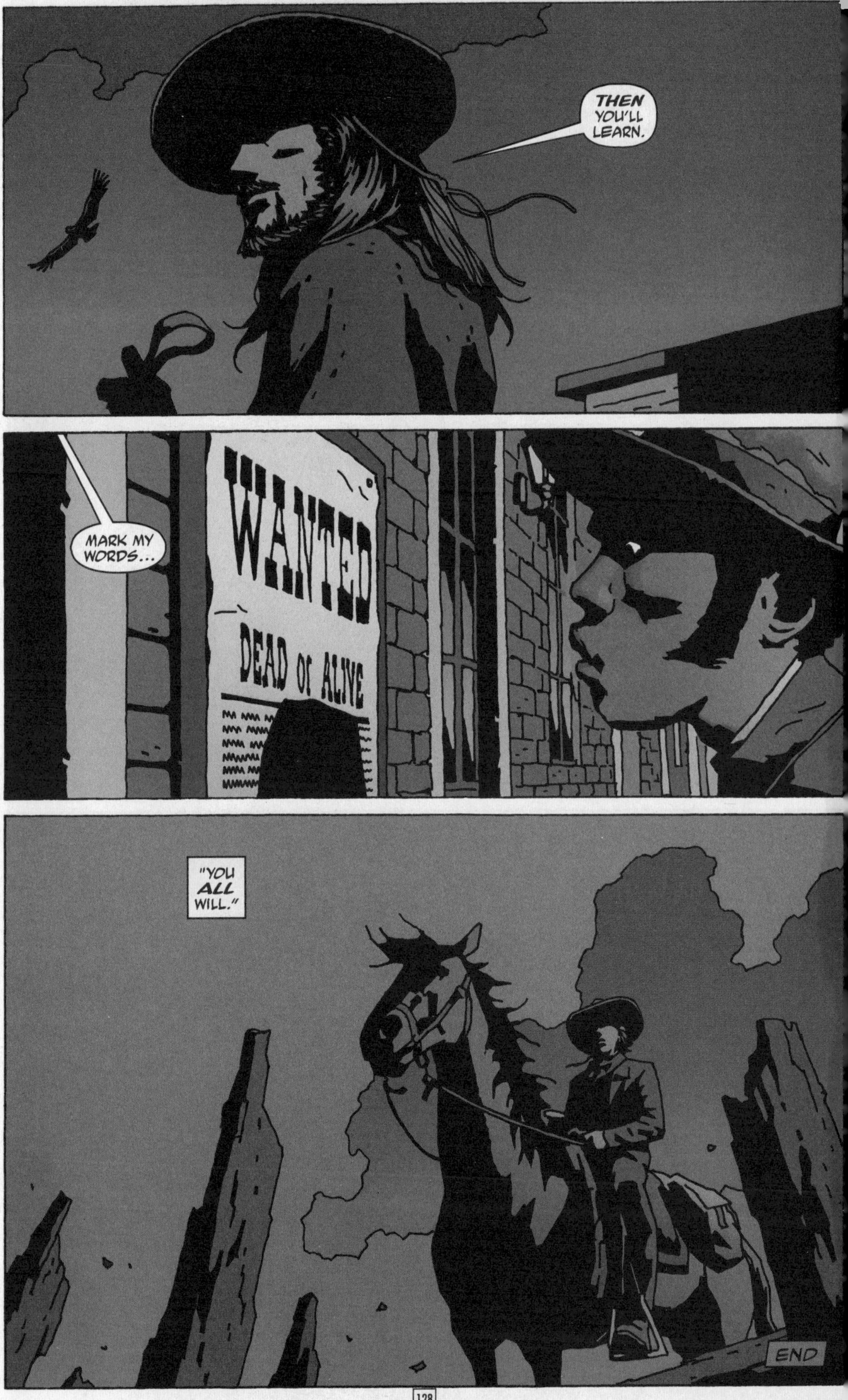
THEN YOU'LL LEARN.
MARK MY WORDS...
WANTED
DEAD OR ALIVE
"YOU ALL WILL."
END

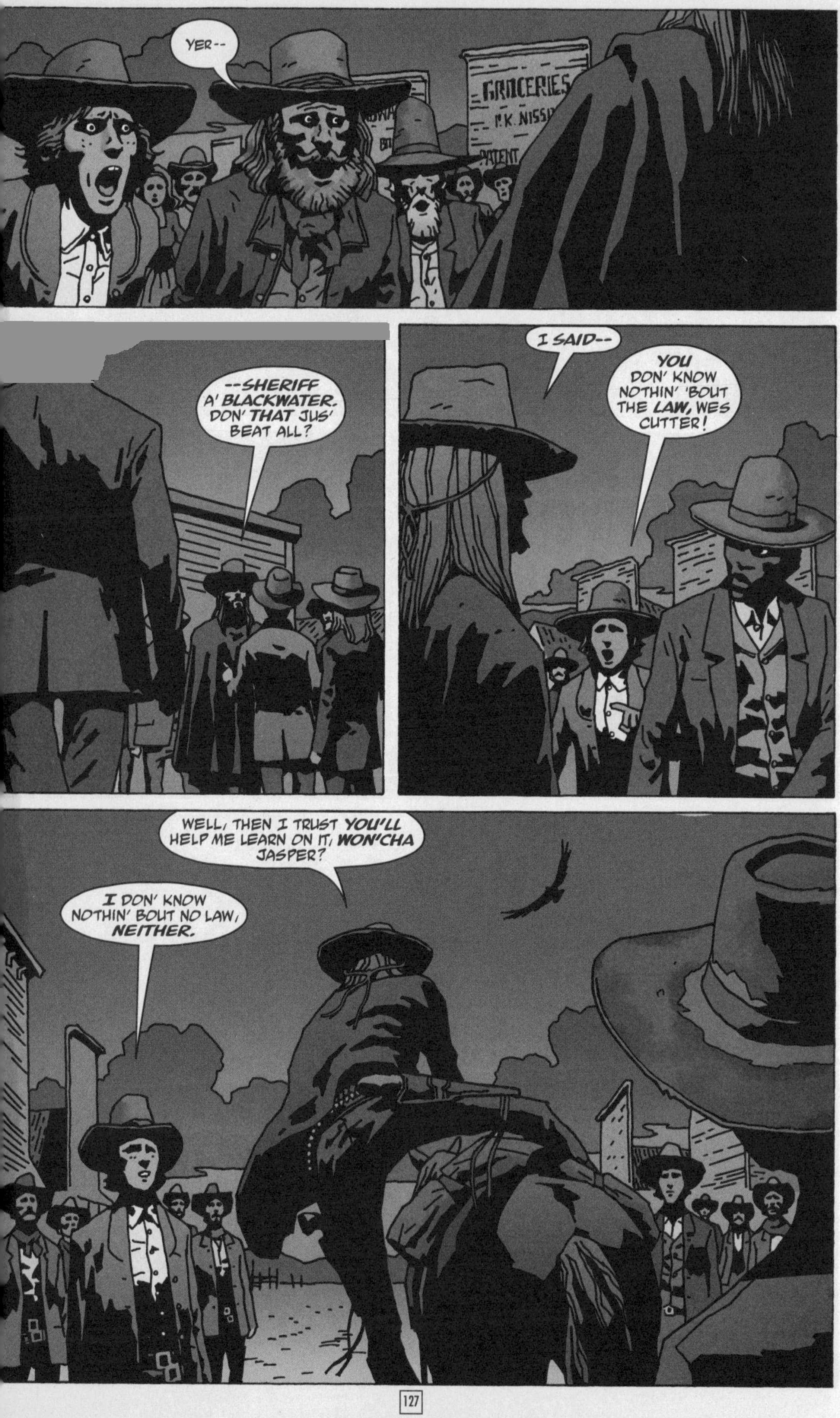
YER--
GROCERIES
P.K. NISS
PATENT
--SHERIFF A' BLACKWATER. DON' THAT JUS' BEAT ALL?
I SAID--
YOU DON' KNOW NOTHIN' 'BOUT THE LAW, WES CUTTER!
WELL, THEN I TRUST YOU'LL HELP ME LEARN ON IT, WON'CHA JASPER?
I DON' KNOW NOTHIN' BOUT NO LAW, NEITHER.